11 Things You <u>Must</u> Do Right

To Keep Your Dog Healthy and Happy

MICHELE WELTON

Published by Petbridge LLC in the United States of America

ISBN: 978-0-9797091-5-9

Disclaimer

This book is intended to provide general information about dog health care. It should not be your sole source of information for caring for your dog, as the information contained in this book may not be applicable to your particular dog.

This information is not intended to diagnose or treat any animal and should not be used as a substitute for obtaining professional veterinary advice.

The author and publisher make no representations or warranties about the accuracy, applicability, or completeness of the information in this book, and assume no liability for any consequences, loss, or damage caused or alleged to be caused by the information in this book.

About the Author

Hello! I'm Michele Welton and I have over 40 years of experience as a Dog Trainer, Obedience Instructor, Dog Breed Consultant, founder of three Dog Training Centers, and author of more than a dozen books about dogs.

I've trained and shown dogs in competitive obedience, agility, herding, tracking, and Schutzhund.

My advice on choosing, raising, and training dogs has been featured on the Orange County TV News Channel and in the *Orange County Register* in Southern California.

Visit my website at
https://www.yourpurebredpuppy.com

Table of Contents

What People Are Saying...

"This book is spectacular, really opened my eyes. I love my Westie pupper and my Whippet doggo and I'm grateful that you've packed so many helpful tips into this book. What a treasure chest of valuable advice. Dog owners, grab this book!"

— Bill Linscotti

"Michele, this is the best health care book I've ever read. Bar none. I love your honest writing, how easy it is to follow and understand. Everything is laid out step by step so I know exactly what to do, what to change, what to fix."

— Chris Hewitt

"I highly recommend this book. It has a tremendous amount of advice that will keep your dog as healthy and safe as he could be. I'm especially stunned at the large number of little things you mentioned that I had never thought of. I would never have known to watch out for these things if I hadn't read your book."

— Laura Madsen

"You've laid out so many things I can DO for my dogs and I love feeling like I'm doing things to make them happy and healthy. It puts me in control of my dog's health, instead of the vet."

— Patrick Bowen

"I've bought all your books and love them all. Nobody else writes the way you do, it's most enjoyable to read. Your books have helped me raise and train my Lab Shepherd puppy and I am proud of the way he looks and acts when I take him anywhere. My honest opinion is, no dog owner can go wrong with your books."

— John Nichols

Introduction: Why Do Dogs Have Health Problems?

There are three major causes of health problems in dogs:

- heredity
- abnormal structure
- environment

Your dog can INHERIT health problems.

Joint disorders, eye diseases, epilepsy, heart disease, thyroid disease, kidney disease, liver disease, certain types of cancer… many health problems in dogs are hereditary.

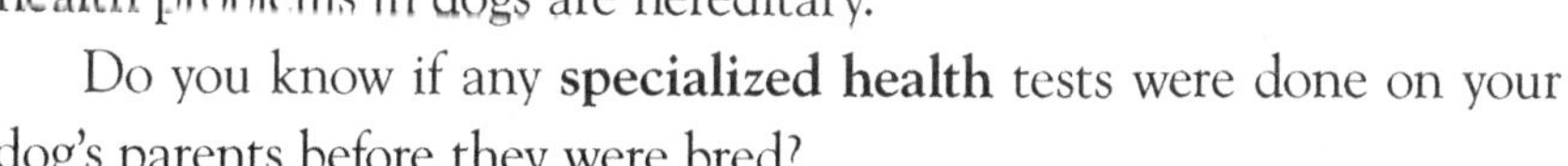

Do you know if any **specialized health** tests were done on your dog's parents before they were bred?

Now I don't mean an examination and health certificate from the vet! Those seldom mean anything.

Specialized health tests include X-rays of the hips and elbows, a professional eye exam by a licensed canine ophthalmologist, a cardiac exam by a board-certified cardiologist, and specialized blood and DNA tests that can detect certain hereditary health problems.

Each breed has a different set of tests that should be done before breeding.

✓ If those tests were done on your dog's parents, with normal results, your dog is less likely to develop those problems.

✗ If those tests were not done… that's unfortunate, because over 500 hereditary defects occur in purebred dogs. (About 100 hereditary defects occur in mixed breeds.)

Now, do you also know how ***closely related*** your dog's parents are (or were)?

If your dog is purebred, the answer is that his parents were more closely related than you might think. You see, within each breed, ALL the dogs are related to some degree—and the closer that relationship is, the greater the risk of health problems.

If you're a science-fiction fan, you've probably seen a movie or read a novel where a small population on some isolated planet has been breeding among themselves for generations. Now the people are developing mental and physical defects and are in desperate need of an influx of new genes to strengthen their gene pool so they don't all die off.

Those plots are based on fact. In a population of any living creatures, re-combining the same genes over and over, without the regular introduction of new and unrelated genes, is not good. It leads to an insidious condition called "inbreeding depression."

> In purebred dogs, each breed has a "closed" gene pool (Pug is bred only to Pug) that never allows any new genes. From a scientific genetic/health perspective, this "pure" breeding is unwise.

Close breeding increases the risks of a weaker immune system, chronic infections, a shorter lifespan, and behavioral abnormalities such as shyness, aggression, or a high-strung temperament.

Now, if your dog is a mixed breed, his parents were probably unrelated. Thus a mixed breed enjoys a sort of "hybrid vigor" that comes from greater genetic diversity, which translates to fewer potential health problems.

Your dog's STRUCTURE can cause health problems.

Breeders have pushed Mother Nature beyond the breaking point by deliberately producing unnatural features in dogs.

Flat faces that must snort and snuffle through life… large protruding eyes vulnerable to injury … bowed legs … long bodies … wrinkled skin … loose lips … long ears with narrow ear canals … massive bodies … tiny bodies … and so on.

All of these exaggerations in structure are ***deformities.***

Did you know that a "natural" dog (breeding without the influence of man) is about 15 to 22 inches at the shoulder, 30 to 50 pounds, with an agile build, shortish hair, and a longish nose?

The more a dog varies from this natural size and build, the more likely the chance of health problems.

Your dog's ENVIRONMENT can cause health problems.

Once you HAVE your dog, you can't do anything about the first two causes of health problems.

> If his parents weren't tested for specific hereditary health problems or if he is inbred to a high degree, or if he has an exaggerated/unnatural build… the risk is greater that he will develop health problems at some point in his life. We can't get around that now.

So in this book, we're going to focus on the ***LAST*** cause of health problems—the one you CAN do something about at this point—your dog's environment.

By environmentally-caused health problems, I mean accidents and injuries, infections, parasites, allergies, digestive upsets, some autoimmune diseases and cancers, side effects of medications or excessive vaccinations… the good news is that there's a long list of health issues you can minimize or prevent simply by controlling, adjusting, and monitoring your dog's environment.

> ***YOU*** (not your veterinarian) are the primary driver of your dog's health.

The things **YOU** do with your dog at home will make all the difference in his short- and long-term health and lifespan.

In this book, you'll learn how to make ***everything*** in your dog's daily life health-promoting.

Outline—11 Things You Must Do Right

1. Feed the right food.

This is the most important foundation for your dog's future good health. I'll recommend 3 different ways to feed your dog exactly what he needs to eat.

2. Allow minimal vaccinations.

Your vet may not have told you this, but vaccination requirements have changed drastically. Your puppy needs only a ***couple*** of vaccinations for only a ***couple*** of diseases—he does not need a whole "series" of shots. And your adult dog doesn't need booster shots every year. In this chapter, cutting-edge veterinarians will tell you how to vaccinate your dog sensibly.

3. Provide a non-toxic environment.

When your dog breathes in something other than pure air (for example, chemical droplets from an aerosol can of hair spray), his immune system recognizes an "intruder" in his respiratory tract and tries to fight it. Frequent battles like that exhaust his immune system and leave it vulnerable to real illness.

> In this chapter, we'll walk through your house and yard, looking for everyday substances that might stress your dog's immune system and (hopefully) replace them with something safer.

4. Prevent fleas, ticks, and heartworms.

Flea and tick collars are outdated—don't put one on your dog. Ditto for flea and tick sprays, dips, and foggers. I'll recommend the products I find safest and most effective for fleas and ticks. As for heartworm, that dreaded parasite carried by mosquitoes, I'll tell you about the chances of your dog being infected and what you can do to prevent it.

5. Provide physical exercise and mental stimulation.

Your dog needs regular exercise to keep both his ***body*** and ***mind*** healthy. Did you know that dogs are vulnerable to a form of dementia like Alzheimer's disease? In this chapter, I'll tell you about interesting activities and exercise options that will keep your dog both physically fit and mentally stimulated.

6. Provide emotional security.

When we feel anxious or insecure, our body responds by producing biochemicals that can throw our physical systems out of whack.

> In other words, ***emotional*** stress leads to ***physical*** stress—headaches, digestive upsets, muscle tension, etc. The same is true for dogs. In this chapter, you'll learn 12 things you can do to keep your dog feeling happy, relaxed, and stress-free.

7. Emphasize safety.

Many dogs are injured or killed due to accidents that could have been prevented. In this chapter, we'll talk about all sorts of things that you might never have realized are risk factors for dogs. Most importantly, we'll learn how raising a dog is like raising a toddler who never grows up.

8. Groom your dog for maximum health and comfort—not for appearance.

A clean and tidy dog is one more step toward being a healthy dog. In this chapter, we'll brush and bathe your dog, clean his eyes, ears, and teeth, clip his nails, and trim or clip his coat. All based on maximum comfort, not for appearance.

9. Control reproduction.

I'll tell you the pros and cons of breeding, spaying, and neutering. If you do spay or neuter your dog, you'll learn ***WHEN*** to do it and ***HOW*** to have it done safely.

> Too many dogs are lost under anesthesia or end up with future health problems because the surgery was done at the wrong time or without specific safety precautions.

10. Find the right vet.

All the effort you've put into keeping your dog healthy can be undone in the blink of an eye by a vet who scoffs at your choice of foods, who warns you that your dog may die because you haven't vaccinated him "enough", or who tries to dose your dog with powerful meds for minor ailments, even when there are safer treatments available.

In this chapter, we'll talk about the vast differences between virtually all of the vets listed in your phone book versus the vets I recommend using. Your choice between the two can make all the difference in the world to your dog's long-term health and happiness.

11. Recognize when something is wrong with your dog.

The quicker you notice something wrong with your dog, the quicker the problem can be resolved. Observe and examine your dog on a regular basis, looking at each part of his body and noting whether it looks normal or abnormal. These little observations can pick up the very beginnings of health problems when treatment will be most effective. This chapter will walk you through a quick list of things to look for on your dog.

Follow these 11 principles with your dog, these 11 things you must do right… and you'll ***minimize*** his chances of developing health problems and ***maximize*** his chances of living the longest, most comfortable, and happiest life possible.

Chapter 1

The 1st Thing You Must Do Right: Feed the Right Food

Introduction—don't skip!

You can dramatically increase your dog's chances of living a long, healthy life by making one simple choice.

In this chapter, I'm going to tell you what that choice is... and exactly how to get your dog started on the path to a l-o-o-o-n-g, healthy life.

Cutting right to the chase, the best food for your dog is....

> Real food. Real chicken, turkey, beef, bison, venison, lamb, fish. Carrots, broccoli, zucchini, pumpkin, apples. Eggs, cottage cheese, plain yogurt.

No, this is not "people food" or "table scraps." Real meat, real veggies, real eggs, etc. are fresh, wholesome, nutritious foods.

All living creatures deserve (and thrive on) real food.

Now understand, when I say real food, I'm NOT talking about deli foods like bologna, sliced turkey, or processed cheese. No hot dogs or bacon, or macaroni and cheese. No french fries, pizza, or spicy tacos.

That kind of "people food" is terrible for dogs. And honestly, we all know that most of that stuff isn't particularly good for us either.

Feeding real, fresh, whole foods will make a huge difference in your dog's future health. That's why a multitude of veterinarians are in full support. World-renowned veterinarian Dr. Martin Goldstein, DVM, says...

"You can boost your pet's health profoundly by making one simple decision. All you have to do is change his diet ... to something you may never have imagined giving him—real food."

Top breeders and trainers have been feeding real food for many generations of their dogs.

> A growing number of veterinarians also recommend feeding real food—that is, vets who aren't profiting from selling dry kibble and canned food.

Vets who are still banking those profits might warn you, "Don't feed homemade! You won't be able to balance each meal."

But each and every meal doesn't need to be balanced, you see.

We don't compute the calories and proteins and fats of each and every meal ***we*** eat, do we? We just eat a variety of wholesome foods, and balance occurs over days and weeks.

Same is true for our dogs. You just need to provide overall balance, which looks like this:

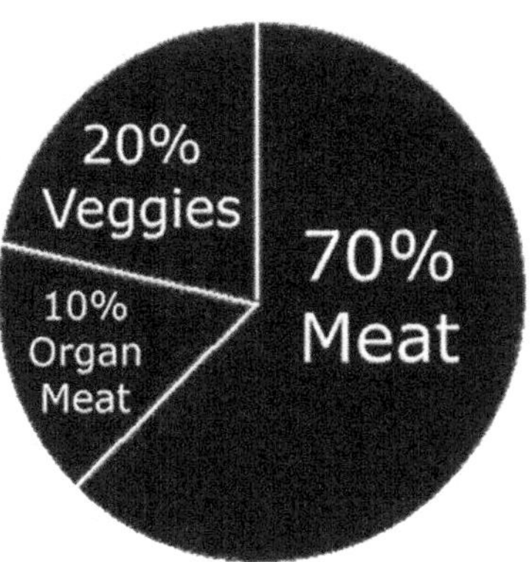

- ✓ 70% meat or fish
- ✓ 10% organ meat (liver, kidney, spleen)
- ✓ 20% vegetables and fruits
- ✓ Bone (either attached to the meat, or ground/powdered bonemeal)

There are 3 best ways to provide this balanced diet of real food to your dog....

3 best ways to feed your dog real food

These are not in any particular order. They're all good options. I like to rotate and combine them. Variety is good!

1. Homemade (prepare it yourself, either raw or cooked) page 33
2. Commercial ***raw*** (available in frozen or freeze-dried packages) page 50
3. Commercial ***cooked*** (delivered to your house) page 54

Notice that there are RAW options and COOKED options. To decide which you prefer, keep reading!

Should your dog's food be raw or cooked?

Most people who feed real food to their dogs **cook** the food. And that's fine. Your dog is going to love it.

But an increasing number of owners, breeders, trainers, even veterinarians, have gone back to the traditional practice of feeding ***raw*** food to their dogs.

> Dogs have been fed raw food (meat, fish, eggs) for more than 15,000 years.

It's only comparatively recently that people began offering cooked food. A dog's digestive system isn't designed for digesting cooked food, but it can usually adapt pretty well to simple cooked foods like meat, fish, eggs, and veggies.

At least... many dogs can.

So if you've decided you want to try feeding **real food,** your first decision should be: raw or cooked?

	Raw	Cooked
Digestibility	✓ dogs absorb raw nutrients to the max	✗ cooked nutrients are not as well-absorbed
Exercises your dog's digestive system	✓ yes	✗ not very much
Amount of poop	✓ less	✗ more
Includes vitamins, antioxidants, amino acids, enzymes	✓ lots	✗ many are killed or damaged by cooking
Risk of bacteria in the food	✗ small amount is sometimes present	✓ most are killed from cooking

As you can see, raw wins on all counts except for the risk of bacteria. In just a moment, I'll answer the controversial question, "Is raw food safe to feed a dog?"

But first ... why is raw food better than cooked?

Reason #1:

Dogs are designed to eat raw food, to completely digest raw food, and to draw the maximum nutrients from raw food.

A dog's digestive tract is tailor-made for raw food. The shape of his teeth are perfect for tearing meat and crushing bone. The powerful hydrochloric acid in his stomach breaks down tough food material and kills bacteria. His short, straight intestinal tract quickly eliminates any questionable food before it can do any harm.

That is the digestive system of a raw meat eater. That is the digestive system of your dog, whether Chihuahua or Great Dane.

The entire canine family (wolves, coyotes, wild dogs, domesticated dogs) has a digestive system designed to eat, digest, and absorb raw meat.

Which makes sense, because they can't roast or bake the rabbits they catch, right? They just eat them raw.

That's why a raw diet is also called a *biologically appropriate* or *species-appropriate* diet.

Reason #2:

Eating raw food keeps a dog's digestive system fit and healthy.

You know the old expression, "Use it or lose it"? When a dog's digestive system goes to work digesting raw food, his digestive system is **exercised,** which helps it stay strong and healthy.

Unfortunately, **cooked** meat makes your dog's digestive system lazy. When you cook meat, the heat breaks down the meat so that what you serve to the dog is semi-digested. Eating semi-digested meat doesn't exercise his digestive system, and this lack of use can open the door to future digestive ailments.

Reason #3:

Raw food is packed with enzymes, vitamins, amino acids, and antioxidants.

Unfortunately, these vital nutrients are damaged by cooking. In the case of essential digestive enzymes, your dog must produce those missing enzymes in his pancreas. Forcing the pancreas to work overtime when it shouldn't need to, can lead to pancreatic ailments.

When you cook your dog's food (or whenever you feed kibble or canned food), always **ADD** synthetic digestive enzymes to the food to help him digest it.

Reason #4:

 Raw foods contain a unique form of moisture that cooked foods don't have.

We all know that meat and veggies are naturally wet. Touch meat and you can feel its juices. Peel a carrot and the inside looks and feels moist and juicy…

> … but I'm not talking here about the kind of moisture that you can see or feel.

There's a more important kind of moisture that raw foods have. It's an ***internal*** moisture packed *inside the molecular cells* of raw meat, vegetables, and fruits.

Internal moisture is only released after the food reaches the intestines. This liquid ***bathes*** the intestines, keeping them moist and slippery, which helps avoid constipation.

Cooked meat and veggies may look and feel moist, but unfortunately, their molecular cells have been broken down by the heat, and their valuable internal moisture has been lost.

Reason #5:

 Dogs are less commonly allergic to raw food, and more often allergic to cooked food.

For example, Cashew is a Cocker Spaniel owned by a friend of mine. Cashew is allergic to cooked beef, and also to kibble and canned foods that contain beef. (All kibble and canned foods are cooked).

But when switched to **raw** beef, Cashew had no problems. This is probably because the *proteins* in raw beef are in their natural form and thus recognizable by the dog's digestive system.

Whereas cooking alters the molecular shape of meat proteins so much that the digestive tract of some dogs don't even recognize it as food.

Their immune system says, "Hey, what's that?" and sends out waves of *histamines* to attack the unrecognized "intruder".

The result can be chronic allergies and digestive upsets.

Is raw food safe?

Whenever the topic of raw food comes up, especially raw meat, the #1 concern that dog owners have is, "Isn't that risky?"

Our mothers and grandmothers have taught us to be careful around raw meat. We wash our hands thoroughly after handling it. We sterilize our countertops.

So how could raw meat be safe for dogs? Doesn't it have bacteria in it? Like e.coli or salmonella?

Yes, pathogens can be present in raw meat.

Pathogens can exist on raw veggies and fruits, too. There have been many supermarket recalls of veggies and fruits for bacterial contamination.

Even dry and canned dog foods (which are all cooked) have been recalled multiple times for contamination from pathogens and other "ingredients" that weren't supposed to be there but found their way in via mass assembly-line processing.

> Unless we keep our dogs in bubbles, we can't keep them away from bacteria. It's everywhere. That's the bad news.

The good news is that a small number of bacteria doesn't bother a healthy dog with a normal immune system. It's gross to think about, but doesn't your dog lick his own behind? He doesn't get sick from that.

Bacteria only become dangerous when they're able to colonize and multiply, and that rarely happens in a healthy dog.

Remember when I said that the canine family has a digestive system designed for raw food? Let's look at how that works:

1. A dog's stomach produces powerful hydrochloric acid. Bacteria die off in acidic environments.

2. A dog's digestive tract is short, which means waste material zips through quickly. Any bacteria that may have escaped the strong stomach acid doesn't have much time to dig in and multiply before getting pooped out.

> In other words, strong stomach acids + quick elimination = very little chance of normal bacteria affecting a normal dog.

Ah-ha! But notice that I said "very little chance of **normal** bacteria causing any problems for a **normal** dog."

You might have some questions about that word *normal.* For example, if you buy raw meat at the supermarket and it happens to contain bacteria, how do you know it's **normal** bacteria?

Couldn't it be **loads** of bacteria?

Or some superform of bacteria?

You've probably seen ugly documentaries about the sorry state of our slaughterhouses and meat processing plants. They're awful.

Could the raw meat you buy at the supermarket be so contaminated that it's too much for even a DOG'S strong digestive system to handle?

That's a fair question. I have the same concern.

> So I don't feed raw meat from the supermarket. I feed organic, grass-fed meat from my local farmer's market.
>
> The livestock is raised on small farms, grass-fed, without hormones or antibiotics, and without being processed

through the giant processing plants that supply supermarkets with their meat.

I can't prove that my meat is safer, but it sure *feels* safer. Plus these farmers are raising their livestock humanely, which is always a good thing.

Can domesticated dogs really eat raw?

Just as we might ask what "normal" bacteria is, we might ask what a "normal" dog is.

Obviously our dogs aren't wolves and they're not wild. Is the digestive system of a domesticated dog still able to handle raw?

Yes. Thousands upon thousands of owners, breeders, trainers, and veterinarians feed raw. They feed raw to Chihuahuas and German Shepherds and Labradoodles and mixed breeds.

> The digestive system of a domestic dog is not appreciably different from that of a wild dog.

However...

> The longer your dog has been eating cooked food (or dry kibble or canned food, which are also cooked), **the more slowly** you should transition him to raw.
>
> This is because his digestive system has become lazier and less functional from the unnatural diet. It needs a few weeks to build up the proper enzymes for a natural diet.

What if a dog is unhealthy? Suppose he already has a digestive disease or a compromised immune system?

Interestingly, sometimes those dogs are the best candidates for switching to a raw diet. It might even be a **game-changer** in curing or improving his ailment.

Talk it over with a vet who either recommends raw or at least has an open mind about it.

> On the other hand, there are some dogs for whom a *cooked* homemade diet might be the best choice. Now, if your vet doesn't even recommend *cooked* homemade, I would look for another vet. Honestly. Because that's not an open mind at all.

Have you decided whether you want to feed raw or cooked?

Next, you should decide whether you want to feed homemade or commercial. I'll talk about those options next!

Option #1: Homemade

There are 3 steps to making homemade food.

1. Decide how much food your dog needs per day.
2. Decide how much food to make at one time.
3. Make the food.

Let's look at those three steps!

How much homemade food does your dog need per day?

If your dog is an ADULT (has reached his adult weight), he should eat 2–3% of his body weight each day.

For example, if he weighs 50 lbs, multiply 50 lbs by 2% and you get 1 lb. Then multiply 50 lbs by 3% and you get 1.5 lbs. Your 50 lb dog should eat between 1 and 1.5 lbs of homemade food each day.

- ✓ More sedentary dogs or very large dogs (100 lbs) can be fed the lesser percentage, as they have a slower metabolism.
- ✓ Very active dogs or very small dogs (up to 10 lbs) can be fed the higher percentage, as they have a faster metabolism that burns calories more quickly.
- ✓ The average dog usually does best in the middle, eating about 2.5% of his body weight each day.

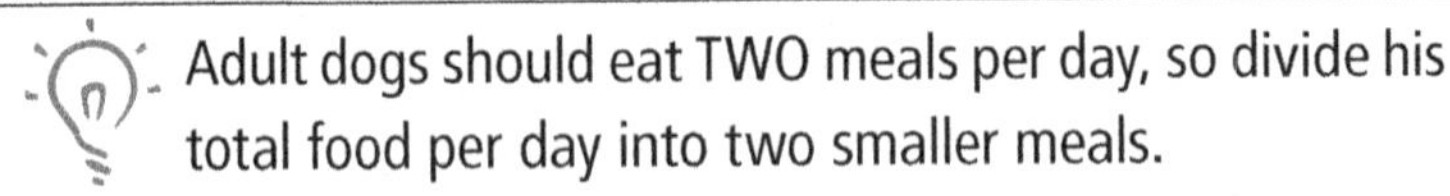
Adult dogs should eat TWO meals per day, so divide his total food per day into two smaller meals.

Dogs who eat only once a day experience an empty stomach and may even spit up white froth or bile. Think of how our own stomachs growl and how we feel irritable when we've gone many hours without eating.

ADULT DOGS ONLY	
5 lb dog	1.5 to 2.5 oz daily
10 lb dog	3 to 5 oz daily
15 lb dog	5 to 7 oz daily
20 lb dog	6.5 to 9.5 oz daily
25 lb dog	8 to 12 oz daily
30 lb dog	9.5 to 14.5 oz daily
35 lb dog	11 to 17 oz daily
40 lb dog	13 to 19 oz daily

ADULT DOGS ONLY	
45 lb dog	14.5 to 21.5 oz daily
50 lb dog	1 to 1.5 lbs daily
75 lb dog	1.5 to 2 lbs daily
100 lb dog	2 to 3 lbs daily

If your dog's weight falls between those listed on the chart, just use your calculator to multiply by 2% and 3%. For example, 65 lbs × 2% is 1.3 lbs, and 65 × 3% is 1.9 lbs. That's the range for your particular adult dog.

If your dog is a PUPPY (weighs less than his estimated adult weight)

Start with this…

1. What does your pup weigh now?
2. What should he weigh, roughly, as an adult?
3. Compare the two numbers.

If the puppy is currently less than half his adult size…

…he should be eating (total food per day) between 6 and 10% of his **current** weight.

For example, if your male pup weighs 20 lbs, and males of his breed typically mature at 60–70 lbs, your pup is less than half his adult weight.

Multiply his 20 lbs by 6% (equals 1.2 lbs of food per day) and also by 10% (equal 2 lbs of food per day). Within that 1.2 to 2 lbs range, you'll need to experiment.

Large-breed pups should eat at the lower end of their range, to slow down their growth. Large-breed pups who grow too quickly are more vulnerable to bone and joint problems.

Also generally, a pup whose weight is getting ***close*** to the halfway point needs **less** food, while a pup whose weight is still far away from the halfway point needs more.

But every pup is different in metabolism and activity level!

> And remember, his current weight will keep changing, so you should monitor his weight on a weekly basis and adjust your food quantity as he grows.

Also… that daily amount shouldn't be fed all at once. Divide it into three or four smaller meals. Most puppies over 8 weeks old should eat three meals per day until they're about 6 months old, then two meals per day thereafter.

Toy breed puppies (because they can have problems regulating their blood sugar) should eat four meals per day until 4 months old, three meals per day until 6 months old, then two meals per day thereafter.

If your pup's current weight is MORE than half his adult size, but LESS than 80% of it...

...he's getting closer to maturity, but still has a ways to go. He should probably be eating 5 or 6% of his current weight, per day. But always keep puppies on the slim side, and this is doubly important for large-breed pups!

If his current weight is close to his adult weight, say 90%...

...try dropping the percentage down to 4%.

And when he reaches his adult weight...

...you just need to **maintain** it now, using the ADULT chart you saw on page 34. Adult dogs will be eating about 2–3% of their body weight.

> Important! These guidelines are only a starting point. Every dog is different. You MUST monitor your pup's shape and energy to make sure he's getting enough food, but not too much food. Always keep your dog on the slim side!

How much food should you make at once?

You don't need to make one meal and immediately feed it. You can make up a batch of food (say, 6 meals) and store them in the refrigerator for 3 days.

So once you know how much food your dog needs each day, multiply that by 3 days and make up a batch of that amount.

For example, if your 50-pound dog eats 1.5 lbs daily, make up a batch of 4.5 lbs, which will serve him for 3 days (6 meals). All you need to do is take it out of the fridge, scoop a meal's worth into his feeding bowl, and warm it up by floating the bowl in a larger bowl of very hot water. It will quickly warm up to room temperature. Dogs digest food best at room temperature.

> For even more convenience, make up a week's worth or 2 weeks worth. Store 3 days worth in the fridge, and freeze the rest. But don't freeze it in one huge chunk—separate into 3-day quantities in individual freezer bags, so it will be convenient to thaw.

Homemade dog food recipe

There are hundreds of dog food recipes. But honestly, you need only one basic recipe. Then you can swap out the ingredients for variety. That's what I do.

When you first start preparing food for your dog, you should have a good postal or kitchen scale. But don't worry, you'll quickly learn to eyeball the food so that it comes out (roughly) in the right proportions. Perfect accuracy is not required.

Basic recipe for a homemade diet for dogs

This recipe makes 1 pound (16 ounces) of homemade dog food. For details, see *Frequently Asked Questions* below the recipe.

You need	Preparation	Amount
meat (chicken or turkey breast, ground beef or chicken, etc.)	ground or chopped; fed raw or lightly sauteed	11 oz (a little less than ¾ lb or 1.5 cups)
organ meat (liver, kidney, spleen…)	same as above	1 oz (roughly 2 tbsp; half should be liver)
veggies (broccoli, cauliflower, zucchini, asparagus…)	lightly steamed	3 oz
fruits (apple, banana, pear…)	raw, finely chopped	1 oz (roughly 2 tbsp)
calcium citrate or bone meal (human-grade, not garden-grade!)	powder	750mg bone meal or 600mg calcium citrate
fatty acids (salmon oil or ground flaxseeds)	liquid or powder	see *Frequently Asked Questions* below
digestive enzymes—only if the meat is cooked	powder	follow manufacturer's recommendation

Frequently asked questions about feeding homemade

What kind of meat should dogs eat?

Chunks of stew beef. Ground beef (hamburger). Boneless chopped chicken or turkey breast. Ground chicken/turkey. Try to include bison, venison, lamb, rabbit, and/or duck, from time to time. You can often get these at farmer's markets.

Can dogs eat regular meat from the supermarket?

Yes, although most supermarket meat comes from livestock that were raised inhumanely and fed crappy, processed, corn-based diets, instead of being allowed to free-feed on natural grass. That can affect the quality of the meat.

> So if you can find it and afford it, I highly recommend "organic" meat from local, free-range, grass-fed livestock. This is even more important if you're going to feed it raw.

Should dogs eat lean meat (90–95% lean) or is fattier meat (80–85%) okay?

I prefer lean for most dogs. It's easier to keep a meal's overall fat content down if you don't feed fattier cuts of meat.

Can dogs eat fish?

Yes, although I don't recommend fish more than once or twice a week because so many species contain toxins such as mercury. We've polluted our oceans, sad to say. The lowest-mercury fish seems to be Wild Alaskan Salmon.

> I prefer to cook fish, as cooking kills a particular type of worm in fish that could make a dog sick.

What is organ meat and why is it in the recipe?

My least favorite part of making homemade food is the *organ meat.* Organ meat includes liver, kidney, spleen, and "sweetbreads" (pancreas or thymus). Those all sound icky enough, but there are other organ meats (like brains) that even I'm too squeamish to feed.

> But dogs need the rich nutrients in organ meat. In fact, organ meat is so rich that dogs should only eat a little bit at a time, else they might get diarrhea.

The most essential organ meat is liver. It's incredibly nutritious, providing iron, B vitamins, minerals, and a huge amount of vitamin A, and yet… vitamin A can be toxic if your dog gets too much of it, so you mustn't over-do the liver.

> Organ meat should make up about 10% of your dog's daily diet. Of that 10%, liver should make up HALF of it. The other half should be one or more of the other organ meats.

Finding organ meat can be tricky. Most large supermarkets carry liver (usually chicken liver or beef liver), so that one's easy. But the other organs may only be available from butchers, farmers' markets, ethnic grocery stores, or online retailers.

> Or buy a complete blend of organ meats online: for example, Monster Mash Organ Grind. There are others.

Can dogs eat vegetables?

Yes, although technically they don't ***need*** vegetables. Vegetables are full of carbohydrates, which have only one purpose in life: supplying energy. But dogs can produce their energy from just proteins and fats, so they don't ***need*** the carbohydrates from vegetables.

But veggies have ***other*** pluses that make me happy to include them in my dogs' diet:

- ✓ Vegetables act as *roughage*. The insoluble fiber in veggies passes through the digestive tract mostly intact, carrying the waste along with it. Thus veggies help keep the bowels moving. In fact, a dog who catches a rabbit will eat the stomach contents of his prey, which includes digested plants, grasses, and berries. Roughage is good!

✓ Vegetables contain wonderful antioxidants.

✓ Vegetables are especially useful when your dog needs to lose a little weight, because they make him feel full without adding many calories.

The main thing to remember about veggies:

Their nutrients are tucked behind a tough cellulose wall *which dogs don't have the enzymes to break down.* When a dog eats a prey animal, its stomach contents have already been partially digested so the cellulose wall has been broken down.

So… either pulverize raw veggies in a food processor, or lightly steam/cook them—either of which will break down the cellulose wall so your dog can digest them. Otherwise, veggies may pass through a dog undigested.

Use fresh or frozen veggies, if possible. If you use canned, make sure they're only canned in water, with no salt.

Favorite vegetables are broccoli, cauliflower, zucchini, summer squash, asparagus, carrots, and green beans. Canned pumpkin (not pumpkin pie filling!) helps normalize the stools.

Avoid starchy vegetables such as red or white potatoes, sweet potatoes, yams, butternut squash, and corn. Once in awhile is fine, but don't feed them regularly. They're fattening and can cause blood sugar spikes.

Don't feed onion, as it can cause anemia. As can garlic *in large quantities,* but a little bit of pulverized raw garlic is fine.

Can dogs eat fruit?

Yes, but in moderation. Fruits are sugary and cause loose stools in some dogs. Especially don't feed canned fruit packed in syrup!

Like a vegetable, a fruit has a *cellulose wall* that you should break down before offering it to your dog. Chop the fruit into small pieces (or break small berries in half to expose the juicy center).

> Favorite fruits include slices of apple, pear, banana, or melon. Blueberries and strawberries are usually loved. Many dogs don't like acidic citrus, while others love it.

DON'T FEED grapes. Don't feed raisins either, which come from grapes. Grapes and raisins can be toxic to dogs. It usually takes a lot more than a single grape or raisin to make a dog sick, but it doesn't hurt to be cautious.

Why is bone meal or calcium needed?

When a dog eats a rabbit, he eats the meat AND the bone. Not every single bone in the carcass, but lots of small bones. Why?

Because meat is high in a mineral called *phosphorus,* while bone is high in a mineral called *calcium*. Since dogs need both minerals in a certain ratio, they instinctively eat both meat and bone.

When living in your home, your dog depends on YOU to give him the right ratio of phosphorus (meat) and calcium (bone).

If all you feed is the meat, his body will be forced to pull the calcium it needs from his own bones… making them weaker and more prone to fracturing.

To add calcium, you can either:

1. add actual bones to his diet—there are articles on the internet about how to do this option; I don't do it myself

2. or add bone meal *powder* or *plain calcium* powder

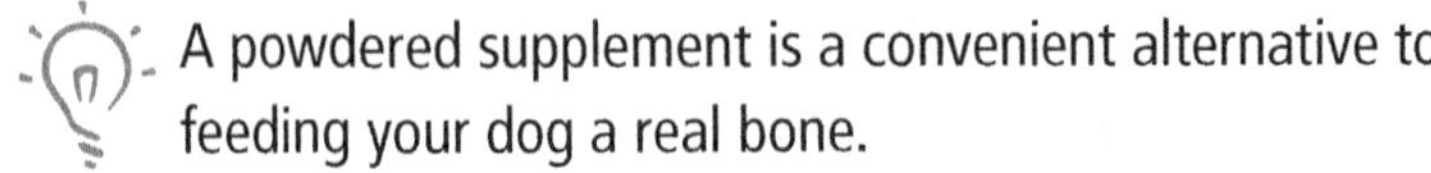

A powdered supplement is a convenient alternative to feeding your dog a real bone.

You can use:

✓ calcium citrate—a human supplement from your health food store

✓ or calcium from natural seaweed—*Animal Essentials Seaweed Calcium* is a good choice

✓ or bone meal (human-grade! not garden-grade!)—Kal is the most popular brand

When NOT to supplement with bone meal or calcium:

✗ When you're feeding a commercial diet. The manufacturer has already added the right amount of bone/calcium.

✗ When you're feeding a commercial diet but you sometimes toss in a little chicken or hamburger, less than 25% of the meal.

With large-breed puppies, too much calcium is just as bad as too little. Too much calcium can mess up the rapidly growing bones and joints of a large-breed pup. So add just enough to balance the meat, no more.

What are fatty acids and why are they needed?

If you've read anything on human health, you've probably heard about the importance of Omega 3 fatty acids. Our human diet tends to have far too many Omega **6** fats and far too few Omega **3** fats, and such an imbalance can lead to chronic health problems.

Same for dogs.

Most doggy diets already have plenty of Omega 6 fats. So usually it's much more important to supplement with Omega 3.

> Omega 3 fatty acids make your dog's skin and coat shiny and healthy, stop itching, calm stress and anxiety, normalize weight, and prevent or improve inflammatory diseases such as allergies and arthritis.

To provide your dog with these benefits, you can add a commercial Omega 3 supplement such as *Zesty Paws Wild Alaskan Salmon Oil* (liquid), *Grizzly Salmon Oil* (liquid), or *The Missing Link* (powdered). You can even rotate them.

How much Omega 3 does your dog need?

The two essential ingredients in Omega 3 fatty acids are EPA and DHA. Generally, you want to give your dog 10–20mg of EPA+DHA (combined) per pound of his body weight. So if he weighs 50 pounds, he needs 500–1000mg of EPA+DHA.

Suppose your bottle of Omega 3 contains, for example, 500mg DHA and 450mg EPA per teaspoon. Add the two together and that bottle contains 950mg EPA+DHA per tsp.

To give your dog his 500–1000mg, you could give him the whole tsp or about half that tsp, and you'd be in the right range for him.

> With fatty acid supplements, start LOW and build up, else your dog might get diarrhea.

Important: if your dog is taking any blood thinners, beta blockers, or diuretics, talk to your vet before giving Omega 3 fatty acids.

What are digestive enzymes, and why are they needed?

If you cooked your dog's meat, add digestive enzymes. The canine digestive system was designed for raw food. If you're cooking the food, your dog needs many more stomach enzymes to digest it.

> Rather than forcing his pancreas to work overtime making more digestive enzymes, add them yourself.

Otherwise your dog may be gassy or have loose stools. He might even eat his own stools trying to get the nutrients that he missed the first time around because he didn't have enough stomach enzymes to digest them.

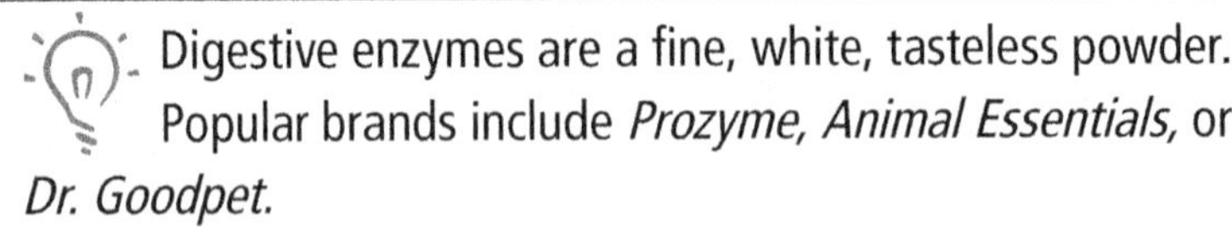

Digestive enzymes are a fine, white, tasteless powder. Popular brands include *Prozyme, Animal Essentials,* or *Dr. Goodpet.*

Should dogs eat grains?

Grain means wheat, corn, soy, barley, millet, rye, quinoa, brown rice, white rice, oats, pasta, bread, and so on.

Dogs are not designed to digest grains.

- ✗ Much of it goes right through them, resulting in lots of waste to clean up.
- ✗ Many dogs have loose stools or gassiness.
- ✗ Many dogs develop itchy skin, where the dog tries to soothe the itch by licking his front feet, or rubbing his face against the carpet, or rubbing his body against the furniture.

✗ Grains and cereals contain lots of carbs. Carbs have one purpose only—they're used for energy. When not used for energy (and the typical family dog doesn't expend a lot of energy), carbs are stored in the body as fat, making them the leading dietary cause of overweight dogs.

On the plus side, there's one good thing about grain: cost.

✓ People on a tight budget might need to substitute some grain for meat. If so, choose quinoa or oatmeal, which are higher-quality grains that are less likely to cause allergies.

Can dogs eat legumes?

Legumes include peas, lentils, chickpeas, kidney beans, pinto beans, etc.

As with grains, dogs don't have the digestive system needed to properly digest legumes and the result can be intestinal distress and flatulence. But tossing a handful of cooked peas into your dog's meal once in a while is fine.

However, some human vegetarians use legumes as meat substitutes in their own diets. Don't do that with your dog. There is currently an investigation into whether feeding too many legumes might be triggering a specific form of heart disease in some dogs.

Can dogs eat cheese?

Most dogs are fine with a little bit of hard cheese, such as mild cheddar or feta.

Cottage cheese is better. Some dog food recipes reduce the quantity of meat and substitute low-fat cottage cheese.

If your dog likes it and doesn't get loose stools, it can be a good variety meal once in a while.

Can dogs drink milk?

I avoid feeding milk. Just as many people are lactose-intolerant, many dogs end up with soft, mucousy stools from cow's milk. Some dogs do better with raw goat's milk, but there really isn't any reason to feed any milk.

Of course if you're eating ice cream yourself, your dog might appreciate licking the spoon clean. My dogs certainly do! Just make sure it isn't chocolate or coffee, which can be toxic to dogs.

Can dogs eat yogurt?

Yes, a tablespoon of **plain** yogurt is good for dogs. It contains "friendly" digestive bacteria *(lactobacillus acidophilus)*, which is good for the digestive tract. Yogurt is especially recommended if your dog has diarrhea or gas. Remember, it should be plain—no sugary yogurt for dogs.

Can dogs eat eggs?

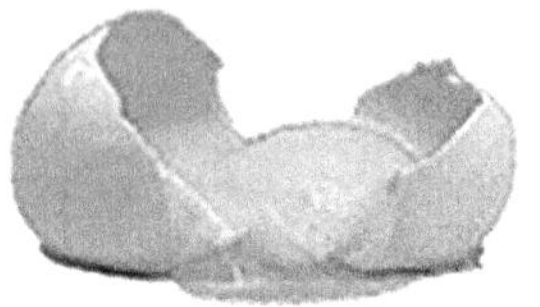

Yes, eggs are good for dogs and can be given once or twice a week. Look for organic eggs from free-range, pasture-fed hens. Most supermarket eggs come from hens that were raised inhumanely and fed a crappy, artificial diet.

You can feed an egg raw or you can soft-boil or lightly scramble it.

Can you feed food straight from the refrigerator?

Yes, but it's better if it's closer to room temperature. So if you're feeding raw, leave it on the counter for 15 minutes, or put it in a plastic bag or a smallish dish, and float the bag/dish in a larger bowl of hot water, until it's room temperature. If you're feeding cooked, I still prefer the methods above, but you can warm that up in the microwave if you're in a hurry.

Foods NOT to give your dog

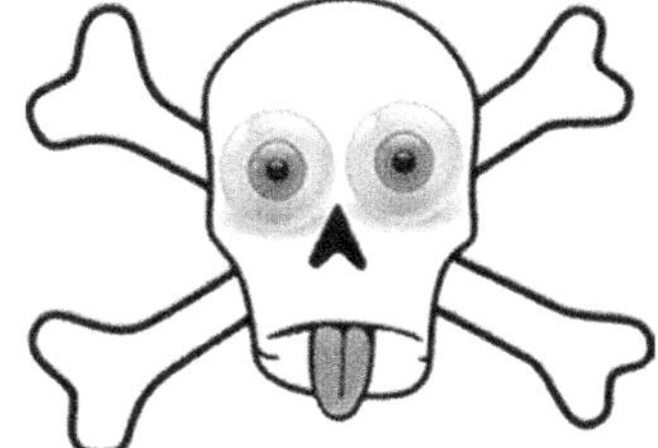

- ✗ Chocolate—can be toxic to dogs
- ✗ Grapes—can be toxic to dogs
- ✗ Raisins—can be toxic to dogs
- ✗ Onions—can cause anemia in dogs
- ✗ Mushrooms—can be toxic to dogs
- ✗ Legumes (peas, chickpeas, lentils, kidney beans, etc.)—cause intestinal discomfort, too much can possibly trigger a specific heart disease in some dogs
- ✗ Garlic—a whole bunch can be toxic, but a little is just fine
- ✗ Deli meats (baloney, sliced ham, etc.)—bad for dogs
- ✗ Hot dogs—bad for dogs
- ✗ Anything deep-fried
- ✗ Anything "rich", i.e. Thanksgiving turkey with all the fixings
- ✗ Anything with hot spices
- ✗ Anything with a lot of salt or sugar
- ✗ Anything alcoholic
- ✗ Anything caffeinated (coffee, tea, soda)

Option #2: Commercial RAW

If you want your dog to eat raw, but don't want to prepare the food yourself… you're in luck.

> In recent years, a revolutionary new concept of feeding dogs has emerged. It provides dogs with the raw food they thrive on, while also making it simple and convenient for their owners to provide it.

It's a win-win situation.

Many dog owners would love to join the burgeoning ranks of top breeders, trainers, and enlightened veterinarians who are feeding raw food.

But for some of those owners, it's hard to find the time.

To feed a good raw diet from scratch, you do need to spend some time preparing it. Shopping for ingredients. Measuring, chopping, mixing, grinding, blending the meals. Packaging and freezing them in ready-to-thaw portions.

It's a bit of work. But definitely worth it for so many owners who look with satisfaction and delight at their happy, healthy, long-lived, raw-fed dogs!

> If you don't have that kind of time, or just can't do it, you no longer need to feel like your dog is being cheated out of all the benefits of eating raw. Now it's easy to feed him the healthy diet he deserves.

Frozen raw dog food

If you made homemade food in your kitchen, then put it in the freezer, that's frozen raw dog food.

Now think of someone else doing that for you. Just as there are companies that make kibble and canned food, there are companies that make frozen raw food. Some of these companies make frozen in addition to kibble and canned, while other companies specialize in frozen.

> You can buy frozen raw food from the freezer section of your local pet store or health food store. Or you can order it online and have it shipped to your house.

Obviously you store frozen food in your freezer. The day before you feed it, you move it from the freezer to the fridge to thaw. Once thawed, you put it in your dog's bowl.

Oh, wait! It's cold!

Some owners don't care. They feed it cold and most dogs gobble it right up. That's usually fine.

But I try to be kind to my dog's digestive system by taking the edge off the cold before I feed it.

I put a large pan in the sink, fill it with hot water, and float my dog's bowl (obviously with the food in it!) on top of the hot water for a few minutes until it warms up a bit. Then I serve it.

Freeze-dried raw dog food

As the name suggests, this is both *frozen* and *dried*. The manufacturer applies a very cold, high-pressure vacuum process that sucks out the moisture.

> Water is surprisingly heavy! So when it's removed, the resulting food is a lightweight, dry substance that can be stored in a bag on your pantry shelf instead of in the freezer.

Do you need to worry about bacteria? No. Since bacteria need moisture to feed on, any bacteria in the raw food are deactivated and can't grow.

In effect, freeze-dried food has been put into ***suspended animation*** until you're ready to rehydrate it by adding water and letting it sit for a while. Then stir and serve.

One thing I should mention…

Freeze-dried food has been processed MORE than frozen food.

The freeze-dry and rehydration process slightly alters the raw nutrients in the food. But it still retains about 97 percent of its nutrients.

> Practically speaking, that probably won't make any difference, so I encourage you to compare and consider both frozen raw and freeze-dried raw.

Comparing frozen and freeze-dried raw dog food

	Frozen Raw	Freeze-Dried Raw
Storage	freezer	pantry shelf
Easy to travel with?	no	yes
Preparation	thaw in fridge, warm to room temp, serve	add water, let soak, stir, serve
Cost	less expensive	more expensive

What about dehydrated dog food?

With all this talk about moisture and rehydrating, perhaps you've seen something called ***dehydrated*** food at the pet store. *The Honest Kitchen* is a common brand of dehydrated food.

Dehydrated dog food is not raw. Instead of using a ***cold*** process, the manufacturer of a dehydrated food ***heats*** it. That's cooking, which changes the nature of the nutrients.

> Now, a dehydrated dog food might (or might not) be okay if you're interested in cooked food, but not if you're interested in the benefits of raw.

Are frozen and freeze-dried foods safe?

If you're asking about safety simply because the food is ***raw,*** I talked about that concern on page 30.

Another way to increase safety is to buy a commercial frozen or freeze-dried raw food that has been subjected to a safety process to eliminate bacteria.

> The process is called *High Pressure Pasteurization.* HPP applies extremely high water pressure that kills bad little buggers like e.coli, salmonella, and listeria. It's been described as "putting the squeeze" on pathogens without destroying vital nutrients as would occur with heating.

> If you're still doubtful, you might start out lightly cooking the food. After awhile, you might decide to cook it less, and finally to just serve it raw. That's what I do, with all breeds from Chihuahuas on up to German Shepherds.

If, instead, you're asking about safety from dog food recalls (page 56), most of the commercial foods that have been recalled due to contamination are *dry kibble and canned foods.*

> But some frozen and freeze-dried foods have also been recalled for contamination.

Any dog food made by any company can end up contaminated.

That's why I recommend making your dog's food yourself, if possible. Otherwise, you're placing his health (often his very life) into the hands of some company.

> I definitely pay attention to a company's recall history when I feed anything commercial to my dogs, and also when I recommend commercial dog food brands to anyone else. That doesn't mean I'll never use a brand that has been affected by a recall. There are many factors I take into account.

Recommended brands of frozen and freeze-dried raw dog food

These are commercial raw foods that I feed (or would feed) to my dogs. They're not 100% what I think a dog food should be—definitely not. And they're not 100% safe—nothing is. I've simply weighed and evaluated as many factors as possible and feel most comfortable with these particular foods.

Visit my website (yourpurebredpuppy.com/health/) for my current recommendations. Dog food companies can and do change their ingredients and formulations, and if I don't like what they've done, they come off my list.

Option #3: Commercial COOKED

If you love the idea of a delicious, cooked meal for your dog, but don't have the time or inclination to cook it….

> there are companies that will make homemade meals (from recipes created by veterinarians) in restaurant-grade kitchens and deliver those meals right to your door.

Usually you fill out a questionnaire on the company's website, telling them about your dog and choosing from a variety of recipes.

Then once every 2–4 weeks you receive a box in the mail, filled with cooked meals. Each meal comes in a sealed packet that contains exactly the amount of homemade food your particular dog needs to eat.

Keep a few packets in the fridge, ready to warm and serve. Store the rest in the freezer.

On my website (yourpurebredpuppy.com/health/) you can read more about the current companies I recommend for cooked, homemade food delivered.

Dry kibble or canned food?

You might be wondering why kibble or canned foods didn't make my list of the best ways to feed your dog healthy food.

Like most dog owners, I started out feeding kibble. Thirty years ago, I fed kibble to my German Shepherds.

I couldn't put my finger on why it made me so uneasy to do so, but it did.

It didn't seem to make sense that the food they depended on for their health and vitality consisted of heavily processed, crunchy, boring, brown pebbles that clattered and clunked into their food bowls.

It felt like I was feeding a hamster.

I tried adding water and canned food to make it look better. But when I read the ingredients on the can, there was precious little meat and lots of weird stuff I had never seen on a grocery shelf anywhere: beet pulp? corn gluten? **That's** what dogs should eat?

Made no sense.

My dogs also produced a lot of waste, as though much of the food was going right through them. That wasn't much fun to clean up.

I even wondered if their food might be a contributing factor to their itchy allergies and softish stools. So I dug into the research... and discovered that there were much better ways to feed my dogs.

3 huge problems with kibble and canned dog food

- ✗ **Questionable safety.** You simply don't know what else might be in that bag or can. Brand after brand keeps getting recalled by the government or pulled off the shelves because of contamination, which often results in the sickness or death of someone's beloved dog.
- ✗ **Inappropriate ingredients.** In ALL kibble and canned foods, your dog ***isn't*** getting what he ***should*** be getting—and he ***is*** getting what he ***shouldn't*** be getting. And that affects his long-term health and lifespan.
- ✗ **Poor quality of ingredients.** Kibble and canned dog foods use cheap, low-quality ingredients that fail USDA inspection for human consumption.

Let's look carefully at these issues, because they can cause a world of hurt to your dog's future health.

Is your dog's food safe?

You've probably heard about pet food recalls, where one manufacturer after another is forced to recall their kibble or canned food because it's contaminated with something dangerous.

Usually it's for bacteria (e.coli or salmonella), but sometimes it's for strange things that you wouldn't think possible if these companies were really serious about quality control: bits of plastic, for example, or sharp shards of bone.

In December, 2018, the FDA issued a warning to pet owners that numerous dog food brands, including Hill's Science Diet (available from veterinarians), contained dangerously high levels of vitamin D, which can cause fatal kidney failure… which, sadly, it already had.

> Hill's Science Diet… Abound… Evolve… Triumph… Nutrisca… Natural Life… Sportsman's Pride… ANF… Nature's Promise… all recalled for vitamin D toxicity.

Over the past dozen years, millions of pet food products have been recalled, including other "famous" names like Purina, Iams, Eukanuba, Solid Gold, Stella & Chewy's, Wellness, Wysong, Canidae, Innova, EVO, California Natural, Blue Buffalo, Royal Canin, Merrick, PetSmart, Nutro, Alpo, Mighty Dog, Breeder's Choice, Diamond, Bil-Jac, Natural Balance, Pedigree, and more.

In one gigantic recall, an industrial chemical called *melamine* made its way into millions of dog food products via a cheap supplier from China.

> Over 3,000 dogs and cats died, and over 14,000 were sickened with life-threatening kidney disease.

? Grieving owners demanded answers. How could so many different brands get contaminated with the same thing?

The answer turned out to be that those "different" dog food brands were not so different.

Many pet foods, it turns out, are assembled on the same central assembly lines—using the same ingredients from the same sources.

In fact, a huge number of canned dog foods are made by just one company, whose name you would never recognize. This one company makes the food for many familiar brand names.

> So when one thing goes wrong at the central plant, hundreds of brands and millions of bags and cans of food can be affected.

And things do go wrong. Most dog food brands, you see, are owned by mega-corporations like Proctor & Gamble and Nestles.

We all know that giant corporations have the reputation of focusing relentlessly on their bottom line, squeezing every last cent of profit from every bag and can.

So they need cheap ingredients.

And the cheapest ingredients come from foreign countries whose food safety practices are (at best) suspect and (at worst) nil.

China is a major offender here.

> This might shock you, but pet foods are not covered by the U.S. government's food safety laws. The FDA doesn't consider pet food to be ***food,*** you see—it's ***feed,*** just like livestock feed, which also isn't protected by safety laws.

Needless to say, the manufacturers of livestock feed and pet feed are very happy with this state of affairs!

It means they can gather up the cheapest ingredients from all over the world, truck it into gigantic food processing warehouses, and shovel it together into huge, steaming vats. Yes, it's gross.

So if you feed your dog any brand that comes off these assembly lines, there's no way you can know if it's safe. And most brands come off those lines.

Of course, the argument can be made that if you feed homemade, your meat and veggies from the supermarket might also be contaminated. While that's true, there are FAR more inspections, regulations, and safety laws protecting human-grade food.

And if you feed homemade, you can increase safety even more by skipping the supermarket and buying your ingredients from local sources who are farming organically and raising grass-fed livestock and free-range poultry.

Using local sources means fewer chances for things to go wrong. And if something does, it's not going to be a deadly industrial chemical from China that's supposed to be found in plastics and countertops—not in millions of cans of dog food.

> **Summary:**
>
> When anyone else makes your dog's food, you have little or no control over its safety. This is especially true when the food is made with ***feed***-grade ingredients (rather than human-grade) and from livestock raised inhumanely (instead of pasture-raised, grass-fed, free-range livestock).

What your dog needs to eat—and why it's not provided by kibble or canned dog food

I told you there were three huge problems with kibble and canned foods. We just looked at the first problem: ***safety.***

The second problem is the ***ingredients.*** In 99 percent of kibble and canned foods, your dog is not getting what he needs (which is lots of meat) and he IS getting stuff that he doesn't need and shouldn't be eating: grains (corn, barley, rice...), legumes (peas, lentils...), starchy vegetables (potatoes...), and all manner of junk fillers.

In the Introduction to this book, I showed you this pie chart. This is what your dog should be eating:

- ✓ 70% meat or fish
- ✓ 10% organ meat (liver, kidney, spleen)
- ✓ 20% vegetables and fruits
- ✓ Bone (either attached to the meat, or ground/powdered bonemeal)

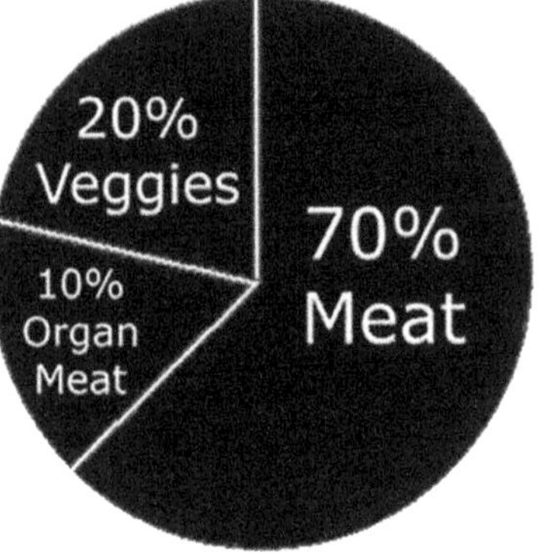

To stay healthy, your dog needs to eat **meat.**

Eighty percent of his food should be **meat.**

His digestive tract is tailor-made for eating **meat.**

The shape of his teeth, the hydrochloric acid in his stomach, his digestive enzymes, his short, straight intestinal tract… that's the digestive system of a **meat** eater.

People who claim that dogs have "evolved" to eat grains and carbohydrates know very little about how evolution works.

> The entire canine family (wolves, coyotes, wild dogs, feral dogs, domesticated dogs) has a digestive system designed to eat, digest, and absorb nutrients from **meat.**

That's why in any acceptable commercial dog food, the primary ingredient AND the next few ingredients should be **meat.**

A specified type of meat. Beef. Chicken. Turkey. Lamb. Duck. Bison. Venison. Salmon. Whitefish.

For example:

✓ Chicken, chicken liver, chicken heart…

✓ Beef, beef liver, beef heart, beef kidney…

✓ Duck, duck necks, organic kale, whole sardines…

✓ Turkey meal, chicken meal, eggs, whitefish meal…

NOT this:

✗ Chicken, tapioca, chicken fat, lentils, squash… not enough meat

✗ Turkey, oatmeal, brown rice, peas, turkey meal… not enough meat

✗ Chicken, whole grain wheat, cracked barley, whole grain sorghum… garbage

✗ Corn gluten meal, meat and bone meal, turkey meal, soybean meal… complete garbage

Why don't kibble and canned diets provide more meat??

Because meat is expensive, and expensive ingredients eat into the pet food company's profits.

Which is why virtually all dog food companies go light on the meat and heavy on everything else, such as…

Grains and cereals

Wheat, corn, soybeans, barley, rice, oats, sorghum… the makers of kibble and canned foods love to substitute these cheap sources of protein for meat.

Unfortunately, dogs are not designed to digest grains and cereals.

✗ Much of it goes right through them, resulting in lots of waste to clean up.

✗ Many dogs have loose stools or gassiness.

- ✗ Many dogs develop itchy skin, where the dog tries to soothe the itch by licking his front feet or rubbing his face against the carpet or by rubbing his body against the furniture.
- ✗ Grains and cereals are loaded with carbs. Carbs are only needed for energy. When not immediately converted to energy (and the typical family dog doesn't expend a lot of energy), carbs are stored in the body as fat, making them the leading dietary cause of overweight dogs.

On the plus side, there's only one good thing about grain: cost.

- ✓ People on a tight budget might need to substitute some grain for meat. If so, choose quinoa or oatmeal, which are higher-quality grains that are less likely to cause allergies.

Legumes

Now that more dog owners are shying away from foods with grain, companies need a *different* cheap meat substitute to sneak past you.

They've chosen legumes. Green peas, pea starch, pea protein, pea fiber, pea flour, chickpeas, soybeans, kidney beans, lentils… yes, they're high in protein, but it's not the kind of protein that your dog can easily digest or absorb

> Legumes can cause intestinal discomfort and flatulence (gassiness). Legumes are high in unnecessary carbs. And legumes are being investigated as triggering a specific type of heart disease in some dogs.

Starchy vegetables

Manufacturers have also begun throwing potatoes, sweet potatoes, and butternut squash into dog food. These starchy, high-carb foods quickly get converted into sugar, which causes your dog's blood sugar to spike, predisposing him to *insulin resistance* or diabetes. A ***little bit*** of sweet potato or squash is okay from time to time—but NOT regularly and NOT ***replacing*** meat.

Synthetic vitamins

For most kibble and canned foods, starting at about the middle of the ingredients list, you'll see a long list of synthetic vitamins and minerals, like this:

> potassium chloride, dl-methionine, l-lysine, taurine, l-carnitine, beta-carotene, vitamin A, vitamin D3, vitamin E, zinc sulfate, ferrous sulfate, niacin, folic acid, etc....

Those aren't awful ingredients, but the very fact that the manufacturer has to include so many says a lot about the quality of their food. It's much better, you see, for a dog to obtain his vitamins and minerals from the actual FOOD.

✓ When a dog food is truly *canine-appropriate* (lots of high-quality meats and fats and very few carbs), virtually all of the vitamins and minerals he needs will already be there. The company will only need to add the few that are missing.

✗ When a dog food **isn't** *canine-appropriate* (includes grains, cereals, legumes, starchy vegetables), the company has to toss in all the synthetics, which may not be as well-absorbed as the real thing.

Junk fillers and unrecognizable stuff

Beet pulp, rice flour, corn gluten meal, wheat middlings… honestly, raise your hand if you've ever thought of feeding your dog wheat middlings?

What about *animal digest?* This ingredient is defined as "material which results from chemical and/or enzymatic hydrolysis of undecomposed animal tissue."

Doesn't that sound tasty? It's a boiled concoction from the rendering plant, and the "animal tissue" can include (really gross here, sorry) roadkill and dead pets that were euthanized at the animal shelter. Yes. The FDA has found pentobarbital—the chemical used to euthanize animals—in some brands of "dog food". How many of us think that's okay?

Australian veterinarian Dr. Ian Billinghurst says: "If you look at the ingredient list on a can or a bag of pet food—with understanding—you will realize that what is being listed is a heap of rubbish. Definitely not the wholesome nutritious food you would want to feed to a valued member of your family."

> Takeaway: You want LOTS of meat in your dog's food. Meat, meat, meat. No grains, legumes, potatoes, or junk fillers.

So we've just looked at ***inappropriate*** ingredients. Now let's look at the ***quality*** of the ingredients.

Poor quality ingredients in kibble and canned foods

Dogs have been domesticated for about 15,000 years. That's amazing, isn't it? And all through those centuries, until about a hundred years ago, dogs were fed real food. Meat, fish, eggs, stews... on this diet, dogs lived to ripe old ages.

Then about a hundred years ago, in the United States, the USDA began stamping **FAILED** on farmers' wheat and corn that didn't pass inspection for the human market due to mold, rancidity, and other contaminants.

Of course, this annoyed the grain industry, who quickly discovered that the meat industry faced the same dilemma—meat that **FAILED** USDA inspection because it had spoiled or because the livestock was diseased.

The idea of mixing the rejects together and calling it "pet food" was born.

> Marketing firms spent an enormous amount of money planting this awful idea in the public's mind.

Today, kibble and canned diets are aggressively promoted by the multibillion-dollar pet food industry and the veterinary industry, both of whom have a huge financial stake in getting you to feed these concoctions.

Here is some of the clever misinformation "fed" to us by the manufacturers of dry and canned pet foods:

The manufacturers will put a photo of a juicy steak or white chicken breast on the bag.

Unfortunately, this is far from the truth.

✗ 99% of kibble and canned foods don't contain sirloin from a healthy cow raised in a lush pasture.

✗ Nor do they contain a plump chicken breast from a healthy hen who pecked happily around the barnyard.

Unless a dog food specifically says pasture-raised or grass-fed, this is the kind of feedlot the meat in your dog's food comes from. Livestock packed together like sardines in miserable pens and warehouses, eating junky grain as they await slaughter.

In USDA-inspected feedlots and slaughterhouses, the meat that seems safe and healthy passes USDA inspection and goes into the human food bin.

Whatever ***fails*** USDA inspection goes into the pet food bin.

It's called **Feed Grade** meat. The worst of it is called **4D** meat—meaning it came from livestock that were **D**iseased, **D**isabled, **D**ying, or already **D**ead when it arrived at the slaughterhouse.

> Takeaway: If you don't want your dog eating that stuff, the manufacturer would need to specify that their meat and eggs come from pasture/grass-fed beef or free-range poultry. Also that their ingredients are *USDA-approved for human consumption. Not just inspected. Approved.* I can't think of any kibble or canned foods that meet that standard.

Kibble and canned food manufacturers will assure you that they're based right here in the United States.

After the massive pet food recalls where toxins from China sickened and killed *thousands* of pets, owners have become wary of ingredients from other countries. So pet food companies have begun saying, "Manufactured in our facilities in the US."

Yes, okay, but… where are the ***actual ingredients*** from?

Most pet food companies buy their ingredients in bulk on the international open market. Which means their sources change regularly. Which means the quality of their ingredients (sometimes the actual ingredient itself) changes regularly.

Unless the company specifies WHERE each ingredient comes from, you'll never know who has supplied the stuff your dog is eating. You also won't know when that stuff has changed. The manufacturer doesn't need to report those changes.

Often the bag looks exactly the same and you would need to read it carefully and compare it to past bags to discover that the company has reduced its chicken by substituting pea protein, or reduced its protein and increased its (cheaper) fats and carbs.

So when your dog's coat suddenly starts looking scruffy, or he starts throwing up or having loose stools, your vet will ask, "Have you changed his food recently?"

"No," you say. But… how would you know?

> Takeaway: The bag or can should specify that all ingredients are ***sourced*** from the US (or another specifically-named country; for example, "wild-caught salmon from Norway" or "pasture-raised, grass-fed lamb from New Zealand").

Kibble and canned manufacturers will assure you that their food includes essential fatty acids.

Yes, but ***which*** fatty acids? Virtually all kibble and canned diets have far too much Omega 6 and not enough Omega 3.

That imbalance leads to health problems such as:

- ✗ inflammatory ailments
- ✗ allergies and itchy skin conditions
- ✗ weight gain
- ✗ mental issues such as anxiety
- ✗ behavioral issues such as excitability or reactivity

All because of a fatty acid imbalance.

> Why are the fats in kibble and canned foods so unbalanced? Well, as usual, follow the money. Omega 6 is cheaper to provide, while Omega 3 is more expensive.

Some manufacturers do add some Omega 3. It's usually listed as *fish oil.* But what kind of fish? Some fish species (such as Wild Alaskan Salmon) provide high-quality oil, while other fish species provide low-quality oil with high levels of mercury.

> Takeaway: People who feed kibble or canned food (especially kibble) should assume that the food is deficient in Omega 3s and should supplement as I recommend on page 45.

Oh, and another thing about fats... you know that pungent smell that wafts up from a freshly opened bag of kibble?

That's the smell of the greasy fat sprayed onto the hard little pebbles to tempt your dog to eat it. Otherwise, it wouldn't be recognizable to him as food. With the fat sprayed on, dogs gobble up their kibble for the same reason kids gobble up french fries.

Tastes great, yes. Nutritious, no.

Kibble and canned food manufacturers will assure you that their food is only "gently cooked."

Dog owners are catching on about high heat killing nutrients in the food. Hence a new platitude by pet food manufacturers: "Our food is *gently cooked.*"

Sounds great, but it's not true. Nearly all kibble and canned foods are subjected to extremely high temperatures... and often cooked not just once, ***but twice or even three times.***

That's devastating to the nutrients, especially the digestive enzymes your dog needs to digest his food.

> Takeaway: People who feed kibble or canned food should always add powdered *digestive enzymes* to the food to aid its digestion.

Kibble and canned manufacturers will assure you that their food is "Complete and Balanced" and formulated to meet the nutritional levels established by AAFCO.

Well, hooray!

Not.

AAFCO is the Association of American Feed Control Officials. Their expertise is in livestock which are forced to stand shoulder-to-shoulder in small pens and only live ***a few months*** before being butchered for consumption.

> Since dogs are not livestock, I don't consider AAFCO qualified to be determining the nutritional requirements of companion animals who should be living **10–18 healthy, happy years** as part of our family, running around and barking and playing.

More problems with the AAFCO label…

- ✗ A dog food gets "validated" by AAFCO simply by having the right numbers of grams and percentages. The actual ***type*** or ***quality*** of the ingredients that your dog is supposed to pull his nutrients from doesn't matter.
- ✗ AAFCO "feeding trials" are run on eight dogs for 3–6 months, after which limited bloodwork is done. That's it. Doesn't seem

to have much bearing on whether a dog could live a healthy lifetime on that food, does it?

I ignore the AAFCO label and look for this instead...

✓ Calories from protein?

✓ Calories from fat?

✓ Calories from carbohydrates

Now... you might think I'm talking about the *Guaranteed Analysis* label that gives percentages of protein, fat, etc.

GUARANTEED ANALYSIS	
Crude Protein (minimum)	24.0%
Crude Fat (minimum)	20.0%
Crude Fiber (maximum)	5.8%
Moisture (maximum)	11.0%

But I'm not talking about this Guaranteed Analysis label.

The GA label is pretty much useless, as it doesn't really tell you how much protein and fat is in the food. It just gives minimums. And the percentages are by weight, which is less useful than percentages by calories.

Unfortunately, most dog food companies hide their calorie percentages. Very rarely is it on the package or can. Sometimes it's on the company's website. But usually you need to call or email the company and ask:

> "In Brand X, what percentage of my dog's calories come from protein, what percentage from fat, and what

percentage from carbs? Not percentages by weight… percentages by calories."

What responses should you be hoping for?

Well, a dog's natural/ancestral diet (rabbits, rodents, deer, fish…) looks like this:

Calories from protein	45 to 55%
Calories from fat	35 to 45%
Calories from carbs	0 to 20%

Those are the calorie percentages I aim for with my dogs. Sadly, the vast majority of commercial dog foods don't deliver those numbers—they're too low in protein, too high in fat, and/or too high in carbs.

Kibble manufacturers will assure you that it's perfectly natural for dogs to eat hard pebbles every day.

Listen to what Dr. Richard Pitcairn, DVM, has to say about *THAT:*

"The whole concept of Insta-Meals for humans is repulsive. Most people would soon be climbing the walls in frustration, desperate for a salad or some fruit—anything whole and fresh, or just different. Perhaps the thought of eating kibbles for the rest of your own life helps make the point that pets forced to do so are being shortchanged. All of us—humans and animals—should have fresh, wholesome, unprocessed food in our daily diet."

Dry kibble is the exact opposite of what a dog is supposed to eat.

✗ Dry food is hard on your dog's teeth.

No, it doesn't clean his teeth. Just the opposite. Tiny shards of dry food can wedge between the teeth and under the gum line.

Those stuck bits become convenient landing spots for bacteria to build up on.

- ✗ Dry food is hard on your dog's digestive tract.
  A dog's natural diet is packed with moisture (INSIDE the food) which helps bathe his intestines, keeping them slippery and healthy. And no, unfortunately, pouring water on the dry food doesn't help much.
- ✗ Dry food is hard on your dog's kidneys and bladder.
- ✗ Dogs who eat dry food are in a chronic state of low dehydration, which increases the risk of forming urinary stones. Bladder stones are especially dangerous in male dogs because the stones can get stuck and cause life-threatening blockages.

> Dogs were born to eat one thing: real food with lots of natural, built-in moisture that aids in healthy digestion and elimination.

Why are kibble and canned foods so common?

If kibble and canned foods aren't very good, why are they so common?

1. Sophisticated marketing.
2. People's love of convenience.
3. Many dry and wet foods are inexpensive.

> Kibble and canned dog foods are not made for dogs. They're made for dog owners who want convenience and lower price, even at the expense of proper nutrition for the dog.

Two shocking reasons veterinarians recommend kibble and canned dog food

No doubt about it, veterinarians are highly skilled at emergency care, diagnostic testing, and surgery, and I'm very grateful for that. They save dogs' lives.

But giving feeding advice? No. This might come as a shocker, but students in veterinary school receive very little education in nutrition. And what they do receive is largely provided (or sponsored) by… pet food companies.

Conflict of interest, much?

Take the Hill's Company, for example, which makes *Science Diet*. The Hill's Company was the first to spot the lucrative potential of getting their product into vet's offices. They got their foot in the door and kept it there through clever marketing.

To get the medical folks on board, pet food companies have:

- ✗ developed sophisticated marketing programs of sponsorships, discounts, and freebies.

- ✗ nurtured relationships and alliances with influential medical people in high places—"You scratch my back, I'll scratch yours."
- ✗ arranged for "scientific studies" to be performed by people already aligned with the pet food companies. "This just in… the latest study performed by the *National Completely Objective Unbiased Scientific Nutrition Council* shows that kibble and canned diets are the perfect food for dogs of all ages." Surprise!
- ✗ established "nutritionist" classes for veterinary assistants, complete with an impressive certificate to hang on the wall of the vet's waiting room. "Wow, Vet Tech Lisa is a Certified Nutritionist who says this dog food the vet is selling would be good for my puppy." Surprise!

> We all know that the pharmaceutical companies do the same things with doctors. The cigarette companies do it. The soda companies. All massive conglomerations do it.

Pet food is a multibillion-dollar industry dominated by gigantic corporations whose only interest is the bottom line of themselves and their stockholders. Whipping the veterinary industry into line has been child's play to them.

The result is that most vets follow the party line of the pet food companies that trained them.

In *The Whole(istic) Truth About Pet Food* (caberfeidh.com/Truth.htm), Christie Keith says:

> "We [humans] are told that processed foods aren't good for us, and advised to eat whole fresh foods and vary our diets in order to stay healthy. Conversely, we are told to NEVER feed whole fresh foods to our pets, to never vary their diets, and not to upset the careful balance of the

> processed diet they are supposed to eat every day of their lives. Does this make sense? Only to the pet food manufacturers. To them, it makes sense and it makes money. That is why pet food manufacturers finance veterinarian training programs and subsidize vet school clinics. Some vets only know what the kibble makers tell them, and pass that on to their clients: eat the processed diet."

So the first reason vets carry and recommend kibble and canned foods is… the pet food companies have indoctrinated them well.

The second reason is… profits.

According to veterinarian Dr. Ian Billinghurst:

> "The sad truth is that prepared pet foods help provide patients for vets. For the vet in practice, there is an enormous profit to be made from selling a product which is endorsed wholeheartedly by the profession, and which at the same time will actively promote (in a non-obvious way) ill health in our patients. This is a win-win situation for us. We get applauded by our clients and peers for selling the stuff. We bank the profits. We enjoy the kickbacks from the manufacturers for doing so, and best of all, we are quietly brewing up our next crop of patients. It's a perfect system."

Fortunately, an increasing number of veterinarians have been breaking free of the grip of the kibble and canned manufacturers.

These vets are now enthusiastic supporters of feeding dogs what they were born to eat: real food, either raw or cooked. Dogs have been fed this way for 15,000 years. They've only been fed dry kibble and canned junk for a hundred or so years.

Think about that.

Feeding real, fresh, whole food will make a huge difference in your dog's future health. Veterinarian Dr. Martin Goldstein, DVM, says...

"You can boost your pet's health profoundly by making one simple decision. All you have to do is change his diet... to something you may never have imagined giving him—real food."

My Honest Advice

Your dog's daily diet should not be kibble or canned dog food.

For his daily diet, you should feed real food *(page 23)*. You can make it yourself *(page 33)* or a company can make it and deliver it to you *(page 54)* or you can buy a frozen or freeze-dried dog food *(page 50)* which you can feed raw or lightly cooked.

Kibble or canned is okay for an occasional meal.

You can certainly feed a kibble or canned meal now and then!

The convenience is great on a day when your schedule is tight, or when you don't feel well, or when you're traveling with your dog.

There are only a handful of such kibble and canned dog foods I recommend for this occasional use. See my website (yourpurebred puppy.com/health/) for my current recommendations.

> Important… NONE of the brands on my list meets all (or even most) of the criteria on my personal list of what makes a dog food good. For all the reasons I explain in that article, there are no kibble or canned foods that I consider good enough for daily use.

Introducing your dog to real food

There have been times when I've taken in a foster pup with no knowledge of his previous diet. Then all I can do is serve him the same food as my other dogs.

But whenever possible, it's best to gradually phase in a new diet.

For example, when you bring your pup home, keep feeding what he is used to—yes, even if it's the cheapest supermarket kibble on Earth. Give him a couple of days to settle into your home while he eats his familiar food. Sometimes the shock of a new environment can cause digestive upsets, so you don't want to make things more upsetting by adding a new food.

Once he has settled in, begin substituting a very small amount (maybe 10 percent) of the new food for the old food. Do this over a couple of weeks until he is completely switched over to the new food.

"Help! My dog won't eat real food!"

Yes, this sometimes happens. Some dogs are stuck in a rut of processed foods—almost addicted to them, like kids who refuse to eat anything without sugar in it.

If you've introduced the new food slowly, mixing it with his familiar kibble or canned, yet your dog refuses to touch it, you need to take a firmer stance.

1. Put the dish of food on the floor, or in his crate with him.
2. If he doesn't eat within 10 minutes, put it in the fridge.
3. When it's time for his next meal, take it out of the fridge. Let it sit for a few minutes until it's room temperature, stir it up, and put it down again.
4. If he still doesn't eat it, throw it out. Prepare the exact same food for his next meal.

Seriously, that's how you do it.

When he's hungry enough and realizes that you're not going to offer anything different, he'll eventually eat it.

In *The Nature of Animal Healing,* Dr. Martin Goldstein, DVM, reassures us:

"My own strong belief is that unless a pet is quite old or suffering from a degenerative disease like cancer, fasting is a natural way for him to clean out his system, regain his health, and marshal new energy—along with an appetite. The time he goes without food doesn't do him harm."

Just make sure your dog is drinking during this time.

If he's a toy breed, keep his blood sugar up! Buy a tube of a supplement called *Nutrical* from the pet store. Dab a tiny fingerful of it on the roof of his mouth several times a day to make sure he has enough calories while he's on his stubborn hunger strike.

> Of course, use common sense—make sure your dog isn't truly ill.

Don't allow free-feeding

Free-feeding means leaving a bowl of kibble continuously available for your pup to nibble at whenever he wants.

Here are 5 reasons free-feeding is not a good idea for any puppy or adult dog:

1. Free-feeding makes your dog's digestive cycle unpredictable, which means you don't know when he will need to go to the bathroom.
2. Your dog's appetite is a good barometer of his health, and it's easier to keep tabs on appetite when you're offering scheduled meals and watching him eat.
3. Free-feeding can create picky eaters who feel entitled to food rather than appreciative of being given food.
4. If you have more than one dog, free-feeding invites bullying and can create nasty food-guarding issues.
5. Finally, scheduled feeding is a prime opportunity to demonstrate that you are in charge of the food. You make the food appear, you require your pup to be calm and polite before you give it to him, you allow a certain amount of time for eating, then you pick up the bowl.

Scheduled, controlled feeding reinforces a subtle, psy logically-healthy, leader-follower relationship. Whereas free-feeding gives your pup the impression that food is just magically available.

Large-breed puppies: special concerns

A large-breed puppy is one who will weigh more than 70 pounds as an adult.

Large-breed pups are different from smaller-breed pups in that you need to be much more careful with their rate of growth. You want large breeds to grow very s-l-o-w-l-y. Why?

> Because a large breed pup *has so much bone* that needs to grow and so much weight that needs to be supported by that bone. Slow, steady growth is necessary. If a large-breed pup puts on weight too quickly and his skeleton is too immature to provide proper support, the result is microscopic tearing of skeletal tissue and malformed bones and joints. That can lead to hip dysplasia, elbow dysplasia, and osteochondritis.

Now, those ailments also have a strong genetic (inherited) component. But they can be triggered or worsened by improper feeding and/or lifestyle factors such as:

- ✗ taking a puppy ***jogging*** with you
- ✗ allowing a pup to ***jump*** too much or too high
- ✗ allowing a puppy to run around on a ***slippery*** floor
- ✗ allowing a puppy to ***dash up or down stairs***

In truth, NO puppy should be allowed to do those things. But they're doubly dangerous for large-breed puppies.

Don't make these two mistakes feeding a large-breed puppy:

Don't overfeed. Many large-breed puppies are dangerously heavy for their age. A roly-poly, six-month-old Lab might look adorable, and a muscular, thirteen-month-old Rottweiler might look impressive... but you're setting them both up for serious health problems.

> Large-breed pups should be kept ***SLIM*** for their first 18–24 months. Adolescents should look tall and gangly.

Don't supplement with extra calcium. In the past, owners were often told to supplement with calcium tablets because a large pup needed lots of calcium for strong bones.

Well, he does need calcium, but not nearly as much as people thought! *Too much calcium is just as bad as too little.* My homemade recipe specifies the amount of calcium I use to balance the phosphorus in the meat. Add nothing more than that.

> A commercial food suitable for a large-breed pup should contain 1.2 to 1.5% calcium ***and*** less phosphorus than calcium. How much less? The calcium-to-phosphorus ratio should be from 1:1 (same amount of calcium as phosphorus) up to 1.4 to 1

> Are you wondering about protein? You might have read on some internet sites that too much protein is bad for large-breed puppies. That's a myth. ***All healthy canines, large and small, young and old, thrive on high protein.*** Ironically, it's LOW protein that causes so many health issues in dogs today, not high protein.

Does your dog need to lose weight?

Dogs should be kept slim and trim!

Even a little bit of extra weight puts major stresses on your dog's heart, lungs, and joints. These dogs become more vulnerable to arthritis, bronchitis, pancreatitis, diabetes, heart disease, and disk problems.

> One solid way to avoid health problems and lengthen your dog's life is to work really hard at keeping him on the slender side!

How to tell whether your dog is in good condition

Look at his profile

Crouch down to your dog's level and look at him from the side—his profile. His belly should be taut, held firmly up against his body.

Your dog's belly shouldn't sag down toward the same level as his chest and ribs.

Older dogs tend to be saggier in the belly, but you want to minimize this. Extra weight is very bad for aging organs and joints.

Look down on his back

Stand close beside your dog and look down at his torso. You should see sort of an hourglass shape: wide-ish across his ribs, narrower across his waist (called the loin), and wide-ish again across his hindquarters. With long-haired dogs, you'll need to feel with your hands.

> What you don't want is a sausage shape that doesn't vary much in width.

Feel his ribs

Put your hands on your dog's rib cage on each side of his body. You should be able to feel his ribs with your fingers without needing to push hard.

No doubt about it… this little dog is fat, which is dangerous for his short- and long-term health.

But you shouldn't be able to SEE his ribs sticking out—unless your dog is a sighthound (such as a Greyhound). Sighthounds have an extremely streamlined build with more prominent ribs.

How to help your dog lose weight

Stop feeding all snacks, tidbits, cookies, and biscuits. Stop feeding kibble or canned food, especially those marketed as "weight loss" diets. The ingredients in most of those diets are atrocious.

Instead, feed real food, but…

- ✓ Eliminate all grains (rice, pasta, bread, etc.), legumes, fruits, milk and cheese, and high-calorie vegetables like potatoes, sweet potatoes, peas, and carrots.

- ✓ Basically you want to feed only meat/fish (plus bone meal) and lots of low-calorie veggies such as summer squash, zucchini, celery, asparagus, and cauliflower.
- ✓ Increase exercise.
- ✓ If the above tips don't bring your dog's weight down, cut back the amount of food by about 10 percent.

Does your dog have any of these health issues?

- heart disease
- liver disease
- kidney disease
- bladder stones
- colitis
- chronic pancreatitis
- inflammatory bowel disease
- diabetes

If so, don't despair. You can still feed real food—in fact, if your dog is currently eating a prescription food for these health problems, I would definitely want to get him off that. The ingredients in prescription diets are really poor.

So yes, you can feed real food, but… each of the ailments in that list upsets your dog's organ function and overall metabolism, so you'll need to adjust the ingredients and proportions in order to compensate.

It would take up too much space to cover disease-specific diets in this book, but there are good recipes online. For example, do a Google search for: homemade dog food heart disease

Chapter 2

The 2nd Thing You Must Do Right: Minimize Vaccinations

Only a few years ago, it was considered mandatory to bring your dog to the vet every year for his shots.

Fortunately, ***times have changed.***

Listen to what Dr. Christina Chambreau, DVM, has to say about yearly vaccinations:

> "Would you rebel if your doctor told you to have measles, mumps, and rubella shots every year of your life until you died, instead of only a few doses as a child?"

Those core vaccinations protected you for your lifetime. You don't need yearly revaccinations for them.

And veterinary immunological researchers now tell us:

> Neither do dogs and cats.

How a vaccine works

Most people have a completely wrong idea of what a vaccine does. They think a vaccine is some powerful substance that, once injected, hangs around your dog's bloodstream until a disease shows up… and then attacks and wipes out that disease.

- **NO.** A vaccine ***does not attack*** a disease.

- A vaccine **IS** a disease.

1. A *vaccine is a weakened version of an actual disease* such as distemper or parvovirus.
2. When your dog is injected with this weakened disease, his own immune system (if it is healthy) is supposed to react by forming *antibodies* against that disease.
3. The injected vaccine is then done. It has no more role to play. It doesn't "protect" your dog from anything.
4. ***The antibodies created by your dog's own immune system*** are what protect him in case he comes in contact with the real disease. Those antibodies *created by his own immune system* are what wipe out the disease.

Please read those four points again. They're important in understanding why dogs don't need yearly shots.

> A vaccine is simply a one-time catalyst that encourages your dog's immune system to produce ***antibodies.*** Or put another way, vaccines "trick" your dog's immune system into producing antibodies. Then the vaccine is done.

It is your dog's own immune system that protects him against disease. The vaccine's job is simply to show the immune system *what a specific disease looks like* so the immune system can recreate the appropriate antibodies to defeat it, if it ever shows up for real.

The question then becomes:

How many vaccinations are needed...

to "imprint" the memory of a virus like distemper or parvo on your dog's immune system so it will be able to produce antibodies if that virus ever shows up for real?

The OLD answer was: One vaccination every year. The "annual booster shot."

> It turns out that answer was wrong. Which isn't surprising, because it was never based on scientific evidence or studies.

Several decades ago, the vaccine manufacturers themselves (talk about conflict of interest...) chose *one year* as a nice round number. The USDA printed that recommendation on the vaccine label. The vets showed the label to their clients as proof. And the clients (us) nodded "Okay" and wrote the check for our dog's "necessary annual booster." Annual shots became a custom.

Now listen to what *Kirk's Current Veterinary Therapy* (the veterinarians' bible) has to say about yearly vaccinations:

> "A practice that was started many years ago that lacks scientific validity or verification is annual revaccinations. Almost without exception there is no immunologic requirement for annual revaccination. Immunity to viruses persists for years or for the life of the animal."

That was written by Dr. Tom Phillips, DVM, PhD, and Dr. Ronald Schultz, PhD, immunologist and professor/chairman of the Department of Pathobiological Sciences, School of Veterinary Medicine, University of Wisconsin.

And here's what it means…

> The immune system "has a memory."

Yes, our immune system contains memory calls. Once these memory cells see what a particular virus looks like, they remember how to produce antibodies against that virus, probably for the dog's entire lifetime.

Annual reminders are not needed.

The same article in *Kirk's Current Veterinary Therapy* goes on to say:

> "Furthermore, revaccination fails to stimulate a secondary response as a result of interference by existing antibodies."

In plain English, that means…

> Booster shots aren't much use when (1) your dog already has antibodies and (2) when your dog's immune system memory cells have learned how to form those antibodies.

Re-vaccinating an already-immune dog provides no additional immunity.

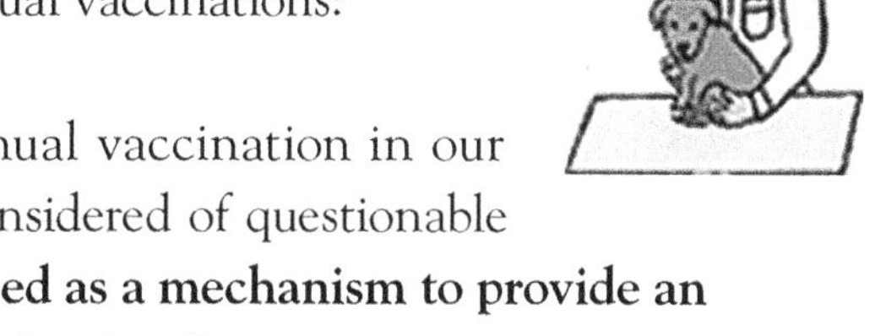

Dr. Phillips and Dr. Schultz end their article with this bombshell—the real reason why so many vets keep insisting that dogs need annual vaccinations:

> "The practice of annual vaccination in our opinion should be considered of questionable efficacy **unless it is used as a mechanism to provide an annual physical examination.**"

"Unless it is used as a mechanism to provide an annual physical examination" is exactly what veterinarians are doing when they insist, against all the scientific evidence, that your dog "needs" annual booster shots.

They want you to come in. They need you to come in. It's estimated that over 60% of vet visits are for vaccinations (the vast majority of which are unnecessary). Vets charge $30 to $50 for the office visit and $60 to $80 for vaccines that cost them a dollar each in bulk.

> Vaccinations account for such a major chunk of a vet's income that it's understandable why they fiercely resist when you tell them your dog isn't getting any more annual booster shots. I do feel for their predicament, but they need to find some other way to generate income other than unnecessary vaccinations.

University of California-Davis veterinary researcher and professor Neils Pedersen is calling on veterinarians to change their unwise vaccination practices. Here's what he wrote in the *American Animal Hospital Association journal:*

> "Current vaccine practices are medically unsound. It is time to question the wisdom of annual booster, multivalent

> products (combination vaccines, the most common being DHLPP for dogs), and unnecessary vaccines. Doing so will return companion animals' immunization to its status as a medical and not an economical procedure."

Now, certainly you should bring your dog in every year for his heartworm test if you live in a high-risk heartworm area. And if your dog is older, a yearly exam, heart check, and bloodwork are very important. In fact, I bring older dogs in every six months.

But vets must stop using the pretext that "yearly shots are necessary" simply to lure us into their offices. Veterinary immunologists have clearly shown that "yearly shots are ***not*** necessary." And your vet knows that.

Annual booster shots–what's the harm?

So now you might be thinking…

"Well, even if yearly shots aren't ***necessary,*** it's not like they do any harm, right?"

On the contrary.

Vaccines are not harmless. Remember, a vaccine is a weakened form of a disease. Repeatedly pumping multiple diseases into your dog can overwhelm and confuse his immune system.

Dr. Richard Pitcairn, DVM, (PhD in immunology), explains that a vaccine may be viewed by your dog's immune system as some sort of bizarre invader.

> "Injecting bacteria and viruses directly into tissues, and within minutes, into the blood system, is highly unnatural. The human or animal body evolved over millennia to watch for and react to organisms that

were entering by the nose, mouth, and intestinal tract. The primary defenses are there, and the process of recognizing invaders and alerting the immune system to their presence is elaborate and well understood. Vaccine injections bypass all of this and shock the immune system by the sudden presence in the blood for which there was no warning. To make it even more unnatural, several organisms are mixed together in vaccines, a condition simply not seen in natural infections. It is no surprise that the immune system gets confused and makes makes mistakes." (drpitcairn.com/books/vaccinations/)

One of the most serious mistakes made by a confused immune system is to suddenly become hyperreactive and begin attacking everything in sight within the dog's body.

That's what we call *autoimmune disease,* where the dog's own immune system suddenly goes on a rampage and destroys its own red blood cells, bone marrow cells, skin and connective tissue cells, thyroid cells, digestive tract cells…

…and the whole tragic process can be triggered by the immune system being overwhelmed and confused by too many vaccines.

Listen to what Dr. Charles Loops, DVM, has to say about the dangers of excessive vaccinations:

"The first thing that must change is the myth that vaccines are harmless. Veterinarians and animal guardians have to realize that they are not protecting animals from disease by annual vaccinations, but in fact are destroying the health and immune systems of these same animals they love and care for."

Dr. Christina Chambreau, DVM, agrees:

"Routine vaccinations are probably the worst thing that we do for our animals. Veterinary immunologists tell us that vaccines need only be given once or twice in an animal's life. First, there is no need for annual vaccinations, and second, they definitely cause chronic disease."

Dr. Roger DeHaan, DVM, has this to say:

"It has become increasingly clear that some vaccines are ineffectual or unnecessary [and] that some vaccines are dangerous, even causing symptoms of the disease they are supposed to prevent." *(The Veterinarians' Guide To Natural Remedies For Dogs)*

> You might breathe a sigh of relief when your dog seems to "breeze through" a vaccination with no immediate reaction. In reality, you have no idea what is going inside him. The real problems may surface in a few months.

Adverse reactions to vaccines include:

✗ **immediate** reactions: occur in the first 2 to 48 hours and include pain, swelling, itchy hives, and (rarely) breathing difficulties that can be life-threatening

✗ **delayed** reactions: occur 10–45 days later and include inflammatory joint stiffness or seizures

✗ **long-term** effects: include permanent damage to the immune system resulting in autoimmune diseases, increased susceptibility to allergies and infections, even neurological changes (fearfulness, anxiety, aggression)

A study of more than 2,000 cats and dogs in the UK showed a 1-in-10 risk of adverse reactions from vaccines. The risk is much higher in smaller dogs than in larger dogs.

Too many vaccines at one time

Along with the unnecessary ***repetition*** of vaccinations, many vets administer an unnecessary ***number of diseases*** given all at once.

Most vets will try to administer 5 or more vaccines in one injection:

- distemper
- parvovirus
- canine hepatitis/adenovirus
- parainfluenza
- leptospirosis

Many vets will also recommend additional injections for:

- coronavirus
- bordetella (kennel cough)
- influenza (flu)
- Lyme
- rabies

Multi-vaccines are bad because the risk of side effects increases (according to a Purdue study) by 12 to 27 percent with each additional vaccine. So does the risk of immune system overload and overreaction, which can result in autoimmune diseases.

Multi-vaccines are also bad because so many of them are ineffective or protect against diseases that your dog doesn't need protecting against.

Which vaccines are really needed?

Let's skim through the ten diseases that your dog can be vaccinated against. It probably won't surprise you to learn that the vast majority of dogs needs only three of them: distemper, parvovirus, and rabies.

Distemper

✓ Needed (but not every year)

Parvovirus

✓ Needed (but not every year)

Canine Adenovirus (CAV-1 and CAV-2)

✗ According to the vets I've referenced in this chapter, this vaccine is not needed by the vast majority of dogs. It's okay to give to adult dogs, but in puppies it causes immuno-suppression for ten days—not a healthy thing to do to vulnerable puppies!

Leptospirosis

✗ According to the vets I've referenced in this chapter, this vaccine is not needed by the vast majority of dogs.

The lepto vaccine has more immediate and acute side effects reported than all other canine vaccines combined. And the more often it's given, the more likely it is to cause a serious reaction. The lepto vaccine is especially dangerous to small dogs. I never give lepto to my dogs.

Parainfluenza

✗ According to the vets I've referenced in this chapter, this vaccine is not needed by the vast majority of dogs.

Coronavirus

✗ According to the vets I've referenced in this chapter, this vaccine is not needed by the vast majority of dogs.

Kennel cough (bordetella)

✗ According to the vets I've referenced in this chapter, this vaccine is not needed by the vast majority of dogs.

There are many different strains of kennel cough and this vaccine is only effective (or semi-effective) against a few of those strains. Worse, a significant number of dogs given this vaccine end up sneezing and hacking for days.

Influenza (flu)

According to the vets I've referenced in this chapter, this vaccine is not needed by the vast majority of dogs. It's a new product rushed onto the market and it doesn't even prevent canine flu, but only lessens the symptoms of it.

IF my dog had a weak respiratory system (say, a dog with chronic bronchitis or collapsing trachea, or a flat-faced dog like a Pug, Pekingese, or Bulldog) and ***IF*** that dog spent a significant time around lots of other dogs, I might consider giving this vaccine. Otherwise, definitely not.

Lyme disease

✗ According to the vets I've referenced in this chapter, this vaccine is not needed by the vast majority of dogs.

Lyme is an inflammatory bacterial disease transmitted by ticks. It's serious in humans, but though it can cause debilitating illness in some dogs, most dogs experience only a brief acute episode. Unfortunately, ***the vaccine itself*** can cause inflammatory arthritis.

> Hunters who live in brushy areas laden with Lyme-carrying ticks might feel better if their hunting dogs were vaccinated against it. Since that's not me, I don't vaccinate against Lyme.

I'll let Dr. Martin Goldstein, DVM, sum this up:

"No to the Lyme vaccine for dogs, to canine hepatitis and bordetella, parainfluenza and corona, all of which either don't work or aren't needed, and may cause harm.

A big no to the existing leptospirosis bacterin, which has caused more allergic reactions than any other single ingredient in the standard canine DHLPP combo." *(The Nature of Animal Healing)*

Rabies vaccination

Now we come to the vaccine that's probably responsible for ***more long-term health problems*** than any other vaccine.

According to numerous vets and immunologists, the rabies vaccine has been pretty clearly connected to the development of:

- ✗ autoimmune diseases
- ✗ an increase in inflammatory chemicals in the body, leading to chronic infections, allergies, and inflammatory ailments
- ✗ an increase in inflammatory chemicals in the brain, leading to seizure disorders or sudden onset of aggressive, anxious, destructive, or obsessive behaviors

Rabies is the only vaccination regulated by state and local laws. And unfortunately, most municipalities are ignoring the scientific research that shows a single rabies vaccine is good for ***at least 5 to 7 years*** and probably longer.

> Yet all 50 states and most local municipalities still insist that you vaccinate your dog against rabies every 3 years. Some truly backward municipalities insist on EVERY year.

There is no scientific basis for this whatsoever. These communities are acting based on emotional fears ("Eeek! Rabies!") rather than immunological truths. In so doing, they're putting the health and lifespan of our dogs at risk, for no benefit.

> So the choice is whether to vaccinate your dog according to the schedule mandated by law or based on the scientific research.

Of course, I cannot advise anyone to break the law.

Some practical considerations are:

- ✗ You can't take your dog to a boarding kennel, doggy daycare, or obedience class without a "current" (whatever that is in your area) rabies certificate.
- ✗ In some areas, veterinarians won't treat your dog without a "current" rabies certificate. You may not even be able to obtain a dog license.
- ✗ If your dog bites someone and doesn't have a "current" rabies certificate, he must be quarantined for 10 days, to be sure he doesn't have the disease. He may be allowed to stay at home during this period or he may be confiscated and kept at a private facility. You will be subject to a misdemeanor charge and/or monetary fine. The person he bit may be worried enough to undergo preventive medical treatment for rabies, after which you may be sued for medical expenses and pain and suffering.
- ✗ If your dog ***has never had*** ANY rabies vaccination and is bitten or scratched by a rabid animal (usually a bat, skunk, fox, raccoon, coyote, or another dog or cat), your dog will die.

If you decide to follow the rabies law in your area:

- Give the rabies vaccination at late as possible. If the law says 6 months old or 12 months old, don't give it any earlier.
- Don't give the rabies vaccine within a month of any other vaccine. You want to minimize the overload.
- Give the rabies vaccine ONLY when your dog is healthy and unstressed. Don't give it immediately before or after (or during) an illness, a long trip, boarding, neutering, dental cleaning, etc.
- If your dog has ever had a bad reaction to the rabies vaccine, or if he has any serious health issues, ask your vet to give you a medical exemption if one is allowed by your state and local municipality.
- If allowed by your local laws, make sure the vet gives your dog the vaccine labeled *3-years.* Then he'll be able to issue you a rabies certificate that says it's good for *3 years.*

> Ready for some dark humor? The *"3-year"* vaccine and the *"1-year"* vaccine are the SAME vaccine. Only the label is different. It's a farce, especially since ***both*** vaccines are good for at least 5 to 7 years and probably for life.

Vaccination schedule for puppies

Aside from rabies, we just talked about the two necessary vaccines: distemper and parvovirus. ***WHEN*** should those two vaccines be given?

Don't overload puppies

Many veterinarians, ignoring all the scientific and immunological research, will try to tell you that your puppy:

- ✗ "needs" his first shots at 6 or 8 weeks old
- ✗ "needs" the shots repeated four or five times between 6 wks and 18 wks old, then another booster at 12 months...etc.
- ✗ "needs" shots against distemper, hepatitis/adenovirus, leptospirosis, parainfluenza, and parvovirus—all bundled into one shot that's often called the DHLPP or DA2LPP
- ✗ "needs" additional shots against coronavirus, bordetella (kennel cough), influenza (flu), and/or Lyme disease

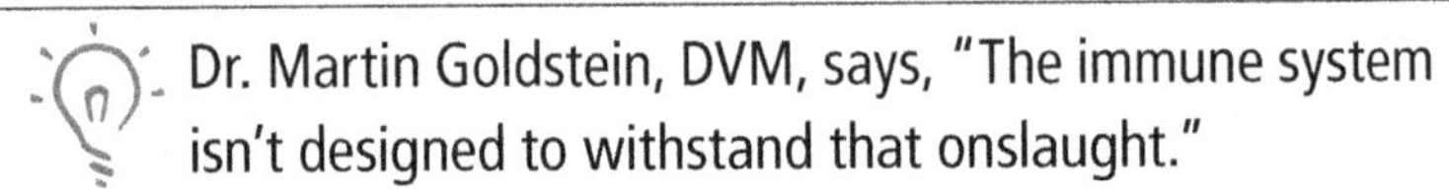
Dr. Martin Goldstein, DVM, says, "The immune system isn't designed to withstand that onslaught."

One dose that works

According to *Vaccines and Vaccinations: Issue for the 21st Century*, written by Dr. Richard Ford, DVM, and Dr. Ronald Schultz, PhD, and published in *Kirk's Current Veterinary Therapy:*

> "A *single immunizing dose* of a modified, live virus vaccine—*in other words, one vaccine that works*—will form long-term, probably lifetime immunity to parvo and distemper."

One vaccine that works.

What do these immunology experts mean by that? They mean that a vaccination only needs to be repeated ***if the pup doesn't respond to the first one.*** In other words, if his immune system doesn't react to the first vaccine by forming antibodies, he needs another dose.

> Why might his immune system not respond? Well, he might have a *defective immune system*. But more commonly, the pup was given a vaccination at such a young age (like 6 or 8 weeks old) that his *maternal antibodies* interfered with it.

Let me explain.

Puppies get protective antibodies from their mother's milk, the rich colostrum milk she produces for the first 36 hours after birth. This natural protection floats around in the pup's bloodstream for many weeks, guarding him against viruses.

If you administer a vaccine when a pup's maternal antibodies are active, those antibodies will neutralize the vaccine (remember, a vaccine is simply a weakened form of a virus). We should be happy about that, because when maternal antibodies attack a vaccine, they've done their job!

But it would seem to make more sense not to vaccinate a puppy until **AFTER** his maternal antibodies have worn off, right? Which is typically by 14–16 weeks old.

It would seem to make sense, but...

No, we shouldn't wait.

> At 10 to 14 weeks old, puppies are most vulnerable to infectious diseases because they have immature immune systems and their only protection is fading away.

That's why it's wise to step in at about 10–11 weeks old and give one dose of distemper and parvo.

Now, maternal antibodies fade away at different rates in different pups, so we can't know (for any given pup) whether his maternal antibodies will be low enough at 10–11 weeks to allow his immune system to respond.

> According to immunologist Dr. Ron Schultz, DVM, PhD, research shows that more than 75% of pups respond to a vaccine at 10–11 weeks. That means their maternal antibodies were low enough that their immune system could make its own antibodies and form the memory imprint that will protect him for his lifetime.

For the rest of the pups, the vaccine will be "wasted" because it gets neutralized by their maternal antibodies before the pup's own immune system has a chance to make antibodies. Which means that particular vaccination wasn't "immunizing" for that pup.

Do you see the difference between *vaccinated* and *immunized?* *Vaccinating* is just injecting the virus, while *immunizing* can only be done by the pup's own immune system if it's healthy enough and not impeded by maternal antibodies.

So to be sure the rest of those pups have a chance to get immunized, we need to give a second dose a few weeks later, when hopefully their maternal antibodies will be gone.

The risky "series" of puppy shots

Now you understand why vets want to give puppies a ***series*** of vaccinations—so that eventually ***one*** of those shots will be given after the maternal antibodies have worn off sufficiently that the vaccine will "take" by jump-starting the puppy's immune system into forming antibodies for life.

The idea is a good one. But...

There's a big problem with repeating vaccinations. And by now, I think you know what that problem is...

> Vaccines are not harmless sugar water that can be pumped into a pup repeatedly with no short-term side effects or no long-term negative consequences.

So if a vet recommends something like "6 weeks, 9 weeks, 12 weeks, 15 weeks, and 18 weeks" (usually with four or five or six vaccines in each injection)... that vet's vaccination protocol is outdated and risky and I would run for the hills, clutching my beloved puppy against my chest.

A more sensible "series" of puppy shots

- ✓ First dose of distemper/parvo at 10–11 weeks old. This will immunize the pups whose maternal antibodies have decreased enough to allow their immune systems to respond properly.

- ✓ Second dose of distemper/parvo three or four weeks later (14–15 weeks old). This dose should immunize the rest of the pups. *Studies show that over 95 percent of pups will have lifelong immunity after this dose.*

This puppy vaccination protocol is recommended by numerous veterinarians today, including world-renowned vets such as Dr. Jean Dodds, DVM, and Dr. Karen Becker, DVM.

Should distemper and parvo be in the same shot... or different shots?

Some truly enlightened vets are so concerned about vaccination side effects that they prefer to give distemper and parvovirus separately, rather than combined in one injection. That's fine.

Here's a good schedule for that protocol:

- 10 wks: parvovirus (I would give parvo first because it's more common than distemper)
- 12 wks: distemper
- 14 wks: parvo again
- 16 wks: distemper again

The only issue with that protocol is that most vets don't keep *monovalent* (single-disease) vaccines in their clinic. If your vet does have them or doesn't mind ordering them, great. Or if he'll let you order them yourself, to be shipped directly to his clinic, great. Or you might decide to buy and give the vaccine yourself. It's easy to give a vaccination; there are quick tutorials on YouTube.

You can buy individual doses of *NeoVac D* (distemper) and *NeoPar* (parvo) from revivalanimal.com

> Remember to order two of each. Total should be around forty dollars, including two-day shipping in a special cold package.

If your vet doesn't even have a combined distemper/parvo shot

Along with not stocking monovalent (one-disease) vaccines, many vets don't even stock *bivalent* (two-disease) vaccines.

This is a serious problem in the veterinary industry. Some vets are so reluctant to change their over-vaccination practices that they stock their clinic only with the *multivalent* (many diseases bundled together) vaccines.

I would absolutely not accept that option.

Your vet can order a distemper/parvo (nothing else) vaccine such as *Merck Nobivac DPv*. If he isn't willing to do that, I recommend that you either order the single-disease vaccines (see the previous page) and administer them yourself, or else find another vet.

Testing your pup's immunity after vaccination: titer tests

After a pup has received his two puppy shots, there's an easy way to check whether his immune system has responded, or not.

The Titer Test

The titer *(TY-ter)* test is a simple blood test that looks for antibodies in the pup's blood. You do a titer test for distemper, and a titer for parvo, looking for antibodies against those viruses.

Since a vaccine is a weak form of a virus, exposure to that virus should have primed your pup's immune system to produce antibodies. Those antibodies will be picked up by the titer test.

To give the immune system ample time to respond (and to give his maternal antibodies ample time to disappear), you should do a titer test 3 or 4 weeks after the last puppy shot.

So if the last vaccination was done at 14–15 weeks old, do the titer tests at 18 weeks or older.

What does a positive titer test mean?

The titer test will be positive if it finds the presence of any antibodies. ANY number of antibodies in a pup older than 16 weeks proves the pup's immune system responded properly. You can consider him immunized against that disease.

Dr. Karen Becker, DVM, says:

"Three to four weeks later, titer. If there's antibody present in the titer test, we know the baby's immune system has responded to the vaccine. This means we've not only vaccinated, but we've actually immunized as well."

Studies show that over 95% of pups will be immunized by a vaccination at 14–15 weeks.

Don't be concerned about the number of antibodies

Some titer tests just say *Positive* (antibodies present) or *Negative* (no antibodies present). Other tests give numbers. The problem with numbers is that it's easy to get hung up on them, fretting about whether the number is "high enough." The labs themselves don't help here, often warning you about a "low" titer.

Immunology experts such as Dr. Ronald Schultz, DVM, PhD, emphasize that the numbers don't mean anything. ANY measurable titer means the immune system responded properly.

I wouldn't let a vet, or the lab that does the titer test, talk me into re-vaccinating a puppy who has produced antibodies in response to a vaccination. I feel confident that he's immunized.

What does a negative titer test mean?

- A negative titer at 18 wks old, three or four weeks after vaccination, might simply be some kind of error. Perhaps the blood wasn't prepared properly when sent to the lab, or perhaps the lab made a mistake processing it.
- Or it might mean the puppy still had maternal antibodies that wiped out the vaccine, which prevented his own immune system from making its own antibodies. A pup who still has strong maternal antibodies at 14–15 weeks old is unusual, but it can happen.

Repeat the vaccine, then re-test the titer a few weeks later. If it still comes back negative…

Dr. Ronald Schultz says that a vaccine at 14–15 weeks old results in a successful immune response in over 95% of puppies—and that most of those pups who don't respond will never become immunized ***regardless of how many vaccinations they receive.***

These pups, usually purebred, are called ***genetic non-responders.*** For whatever reason, their immune system doesn't recognize the virus when it's injected, rather than coming in through the nose or mouth as the natural virus would do.

Oddly enough, non-responsiveness is usually to just ONE of the vaccines (typically parvo). The dog usually responds fine to the other vaccine. Go figure!

Socializing puppies: when is it safe?

Until my puppy is immunized, I keep him away from the park, pet stores, grooming shops, obedience classes, and any other area frequented by unknown dogs.

But that doesn't mean he just sits at home until he's 18 weeks old. In my opinion, this time period in a puppy's life is too valuable to waste it staying in the house and backyard.

After my pup has had his first shot at 10–11 weeks (which will be immunizing in about 75 percent of pups), I wait a week for good measure. At about 12 weeks old, I begin taking the pup for short car rides to the library, the mall, the supermarket… any place with people, but no other dogs. I just sit with him on a bench, say hello to people who pass by, and feed him lots of treats so he comes to associate new places and new people with good things.

To learn how to socialize your puppy, see my book, *Respect Training For Puppies.*

Does an immunized puppy need any more shots?

Dr. Karen Becker, DVM, says no. She says:

"If we follow the protocol as laid out above (distemper/parvo vaccination at 10 wks, then 14–15 wks), titering two to four weeks after the last round of vaccines at 14 to 15 weeks of age, and we confirm the babies' immune systems have responded to the vaccinations, there is no reason to continue to

> re-vaccinate those animals… giving a dog or cat boosters of the same vaccines doesn't mean he's more protected. Many pet owners are led to believe—often by the reminders sent by their veterinarian's office—that vaccines 'expire.' It's frustrating, because these reminders are intended to provoke fear in responsible pet owners."

Dr. Jean Dodds, DVM, says no. According to studies, she says, the initial puppy vaccinations provide lifelong immunity in the majority (97%) of dogs. She does not recommend any "boosters."

And we already know that Dr. Schultz says in *Kirk's Current Veterinary Therapy:* "Immunity to viruses persists for years or for the life of the animal."

> After thoroughly studying the research, I'm satisfied that this conclusion of the immunological experts is correct. I personally give no more vaccinations.

My vet says to give a booster at 1 year, and then every 3 years

Yes, this is also the opinion of the American Animal Hospital Association. But I don't put a lot of stock in an organization whose website tagline says: *"For veterinary professionals and their practice teams."*

Such organizations, in my experience, are focused on what's best for its veterinarian membership (especially regarding income) and not necessarily on what's best for the dogs.

> For example, veterinary associations have long insisted that dogs needed annual vaccinations, even in the face of immunological research that showed otherwise.

Now they've backed off from their "annual" stance. And yet "every 3 years" is still a far cry from the statistics that show this:

> A puppy vaccination at 14–16 weeks provides lifelong immunity in 97% of dogs, especially if you've done titer tests at 18 weeks old that *confirm* immunity.

What about boosters every 5 years?

Some owners choose to do a booster every 5 years. That's okay, if you like. For most dogs, it works out to ***only one booster*** (two at the most) in their entire life, because...

You shouldn't re-vaccinate an elderly dog.

A large dog might be considered *elderly* at age 8 or 9, which means that if you did decide to booster during his lifetime, you might do so at age 5... but no more. Small breeds aren't elderly until age 10 or 12, so you might booster a small dog at age 5 and again at age 10... but no more.

Why no more?

Because a dog who has successfully reached old age most likely has a fine, functional immune system that has been effectively dealing with infectious diseases all along.

Here's how... Has your dog ever sniffed at another dog's stool, or snuffled around in the grass where another dog might have gone to the bathroom? If that other dog harbored a virus, or was recovering from a virus, your sniffing dog came into contact with it.

> But it didn't ***infect*** him, did it? Because his immune system memory cells said, "Ah-ha! I recognize that!" and created the right antibodies.

In fact, even if that other dog who went to the bathroom on the grass didn't ***have*** a virus, but had recently been ***vaccinated*** against it, your sniffing dog may still have come into contact with it. How can that happen?

From "shed" particles. For several weeks after being vaccinated, a dog may "shed" particles of the vaccine into his environment. Sort of like how we shed some of our skin cells when we walk around.

When a recently vaccinated dog sheds virus particles, other dogs may inhale or ingest them. If their immune system is healthy, it says "What's that?!?" and makes antibodies. In a sense, shed particles can act like a vaccination to other dogs, essentially kicking their immune systems into gear.

> Therefore, when I have an older dog who had proper puppy shots (or at least one vaccination as an adult), I feel plenty confident about his immunity as an older dog. Because he probably wouldn't have reached this age without a functioning immune system.

I never risk confusing or overloading the immune system of an aging dog by subjecting it to vaccination risks for no reason.

Other dogs I *won't* vaccinate

A dog who has had a bad reaction to a vaccine

I don't just mean a bit of tenderness around the injection site. I mean swelling of the face or head, hives, itching, repeated vomiting or diarrhea, fever, etc.

A dog with a serious illness

If my dog has any serious illness (for example, cancer or any ailment that would interfere with his immune system's ability to make antibodies), I would never vaccinate him again.

Dr. Martin Goldstein, DVM, tells this sad story of a Jack Russell Terrier with cancer:

> "While under general anesthesia, Wesley had been given a combo vaccine of DHLPP, plus a coronavirus vaccine, plus rabies. Seven agents in all, while the poor dog's immune system was already struggling with the general anesthetic and cancer!" *(The Nature of Animal Healing)*

For Pete's sake, every vaccine label says it should be given *ONLY to healthy dogs.* How is a dog with cancer healthy?

Dr. Donna Starita Mehan, DVM, says: "Never vaccinate an animal with symptoms of acute or chronic health problems, or at the time of surgery or any other physical or emotional stress."

Dr. Jean Dodds, DVM, says: "I do not recommend vaccinating females during estrus [heat periods], pregnancy, or lactation."

Titers INSTEAD of boosters?

Earlier I recommended doing a titer test after a puppy's final vaccination, to ensure that he was truly immunized. A titer test is a simple blood test that checks for antibodies in the blood. If the pup's immune system has made antibodies, he's immunized.

Can you also use titer tests to ensure that your ***adult*** dog is protected? Because if you knew he was protected, you wouldn't need to re-vaccinate. If he isn't protected, you could go ahead and give him a booster.

Titer tests sound like a great way to prevent dogs from being overvaccinated, don't they?

Except...

There's a problem with using titers in adult dogs

✓ A ***positive*** titer test proves that your dog has antibodies. Great! Plus a positive titer test provides documentation for boarding kennels, training classes, etc.—at least those that are willing to accept titers in lieu of vaccination.

✗ However... a ***negative*** test doesn't mean your dog ***isn't*** protected.

A titer test, you see, only measures the number of antibodies ***currently*** circulating in the blood.

"But shouldn't antibodies be circulating in the blood ALL the time?" No, that's not necessary.

> Immunity isn't just based on how many antibodies are ***currently*** circulating, but on how ready and able his immune system is to ***produce*** those antibodies when necessary.

Remember, the immune system has a memory. Memory cells prompt the immune system to form antibodies when a familiar virus infects the body. The antibodies don't need to be there all the time.

Dr. Donald Hamilton, DVM, compares antibodies to fire engines. Just because the fire engines aren't racing around all day, he says, just because the firefighters are back in the firehouse sleeping or playing cards, doesn't mean they aren't ready to jump in their trucks and head to the fire when the alarm sounds.

Dr Will Falconer, DVM, confirms this:

> "...there is no reason for the immune system to keep producing antibodies against an invader forever, so over time, these levels of antibody will wane. The fight is finished, there's no more invader showing up, so there's no need to keep a titer high.
>
> What is not measured by the titer test is any part of the cell-mediated immunity, especially the memory cells. So, while antibody levels will wane over time, these long-lived memory cells lie quietly in the recesses of the immune system, awaiting further signals that the invader is back. It is

> these cells that are responsible for the *duration of immunity* that cannot be measured by a titer test." (vitalanimal.com)

So a negative titer test doesn't tell you whether an adult dog is immune because it only measures circulating antibodies, not memory cells. If your dog's immune system has not recently been "challenged" (exposed to the virus), there is no need for antibodies against that virus to be circulating in his blood.

> Hence a perfectly plausible explanation for a negative titer test in an adult dog who was properly immunized at 14–15 weeks old, especially when that was confirmed by titers at 18 weeks. *If you didn't do puppy titers* and the adult one you just ran is negative, I would re-vaccinate, then repeat titers in a few weeks. So soon after a vaccine "challenge", the titer should be positive or something is not right.

What about vaccinations for a dog adopted as an adult?

Suppose you've adopted a dog and you don't know whether he had any puppy shots. You might not even know if he's had any shots as an adult.

You could do a titer test. If it's positive, he's all set. If it's negative… well, we've already covered that it's not abnormal for titers to be negative in an adult dog who hasn't recently been "challenged" by the virus.

> You can always go ahead and vaccinate him now, just once, and test titers in a few weeks to make sure it "took."

Vets give you some closing thoughts on vaccines

The AVMA *Journal* says:

"There is no scientific data to support a recommendation for annual administration of vaccines. Furthermore, repeated administration of vaccines may be associated with a higher risk of anaphylaxis and autoimmune diseases."

In the same issue:

> "There is little scientific documentation that backs up label claims for annual administration of most vaccines. In the past, it was believed that annual vaccination would not hurt and would probably help most animals. However, concerns about side effects have begun to change this attitude. The client is paying for something with no effect or with the potential for an adverse reaction."

Dr. Martin Goldstein, DVM, says:

> "Initially, [pharmaceutical] companies may have responded to health epidemics in an admirable fashion. But over time, they've evolved as any business does, pushing all the products they can, vying for market share, and creating new markets, sometimes creating a market for vaccines to fight mild diseases better addressed with treatment. And veterinarians, well-intentioned as they may be, have shared in the profits." *(The Nature of Animal Healing)*

Finally, Dr. Don Hamilton, DVM, warns you not to fall for the guilt trip pushed on you by some vets:

"Another trend of the past few years is coercion of guardians into procedures such as vaccination. This coercion may be blatant, such as refusal to provide services, even emergency care, unless the animal is 'current' on vaccines.

Sometimes even critically ill animals are vaccinated upon admission for treatment.

More subtle means include induction of fear and/or guilt by asserting (as an authority figure) that companion animals are at risk if not vaccinated yearly, and that failure to comply is evidence of lack of caring.

Tactics such as this can create feelings of guilt in the guardian, leading to a fear-based decision to vaccinate an animal that is not at risk.

This is unethical, if not outright malpractice, and refusal is an acceptable response."

YOU must take charge of your dog's vaccinations

You might drop your dog off at the vet's for dental cleaning or grooming... and when you pick him up, the receptionist casually mentions that "He was a little behind on his vaccines, so we gave him a DHLPP plus kennel cough."

Specify "No vaccinations!" whenever your dog must be out of your sight for any reason.

> As you continue your research into which vaccinations your dog really needs, don't be afraid to stand up to a vet and Just Say No.

Alternatives to vaccinations?

"Are there are any alternatives to vaccines—natural alternatives without harmful side effects?"

None that I use, no. The only alternatives at this time are called *nosodes,* which are homeopathic remedies intended to sensitize the body to a particular virus.

They're safe. No side effects. They're given by mouth and can be administered even to very young puppies.

> But their effectiveness depends on who you ask. A few vets believe in them. Some vets are non-committal. But most vets don't believe they work at all.

Have I ever used them? No. I prefer giving just the right number of vaccines, which immunological research has proven is very few.

Chapter 3

The 3rd Thing You Must Do Right: Provide a Non-Toxic Environment

We've talked about keeping your dog healthy by feeding real food and minimizing vaccinations.

Let's look now at his environment—your home and yard—to see if anything there might affect his health, for better or for worse.

His environment means:

- the air he breathes
- the floors and carpets he walks on
- anywhere he sleeps
- the yard where he wanders around

How your dog's environment affects his health

When your dog breathes in something other than pure air—for example, chemical droplets from an aerosol can of hairspray—**his immune system recognizes an "intruder"** in his respiratory tract and tries to fight it.

A few sneezes might do the trick. If not, the immune system will delve deeper into its arsenal, altering your dog's body biochemistry in an attempt to oust the intruder. Histamines may be produced to "wash it out." An army of white blood cells may be mustered and dispatched to fight it. And so on.

The immune system usually wins, but the problem is:

> Frequent battles STRESS the immune system and make it hypersensitive, which can lead to chronic allergies.

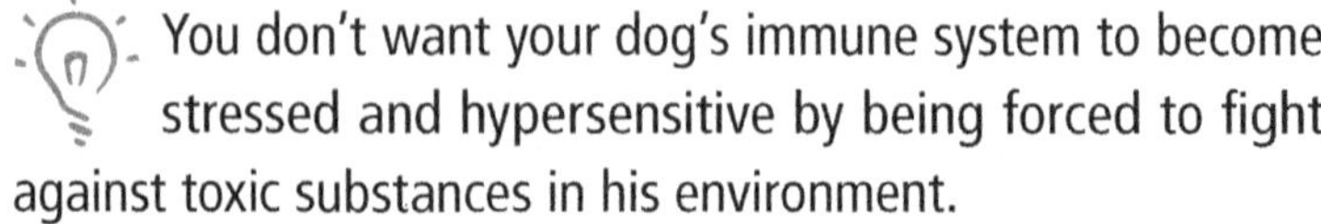

You don't want your dog's immune system to become stressed and hypersensitive by being forced to fight against toxic substances in his environment.

Of course you can't change the pollution levels *in your city*, but you can make sure:

> That there aren't any (or very few) fumes, chemicals, or other toxic substances in your home and yard that will end up in your dog's respiratory system or on his skin or paws, triggering a reaction from his immune system.

You'll need to make some decisions about whether to continue using certain products that make your own life easier and more convenient, but may damage the long-term health of your dog.

Imagine your dog to be an empty barrel

Imagine your dog to be an empty barrel. Each chemical he breathes or absorbs through his skin fills a part of the barrel.

✗ If you hang air fresheners in your house, his barrel will no longer be empty. Air fresheners contain chemicals that affect a dog's eyes, nose, and respiratory system.

✗ If you smoke indoors, you've added more chemicals to his barrel.

✗ If you give him a bath with a typical pet-store shampoo… you wash his bed with a typical brand-name laundry detergent… if you clean your house with a typical brand-name cleaning spray… if you spray your bushes with fungicide… if you let him lick your hands after you've applied skin moisturizer…

How fast his barrel fills up is different for each individual dog, depending upon his biochemical make-up, the strength of the "intruders" that are filling the barrel, and what his past exposures have been.

The furniture polish on the coffee table beside his crate, the mothballs in the linen closet, the weed killer on the lawn… When he smells these substances or walks on them, his nasal passages, skin, and immune system must deal with them.

Chemicals build up. And when his barrel overflows, he will get sick. Either an acute illness or more commonly, chronic ones.

If you can reduce the number of chemicals your dog is exposed to, you'll give his immune system a chance to rest and recuperate.

So let's start "emptying the barrel."

Eliminate products with "fragrances"

If you could do only one thing in your house to protect your dog's immune system, this is what I would recommend:

> Replace products that contain *fragrances* with products that are ***fragrance-free.***

The word *fragrance* on the label of any product is a huge red flag.

You and I might think of *fragrance* as meaning "a lovely scent, like a fragrant flower."

Unfortunately, in the manufacturing industry, a *fragrance* contains hundreds of chemicals and the company doesn't need to disclose any of them to government regulatory agencies or to consumers. Why not? Because of "trade secret" loophole laws.

> So on the label, all you'll see is *fragrance* or *parfum,* but rest assured that behind that simple word is a complex concoction of chemicals that are linked to all sorts of health problems.

Fragrances are one of the top five causes of allergies in both people and pets. The UN Global Harmonized System of Classification and Labeling of Chemicals has identified more than 1,000 chemicals used in fragrances that qualify for a "danger" or "warning" level classification based on associated health issues such as allergies, respiratory problems, and cancer.

> So if you could just remove products that say fragrance and replace them with products that say ***fragrance-free,*** you'd be doing a lot to protect your dog's future health right there.

Products that typically include fragrances are household spray cleaners, floor cleaners, dish detergents, laundry detergents, dryer sheets, hair shampoos, and skin lotions.

You don't want your dog breathing fragrances from these products, or licking them off your skin, or coming in contact with them through clothing or bedding.

And of course, there's perfumes and colognes. I always feel a little sad when I see a small dog carried in the arms or sitting on the lap of an owner who is reeking of perfume or cologne. You and I have 5 million scent receptor cells. Your dog has over 100 million. The canine olfactory system is extremely sensitive, so it's just not kind to overwhelm it with perfumes or colognes.

Unscented vs. fragrance-free

In trying to avoid fragrances, you might think "unscented" products would be just what you're looking for.

Unfortunately, manufacturers have twisted the word *unscented* to mean "You can't smell anything in our product."

> Bah! They accomplished that by adding odor-neutralizing chemicals. So there might be no detectable scent, but the ***chemicals*** are still there! Nice, eh?

So... you want to avoid products with *fragrances* AND products that claim to be *unscented*. Instead, try ***fragrance-free*** products, which means the company used no synthetic fragrances or odor-neutralizing chemicals. Yes, the product might have a smell to it, but it's the natural smell of its ingredients. That's fine.

> Sadly, some manufacturers lie. Their products say fragrance-free, but they're lying. Not much we can do.

Companies I use for fragrance-free products

The Seventh Generation and **Ecos** make a lot of good ***fragrance-free*** products.

I especially like their fragrance-free, vegetable-based cleaning products and detergents.

Most supermarket cleaners are based on harsh detergents, dyes, chlorine, ammonia, and caustic solvents.

Those chemicals irritate your dog's skin and paws, or create fumes that can damage his sensitive eyes, nose, and lungs. His immune system may also launch a protective counter-strike and, if this happens frequently, the immune system becomes hypersensitive, leading to chronic allergies.

Air fresheners

If you get rid of fragrances in your home, you might be tempted to turn to air fresheners to keep the house smelling nice.

Or maybe not.

I was astonished when I first learned how "air fresheners" work. Whether sprays, gels, plug-ins, beads, or hanging cardboard shapes, most air fresheners contain dreadful chemicals such as formaldehyde, petroleum distillates, and *nerve-deadening chemicals* that actually interfere with your ability to smell.

So odors aren't really gone and the "air freshener" hasn't "freshened" the air. Your ability to smell odors has been numbed. Sort of like Novocaine for your nose!

> As you might expect, air fresheners can seriously irritate your dog's eyes, nose, and respiratory system.

A nice-smelling home

Baking soda

I set shallow bowls of baking soda on counters and shelves that my dogs can't reach. The bowls should be wide and shallow so there's a lot of surface area of baking soda. The goal is for odor particles that drift around your house to land on the baking soda to be neutralized.

Slow cooker/crockpot

Combine a few cinnamon sticks, apple peels, orange slices, and whole cloves in your crockpot. Cover the ingredients with water, and set it on Low for eight hours. Experiment with covered vs. uncovered. Makes your house smell like warm apple pie!

Essential oils?

I don't use essential oils. Too many of them are toxic to dogs, and even more are toxic to cats and pet birds. After sifting through the research, there doesn't seem to be a consensus on which essential oils truly are safe for pets. So I don't take chances.

Potpourri? Candles?

I don't use these either. The scents in potpourri and candles come from either essential oils or chemical fragrances.

Cleaning "accidents" on the carpet

When your dog poops or pees on the carpet, it's tempting to break out the heaviest-duty cleaner you can find, complete with its fragrances or odor-neutralizing chemicals.

But the best way to clean up pet waste is with an *enzymatic cleaner,* a cleaner with natural enzymes that break down and "eat" the microscopic particles in waste, removing the odor and stain. I used to love

Nature's Miracle, but the company has reformulated their products with scents and fragrances, so no more! Try *NonScents Stain & Odor Eliminator* on Amazon.

A walk through your house and yard

Let's take a quick walk through your home and yard, looking for everyday substances that you might consider changing.

Kitchen

- Cleaning products, especially general cleaners, floor and carpet cleaners, or upholstery cleaners if he sleeps on the furniture

- Your dog's food bowl. For some dogs, eating from a plastic dish can eventually cause allergic pimples (resembling acne) on their muzzle, chin, or nose. Plastic also develops nicks and abrasions that can be irritating against the tongue, or worse, provide hiding places for bacteria. If possible, switch to a stainless steel, ceramic, or glass feeding bowl.

Bathroom

- Personal care products that your dog comes in contact with when he snuggles up to you or licks your hands or face. Especially look at shampoos (both yours and your dog's!) and skin lotions. If possible, reserve perfumes and colognes for Date Nights rather than everyday use.

Laundry room

- Laundry detergents and fabric softeners that your dog comes in contact with when he sleeps on his bed (or on your bed) or when he snuggles against your freshly-laundered clothes.

- Most laundry detergents contain dyes and fragrances, even when the manufacturer has boldly stamped "unscented" on the front of the box. I like *Ecos* and *Seventh Generation* detergents that are vegetable-based and fragrance-free.

Closets

- I don't know if anyone still uses mothballs. Just in case, the chemicals in mothballs give off subtle fumes that can sicken a dog or cat when they leak from their storage place and permeate the whole house. If possible, better to store woolen goods in a cedar chest. Or stuff socks with cedar chips and tuck the socks around woolens as natural repellents.

Garage

- Antifreeze made with ***ethylene*** glycol is extremely poisonous. If it leaks from your car's radiator or spills on the ground when you're pouring it in, pets may be attracted to its sweet smell. Ethylene glycol causes severe damage to the heart and kidneys and can be fatal.

Safer for a home with pets is antifreeze made with propylene glycol. Your dog would need to drink a lot more of it to get sick.

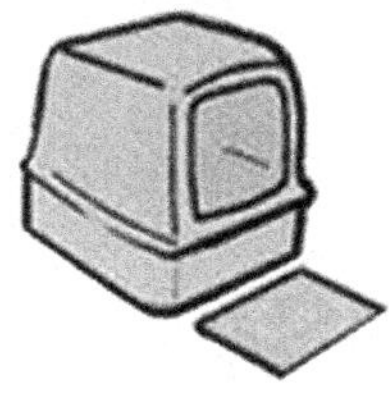

Cat litter box

If your dog ever gets into the cat box, you don't want him ingesting "clumping" kitty litter. When it first came along, clumping litter seemed wonderful. It hardens into a compact little ball when it gets wet, (i.e., when your cat's urine soaks into it.) This *clumping* makes it much easier (and less wasteful) to scoop up.

But when something seems too good to be true… it usually is.

We now know that when a cat licks clumping litter off his paws and fur, or when a dog gets into the litter box and (gross) eats the cat's waste plus a mouthful of litter, that litter gets WET from saliva and stomach fluids, and clumps in the animal's stomach. Now your dog or cat might be in trouble.

Clumping litter also includes chemicals and fragrances that can cause respiratory distress in pets.

> I recommend trying litter made from recycled newspaper. It's non-toxic, dust-free, super-absorbent, and environmentally friendly. A popular brand is Yesterday's News, but there are others.

Your yard

Do you use pesticides in your yard or on your grass or garden?

Pesticides are poisons designed to kill insects (insecticides), weeds (herbicides), fungus (fungicides), or rodents (rodenticides).

Pesticides include active ingredients (the toxic chemicals designed to kill the pest) and inert ingredients (often carcinogens).

Your dog inhales pesticides and absorbs them through his paws and skin. Pesticides can poison a dog or cause severe neurological damage and metabolic diseases.

>  If you're willing to spend some time learning about organic gardening, your dog would surely appreciate it!

Plants

Even when gardened organically, any plant material your dog eats (even grass) may produce mild vomiting or diarrhea. But some plants are truly toxic to dogs, and even more are toxic to cats.

If you're online right now, see the most current list of toxic and non-toxic plants on the Animal Poison Control Center website.

Your dog's drinking water

You have several options: tap water, bottled water, filtered water, and distilled water.

Is your tap water safe? It might be declared safe by your community's standards. But we all know that such standards change as chemicals and additives once declared safe are discovered—surprise!—to cause cancer. City water (and some well water) can contain chlorine, fluoride, heavy metals, and other contaminants. Or your tap water might really be fine.

Some owners give bottled water to their dog. That can be fine, too. But often bottled water is just some other community's tap water poured into bottles and sold. And when bottled water sits on a shelf for a long time, harmful chemicals can seep out of the plastic into the water.

Some owners have a home filtration system and give filtered water to their dog. That can also be fine, depending on how good the filtration system is.

Finally, some owners give distilled water to their dog. This option is controversial because the distilling process removes all minerals, even good minerals. I have some concerns about that, but am not an expert in this area.

> I don't think we can truly know which option is best. Personally, I give filtered water with no chlorine or fluoride.

The air in your home

If your dog has allergies...

> ...consider adding a whole-house HEPA filter to your ventilation system, or a stand-alone room HEPA filter to the rooms in which your dog spends most of his time.

Tobacco smoke

No need for lectures, you're an adult who already knows this isn't good for anyone to be breathing. Please try to smoke outside and away from your dog.

Interior painting projects

If you're repainting your walls, be aware that most brands of paints and adhesives today release *volatile organic compounds* (VOCs), such as formaldehyde, into the air of your home. If possible, choose paints that specify no- or low-VOC on the label.

Chapter 4

The 4th Thing You Must Do Right: Prevent Fleas, Ticks, and Heartworm

We've talked about keeping your dog healthy by feeding real food, minimizing vaccinations, and providing a non-toxic environment by minimizing his exposure to chemicals.

Next, you need to keep him free of fleas, ticks, and heartworm, that awful parasite carried by mosquitoes.

Preventing fleas

There are five things you can do to prevent or kill fleas:

✓ Keep your dog strong and healthy.

✓ Check your dog regularly with a flea comb.

✓ Make your house flea-resistant.

✓ Make your yard flea-resistant.

✓ As a last resort, especially on a flea-allergic dog, use Frontline Plus, a topical drug.

Let's look at these one at a time.

1) Keep your dog strong and healthy.

Like all parasites, fleas tend to infest weaker dogs. So your first step in preventing fleas is to keep your dog strong and healthy by following the 11 steps in this book.

- ✓ For example, a diet comprised mainly of meat, especially with additional Omega 3 fatty acids, keeps his skin and hair healthy and flea-resistant.
- ✓ Minimal vaccinations keeps his immune system "exercised" (which is healthy) but not "stressed" (which would be a magnet for parasites).
- ✓ Providing a non-toxic environment protects his skin, eyes, nose, and respiratory system.

> Dogs who are strong and healthy seem to resist and repel fleas better than dogs who are fed processed food, over-vaccinated, and living their daily life among chemicals.

2) Check your dog regularly with a flea comb.

Use a special, fine-toothed *flea comb* to comb through your dog's hair, especially when you come home from outings in fields or woods where fleas are known to be, or likely to be.

The teeth of a flea comb are very close together, so as you comb slowly through the hair, a flea will inevitably get caught against the teeth and can't escape. Quickly dunk the little bugger in a glass or bowl of soapy water to drown.

> As you're combing through the coat, be alert for flea "waste." These black specks (resembling coffee grounds) are dried flea feces stuck to your dog's hair.

3) Make your house flea-resistant.

Vacuum.

Frequent vacuuming, especially of carpets, baseboards, and upholstery (including between cushions) removes flea eggs and also flea waste (which contains blood) that flea larvae feed on. Remove their habitat and your home is less hospitable to fleas.

Sprinkle borate powder on carpets.

Sodium borate powder kills fleas by dehydrating them, drying out their skeletons until they perish. Popular borate products include Fleabusters and Flea Stoppers. Note that sodium borate powder is different from **hydrogen** borate or *boric acid.*

You work the very fine powder into your carpets with a push broom and leave it for a couple of days before vacuuming. The powder is so fine that particles remain deep in the carpet.

> It can take 2–6 weeks for fleas to dehydrate and die. But it's usually effective and one application lasts up to a year.

Negatives? It's very messy to apply. The fine powder puffs out of the canister in clouds of white flour. Although skin contact is safe, inhaling it irritates the respiratory system. So wear a dust mask and goggles and remove your pets while applying it. Fleabusters also has outlets across the country that will come to your home and do it for you, if you prefer.

> Caution: 20 Mule Team Borax can also work. But it wasn't designed for either fleas or pets, and the company itself doesn't recommend using it as such.

Diatomaceous earth powder

Pronounced *DIE-ya-toe-may-shus,* the name comes from the *diatom,* an ancient aquatic organism. In lake and sea beds, the skeletons of millions of diatoms have fossilized into a soft, sedimentary rock that's easily crumbled into a fine powder.

How does this powdery substance help with fleas? Diatomaceous earth (DE) has razor-sharp edges that scratch the outer layer of hard-bodied insects (like fleas, ants, and roaches) when they walk across it. Those insects dehydrate and die.

> I have concerns about DE. It can be effective, but if you get the wrong kind or use it improperly, it can cause health issues.

DE comes in food-grade, pest-grade, and pool-grade. All three grades contain *amorphous silica,* which is mostly harmless unless you get it in your eyes or nose. Then it's quite the irritant! *Pest-grade* DE adds chemicals to help attract insects into the powder. *Pool-grade* DE (used for pool filtration) is the most dangerous because it also contains ***crystalline*** silica, which causes serious lung disease.

Food-grade is the only safe grade I recommend. But it's not easy to apply properly. If you apply too much (a visible layer), bugs simply walk around it or hop over. Too much powder also tends to puff up into the air when anyone walks past, causing inhalation issues or landing on your kitchen counters or electronics.

Another negative: the powder needs to stay completely dry, so if you wash your floors, you'll need to reapply it.

Flea traps

There are dozens of flea trap designs, most of which fail abysmally.

But there are two I like: the *Victor M230 Flea Trap* and the *BioCare Flea Trap* (also called *Springstar S102*). They cost less than twenty dollars online, or from home and garden stores. You might try both to see which works better for you.

If you're handy, you can build your own and place them all over your house. Basically you want to combine a light source (which attracts the fleas) and a shallow dish or pie plate that the fleas can easily hop into.

For the light source, you can use a battery-powered LED "tea light candle." Tuck it inside a drinking glass and stand the glass/candle in the center of the plate.

In the shallow dish, you can put water plus a few tablespoons of Dawn dish soap. Or skip the water and lay down a sticky substance such as shampoo or cooking oil.

Wait until nighttime to set the traps, so the fleas will be more attracted to the light. The traps usually do best on the floor in high-traffic areas, but keep moving them around to find the best spots. Be sure your pets are kept out of the area or in their crates so they can't drink the water or stick their nose into the sticky stuff!

4) Make your yard flea-resistant.

Many of you may garden your yards to provide sanctuary for wildlife such as field mice, squirrels, chipmunks, skunks, opossums, and so on. I do too.

Unfortunately, those animals are often infested with fleas, as are stray cats who wander through your yard.

So if you're determined not to have fleas, you either need to manicure your yard, or else treat it with some form of flea preventative. The problem, of course, is that flea preventatives are insecticides, and insecticides are almost always toxic to our pets.

> Some owners use *food-grade diatomaceous earth* in their yard. We talked about DE in the previous section. It can work, but its primary problem for outdoor use is that it must be dry to work. Whenever it rains, you need to reapply it.

I recommend nematodes for your yard

Nematodes are teeny-tiny organisms that gobble up fleas (in all life stages), but are harmless to people, mammals, birds, aquatic life, reptiles, amphibians, and plants (even vegetables). They're also harmless to desirable garden dwellers such as earthworms, praying mantises, bees, and ladybugs.

I highly recommend nematodes.

Your soil already contains some of these organisms, so you're not introducing anything alien. You just need more of them to really make a dent in your flea population.

> There are many different types of nematodes. The ones that prey on fleas are called *Steinernema carpocapsae.*

Where to buy nematodes

You can buy SC *nematodes* at garden centers, but there's always a concern about how long they've been kept in storage, because they can die. If you open the sealed package and detect a fishy-like smell, a bunch of them have died.

I suggest ordering online from a reputable company such as Arbico Organics. You need about 5 million nematodes for 1,600 square feet. Order at the beginning of spring.

When they arrive, either deploy them immediately, or store them in the fridge and deploy within seven days. Spray them throughout your garden and expect results in a week or two.

5) Use Frontline Plus or Advantage.

If my dogs pick up a crop of fleas, rather than just a couple, a flea comb might not be enough to get them all, as fleas multiply so quickly. Or if a dog is allergic to fleas, he might engage in frenzied scratching from a single bite. Allergic dogs can tear their skin open, leading to nasty infections.

That's when I apply a single dose of Frontline Plus or Advantage 2, which are flea-killing liquids available from pet stores. You squirt the liquid onto your dog's skin between his shoulder blades and it spreads across his body via the oil layer on his skin.

> Frontline and Advantage work by disrupting a flea's nervous system, wiping out the little buggers within 24 hours. Just coming into contact with the dog's hair is enough to kill them. Frontline and Advantage also break the flea's life cycle, which helps prevent an infestation.

One application works for 4–6 weeks, assuming the flea population in your area isn't resistant to the ingredients.

> Just as bacteria can become resistant to antibiotics, parasites can become resistant to the drugs in flea preventatives. If Frontline isn't working in your area, try Advantage, and vice versa.

Are these drugs safe? Well, nothing intended to kill another living creature can be called safe. Keep in mind that the drug poisons the flea ***by poisoning the dog first.*** Yes, that sounds melodramatic, but in essence, that is what we're doing. We're putting the poison on the dog.

The most common side effect of Frontline or Advantage is a mild skin reaction. Far less common, but much more serious, are neurological side effects such as tremors, uncoordinated movement, or seizures.

> Remember, this is a drug that attacks the central nervous system of the flea. So it's not a surprise that in rare cases, it might affect the central nervous system of the dog.

So why use it? Because I'm not convinced there's anything better or safer for those occasional instances when fleas break through my home- and yard-preventatives and either attack an allergic dog, or are too numerous to combat with a flea comb.

What about competitors of Frontline Plus and Advantage? Unfortunately, my dogs experienced side effects from K9 Advantix and Revolution, so I no longer use those.

Newer competitors include chewables such as Nexgard, Bravecto, Simparica, and Credelio. I haven't tried these because I ***never*** use brand new flea meds on my dogs. Manufacturers run their safety tests for only a few months. Who knows what long-term side effects will come to light in the coming years?

> So I stick with the older, tried-and-true Frontline Plus or Advantage. And remember, I don't use them as ***preventatives.*** I use them as a rapid treatment on an occasional, as-needed basis.

Flea preventatives I DON'T recommend

With all of the effective flea control methods described above, there's really no reason to use any of these:

✗ NO flea shampoos or dips

✗ NO flea sprays or powders

✗ NO flea collars

✗ NO flea foggers

Herbal products

Even though I'm a big supporter of herbal medicine and use it for both my human and animal families, I have not had success with herbal products against fleas.

Some owners report success with pennyroyal and tea tree oil. I have friends and colleagues whose dogs suffered serious reactions to these herbs. The *Merck Veterinary Manual* lists tea tree oil as "especially risky" because it's so difficult to dilute safely for any given dog. Small dogs and cats are especially vulnerable to overdoses.

Essential oils (eucalyptus, citronella, cedarwood) are often touted as flea repellents, and they can be. The problem is that it's frighteningly easy to overdose these oils if you actually put them on the dog, especially a small dog. If you don't put them on the dog, they're still awfully strong-smelling for a dog's sensitive nose.

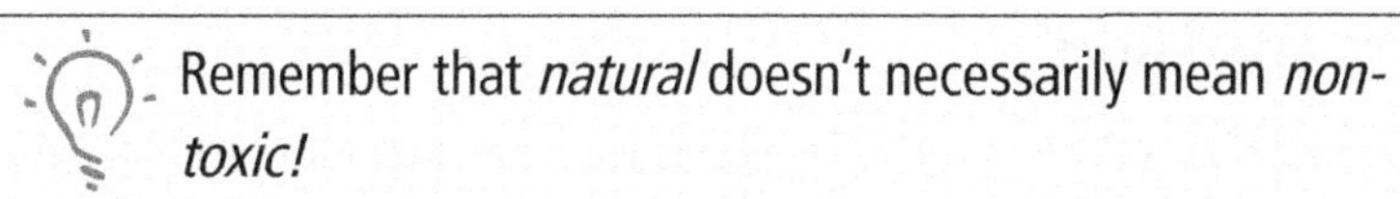

Brewer's yeast and garlic

Finally, garlic and brewer's yeast are sometimes considered flea repellents.

Unfortunately, current research suggests that *yeast* is hard for dogs to digest and can trigger allergies.

Garlic is dangerous to dogs in large quantities, but fine for dogs in small quantities. But I've had no success with it against fleas. They're tough and persistent little buggers!

Preventing ticks

A **TICK** is about the last thing you want to find attached to your dog. These tenacious little arachnids (they belong to the ***spider*** family) insert their head under your dog's skin and gorge themselves on his blood. Gross!

> The worst thing about ticks is the health problems they can cause. The neurotoxins in their saliva can cause allergic skin reactions, while some dogs actually suffer **temporary paralysis.** Certain ticks in certain areas of the country carry Lyme disease, ehrlichiosis, or Rocky Mountain spotted fever.

With ticks, the best offense is a good defense.

In other words… try to avoid them.

How to avoid ticks

You can avoid most ticks by learning how and where they find you and your dog. They can't jump or fly, so they ***climb*** onto tall grass or weeds, or onto a fence. From these advantageous ambush positions, **seldom more than three feet above the ground,** they cling, waiting.

When they detect a living creature nearby (they can smell the carbon dioxide we exhale, and also sense body odor, body heat, and vibrations), the tick stretches out its front legs in an attempt to snag or attach itself to the potential host.

So, to avoid ticks when walking your dog:

✓ Keep him away from overgrown fields, fences in fields, brushy areas, and the edges of woods. That's prime tick country. Don't go off the beaten trail. Walk in the center of mowed trails and keep your dog on-leash and close beside you. **Don't let him brush up against vegetation.**

Ticks can be active anytime the ground temperature is above 45 degrees Fahrenheit, but they're most active when it's warm and humid.

Ticks in your own yard

If you have ticks on your own property, the same habitat issues apply as when you have fleas. You need to make the yard inhospitable to ticks, or use some sort of pesticide, or both.

- ✓ Keep grass mowed, bag the clippings and leaf litter, cut weeds very short. Ticks avoid direct sunlight and will not infest areas that are open, sunny, and well-groomed.
- ✓ Remove wood piles and debris that offer hiding places for wildlife that carry ticks: mice, chipmunks, stray cats, etc.
- ✓ Place a 3-foot wide barrier of wood chips or gravel between your lawn and wooded areas to restrict tick migration into recreational areas.
- ✓ Treat your yard with diatomaceous earth. I talked about this powder in the flea section. Some owners have also used Cedarcide sprays with good results.

Find ticks quickly.

The faster you can get them off your dog, the less time they will have to transmit diseases.

> An infected tick must attach to your dog's skin for 24 to 36 hours before disease-causing microorganisms have enough time to wiggle down to the tick's salivary glands and get injected into your dog's bloodstream.

So if you check your dog before a hike and find no ticks, then check him after the hike and find ticks, those ticks have NOT had time to inject any diseases.

Unfortunately, ***finding ticks quickly*** can be easier said than done!

- The larger species (like brown dog ticks) are fairly easy to see, especially when they're attached to the skin and engorged with blood.

- But the tinier species (like deer ticks) can be a real challenge—depending on their stage of maturity, they can be as tiny as the head of a pin, and these tiny ones cause the worst diseases.

> So don't just rely on your eyes, especially on dark-colored dogs or long-haired dogs. Run your fingers (and a flea comb) through the coat, feeling for the tiniest bump.

Remove ticks properly.

You can use your fingers, but tweezers are better. By far the BEST tool to use is the ***Pro-Tick Remedy*** tick remover, available from Amazon. It's excellent.

Basically, you grasp the tick at the base of its head, as close as possible to the dog's skin. Don't squeeze the tick's body or it will squirt more of its disease-causing bacteria into your dog!

Pull very slowly and in a straight line, trying to "back" the tick OUT the same way it went IN. You want the tick to simply let go and come out intact, leaving an empty hole in your dog's skin. Dab on a bit of 3 percent hydrogen peroxide.

> If you tug too quickly, or if you pull sideways or with a circular motion, the tick's head will break off and remain embedded in the skin. (This is where the Pro-Tick Remedy tool really shines—it usually gets the tick off the dog without breaking off the head.)

Breaking off the head is not an utter disaster, but it can cause further irritation. Just keep an eye on it as it heals.

✗ Don't try to remove a tick by burning it with a match. A dying tick may release its toxins into your dog's skin.

✗ Don't try to remove a tick by "smothering" it with Vaseline, oil, or nail polish. A tick can live for hours covered in these substances, while it continues gorging itself and transmitting its diseases.

Dispose of ticks properly.

Drop the tick into a cup of rubbing alcohol and leave it there overnight. Only when it's dead should you flush it down the toilet. If the tick may have been on your dog for more than 24 hours, preserve it in the alcohol until you identify it.

In the US, the vast majority of diseases are caused by the black-legged or deer tick, the American dog tick, the brown dog tick, the wood tick, and the Lone Star tick. The most common diseases transmitted to dogs by ticks are Lyme disease, Rocky Mountain Spotted Fever, anaplasmosis, and ehrlichiosis.

Should you give your dog tick-killing drugs?

In the section on fleas, we talked about flea preventatives that you apply topically to your dog or give as a chewable tablet. Those drugs are also effective (more or less) against ticks.

The problem is that the manufacturers want you to give them on an ongoing basis (usually once a month). Whereas I use Frontline Plus only on an occasional, as-needed basis.

I'm not in favor of putting my dog on a regular regimen of these drugs unless I lived in a tick-infested neighborhood where tick diseases are common and none of the other tick control methods in this chapter have worked.

Preventing heartworm

Heartworms are large (6 to 12 inches) worms that can find their way into the blood vessels around your dog's heart and lungs. A severe infestation can damage your dog's heart and lungs and result in death.

That's the bad news.

The good news is that heartworm is not the immediate death sentence that pharmaceutical companies and some veterinarians might have you believe. It doesn't strike your dog overnight and require immediate surgery, for example.

How a dog gets heartworms

First, an infected mosquito must bite your dog.

Heartworm is carried by mosquitoes. Actually, that's not quite true. A mosquito obviously can't carry a six-inch heartworm! What mosquitoes carry are tiny organisms called heartworm ***microfilaria*** (sort of pre-heartworms).

Mosquitoes aren't born with microfilaria. They ingest it if they bite another animal that has it. In some parts of the country, that doesn't happen very often because so many people keep their dogs on heartworm medication that there aren't many infected dogs left to bite.

But suppose a mosquito does happen upon an infected dog and ingests that dog's blood. The tiny heartworm organisms called ***microfilaria*** enter the mosquito's body.

Second, inside the mosquito's body, the microfilaria must develop into larvae.

This can occur ONLY:

- IF the weather stays warm enough (above 57 degrees Fahrenheit for 30 consecutive days and nights)

- AND IF the mosquito lives long enough

  If the temperature gets too cool, no larvae will develop. If the mosquito gets swatted, no larvae will develop.

So it takes perfect conditions and luck for microfilaria to become larvae. If they make it, they crawl into the mosquito's mouth parts and wait for their buggy host to inject them into another dog.

Finally, this mosquito, with its surviving larvae, must bite YOUR dog.

Bummer. But still your dog is not yet infected.

When the mosquito bites, it injects a few larvae, but not quite ***into*** your dog. The larvae are deposited in a drop of mosquito saliva ***adjacent*** to the bite. The larvae must swim through the saliva (before it evaporates in the heat) and into the puncture hole left by the mosquito bite, thereby entering your dog's skin.

Now your dog is considered heartworm ***infected*** or heartworm ***positive.***

But he still doesn't have heartworm ***disease.***

Heartworm larvae, you see, don't go directly to the heart. They spend a couple of months living under the skin, continuing to develop. Some of them will die from various causes.

But eventually a few larvae, perhaps two to five, will find their way into your dog's bloodstream and then into the area around his heart and lungs. There they will mature into adult worms and begin producing their own microfilaria—their own "children," if you will.

> At this point your dog is a source of infection for every other dog and cat in the neighborhood.

How is your dog a source of infection? The microfilaria is circulating in his bloodstream. If he gets bitten by a mosquito, the insect ingests your dog's microfilaria, then flies off toward some other (unlucky) dog... and the whole cycle begins again, for that next dog.

> So a heartworm-positive dog, whenever he goes outside where there are mosquitoes, is a hazard to every other dog in the area.

Meanwhile, the adult heartworms in your own dog's pulmonary system (if there are enough of them or if they lodge in a particularly sensitive place) will begin to irritate his arteries or constrict his heart passages. Eventually he'll start to cough.

NOW your dog has heartworm disease.

NOW what do you do?

Now you're looking at a major $500 to $1,000 treatment that will take two or three months to complete.

Your dog will need several injections of a powerful drug, an injected form of arsenic. Your dog must be kept inactive for several weeks so the dying worms don't break off from his heart all at once and form a mass that might block a major blood vessel.

So treatment for full-blown heartworm disease is very serious.

It would be better to prevent it, don't you agree?

The three keys to preventing heartworm

1. Avoid mosquitoes.
2. Have your dog tested annually (a simple blood test).

3. Consider giving heartworm medication every month to kill any larvae that might have been injected by a mosquito.

Let's look at those three keys to preventing heartworm.

Avoid mosquitoes

The best way to cut down on mosquitoes in your yard is to remove all sources of standing water.

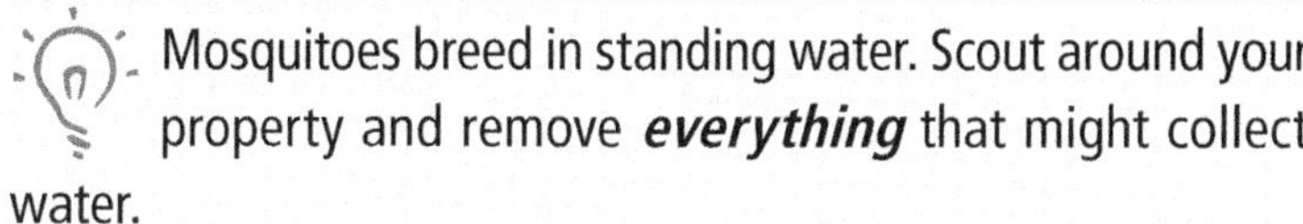

Mosquitoes breed in standing water. Scout around your property and remove ***everything*** that might collect water.

- ✓ Cover trash barrels.
- ✓ Turn over empty buckets, flower pots, and wheelbarrows.
- ✓ Turn over kiddie pools when not in use.
- ✓ Clean gutters of debris so water drains properly.
- ✓ Fill in (or drain) low areas that form puddles.
- ✓ Fill in hollow tree stumps that catch water.
- ✓ Dispose of old tires (drill holes in the bottom of a tire swing).
- ✓ Change the water in bird baths frequently.
- ✓ A garden pond should include a waterfall or fountain to keep the water moving. Healthy ponds attract dragonflies and frogs, both of which devour mosquitoes and larvae.

Next, prune brushy growth, where mosquitoes like to sleep.

Third, repair your screens and make your house mosquito-tight. Consider using an indoor mosquito light such as the Katchy.

Finally, keep your dog INDOORS when mosquitoes are most active.

Have your dog tested annually

A blood test for heartworm should be done about one month before mosquitoes start appearing in your area.

Since it takes a few months for the various stages of heartworm to be detectable by the blood test, you're actually testing ***in the spring*** to see if your dog was bitten by an infected mosquito ***last fall.***

Consider giving monthly heartworm medication

If your dog's annual heartworm test is negative, you might decide to keep it that way by giving him a monthly drug that kills heartworm larvae if there are any in his bloodstream.

> The trade-off, of course, is that you're giving the drug (an insecticide, a poison) for nothing if your dog isn't infected. That's the trade-off you make when you use heartworm medication.

Most vets believe that medication is an absolute necessity everywhere in the US. Other vets believe that medication is only necessary in areas with a lot of heartworm cases or in dogs who spend a lot of time outdoors. A few vets believe that long-term use of heartworm medication can be harmful.

I don't have a strong opinion on this. In the end, only you can decide whether you're more concerned about the risks of heartworm or the risks of ongoing medication.

Which heartworm medication is best?

I prefer Heartguard Plus. It has the longest track record, so we know exactly what to expect from it.

Unfortunately, the ***Plus*** means the company has added another drug to kill roundworms and hookworms. The vast majority of dogs don't need that, so it's simply an unnecessary additional poison.

Other heartworm medications include Sentinel, Trifexis, and Revolution, none of which I feel comfortable with. Too many side effects, and too many other drugs mixed in.

> **Caution:** A few breeds may react adversely to the drug (ivermectin) that's used in Heartgard Plus.

If your dog is a collie-type breed or cross, he ***might*** have inherited a mutant gene called mdr1. The mdr stands for multi-drug resistant, which means the dog can't metabolize certain drugs. The dosage of ivermectin used in heartworm medication is usually okay, but higher doses can result in neurological toxicity.

- 70% of Collies (Rough or Smooth) have inherited the mutant mdr1 gene
- 50% of Australian Shepherds have it
- 10–15% of Shelties and German Shepherds
- About 5% of Border Collies and Old English Sheepdogs

> If your dog is one of those breeds, or a cross or mix of those breeds, you should TEST him to find out if he has this gene.

It's a simple DNA test. You swab the inside of his cheek and send the sample to the Washington State University Veterinary School. Or your vet can draw blood and send that sample.

If your dog has the mutant gene, you should be cautious with the drugs listed on the WSU website.

When should you give heartworm medication?

Your medication schedule should follow the life cycle of mosquitoes in your area.

Here's a map (tibetanmastiff.net/Heartworm.html) that recommends, based on the mosquito season in your area, the ***first*** day you might want to start heartworm medication, and the ***last*** day you might want to give it.

> With this schedule, the goal is to protect your dog with medication during the periods of risk without giving him unnecessary drugs during the periods of little to no risk.

Mind you, following this schedule does not guarantee that your dog will not become infected with heartworms! It's simply a helpful tool that tries to balance the risks on both sides.

Chapter 5

The 5th Thing You Must Do Right: Provide Physical and Mental Exercise

We've talked about keeping your dog healthy by feeding real food, minimizing vaccinations, providing a non-toxic environment, and preventing parasites (fleas, ticks, and heartworms).

Now let's work on his fitness.

Exercise is absolutely vital for dogs. Dogs who don't get enough exercise live shorter, unhealthier lives.

> Exercise keeps your dog's heart, lungs, muscles, and joints strong and healthy, so that he lives longer and more comfortably.

How much exercise your dog needs

✓ As much as it takes to keep his body trim. As we discussed in the feeding chapter, your dog should be on the slim side. He should have a discernible "waist" and a taut underbelly, and you should be able to feel his ribs with your fingers.

✓ As much as it takes to satisfy him and prevent the hyperactivity and destructive behaviors (such as chewing and barking) that occur when a dog has excess energy with no other means to vent it.

Your dog's MIND needs to be exercised, too.

Mental stimulation is as important for dogs as it is for people. When we have nothing to think about, nothing new to look forward to, no hobbies or intellectual pursuits, we're bored. As the saying goes, "Use it or lose it!"

> Dogs are even vulnerable to a form of dementia called *Canine Cognitive Dysfunction,* which is similar to Alzheimer's disease. Help keep your dog's mind healthy by providing interesting activities that encourage him to be attentive, to think, to reason, to figure things out.

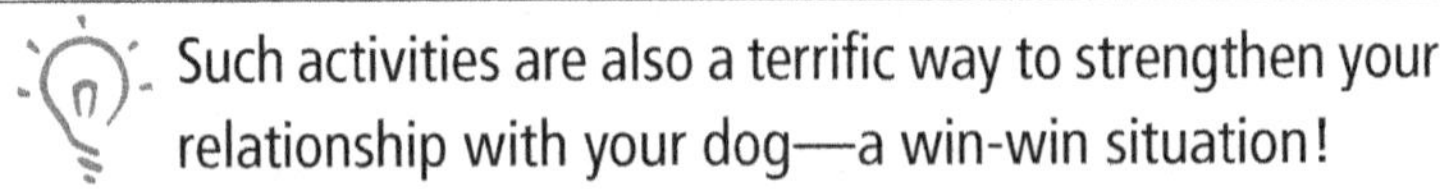

> Such activities are also a terrific way to strengthen your relationship with your dog—a win-win situation!

The myth of "exercising" in the back yard

Some owners think their dog gets all the exercise he needs just by "running around" the yard.

A few dogs will, indeed, run around in a large yard. But most dogs just wander around in a leisurely manner, sniffing, peeing, sniffing, pooping, sniffing... then they sprawl in the sun (or shade) and snooze. Needless to say, this provides zero exercise.

Of course, some dogs do "exercise" in the yard—they're bored stiff, so they run up and down the fence line barking at passersby, or UPS trucks, or the neighbor's dog, or the neighbors. I recommend calling the police or your homeowners' association on these inconsiderate owners.

Also don't make the mistake of thinking that just because you have ***two*** dogs, it's a done deal that they will help keep each other exercised.

Many dogs who live together do just that—they ***live*** together. They may follow each other around, but if they're not actively running and playing, they're not keeping each other exercised.

> Now if YOU go outside and walk (or run) around the yard with your dog, he will get much more exercise, especially if you play Fetch or Tug games. Go ahead: it's fun!

Master list of exercise options

Walking on leash

Walk different routes, especially routes where something interesting is happening (say, a ball game at the park). This will encourage your dog to lift his head and pay attention. If your dog doesn't walk nicely on a leash, see my *Respect Training* books.

Free running

This option is only safe if the area is enclosed, or if your dog always comes when called. The problem is that if he gets too far away or if there's wind or noise, he can't hear you call.

A modern remote collar (like the Mini Educator ET-300) can solve this problem. No, you don't "shock" your dog! You set the level on such a low tingle/vibration that the dog can barely feel it. You don't use it to punish him. Just the opposite! You teach him that when he feels that tingle/vibration, it's the same as a Come command, and when he comes to you, he'll get a reward. Yay!

> This modern use of a remote collar gives your dog freedom to run clear across a field because you can always reach out beyond your voice range and "tap him on the shoulder" to call him.

Fetch games

With balls, sticks, toys, or flying disks.

Tug games

Controlled tug of war is taught in my training books.

Playing with other dogs

Your own or a friend's. I don't allow my dogs to play with dogs I don't know extremely well. I explain why in the next section on *Dog Parks*.

Dog parks

A dog park is a fenced area especially designed for dogs to gather and play off-leash with other dogs. Dog parks have sprung up in many cities and neighborhood developments.

I don't recommend dog parks. In my opinion, letting your dog play with other dogs that you can't control is so risky. It can take only one instance in which your dog is attacked for him to start acting aggressively toward other dogs for the rest of his life. His mentality becomes, "I'll get them before they get me."

> Owners consult with me all the time about these psychologically scarred dogs. "It was just that one time," they say mournfully.

Most owners stand around a dog park chatting, laughing, and talking on their phones while their dog's body language (or some other dog's body language) is flashing bright-red warning signs that a fight might be imminent. Most dog owners haven't a clue about dog behavior when they're in a group/pack situation.

I don't put my dogs' lives in the hands of other owners.

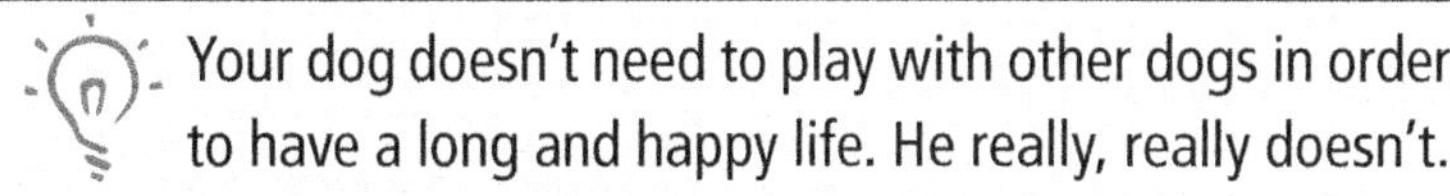

Your dog doesn't need to play with other dogs in order to have a long and happy life. He really, really doesn't.

It's especially dangerous to take a ***small*** dog to a dog park. Larger dogs can view smaller dogs as ***prey.*** A sudden movement, such as your small dog pouncing on a leaf, can trigger dormant chasing instincts even in a nice dog who means well. He can seize your little one instinctively, before he even thinks about what he is doing, before you have time to move or draw a breath. No, I really don't recommend dog parks.

"Pulling" activities

An athletic dog can pull you on a sled (sledding), on a two-wheeled scooter (scootering), on a two- or four-wheeled cart (carting), or on cross-country skis (skijoring). Or your dog can pull a sledge loaded with weights (weight-pulling).

Obstacle course (agility)

Over the hurdles... up the ramp... across the plank... down the ramp... through the tunnel... is this a playground? Yes, a playground for dogs!

Agility is an obstacle course sport for dogs. Agility teaches your dog to pay attention to you, follow your directions, remember the names of the different obstacles, and remember how to negotiate each obstacle. Agility builds your dog's self-confidence, which is especially valuable for a young or timid dog.

You can build or buy obstacles. See my training books or akc.org/sports/agility/

Swimming

Swimming is one of the best physical activities for dogs.

The buoyancy of water allows your dog's muscles and joints to move through a complete range of motion without bearing weight. Thus, his muscles become toned without any impact or concussion from hard ground. Swimming also provides a cardiovascular workout that strengthens his heart and lungs.

For dogs with arthritis or joint problems, swimming (in WARM water) is especially recommended. The warmth relaxes their muscles so they won't be in pain while getting the exercise they need.

Some animal hospitals offer therapeutic swimming sessions in a heated, non-chlorinated pool. Do an online search for: **pet hydrotherapy** and **pet swim therapy**

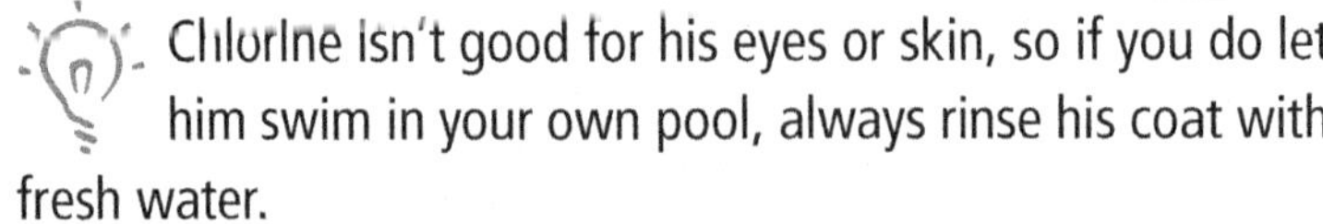

Chlorine isn't good for his eyes or skin, so if you do let him swim in your own pool, always rinse his coat with fresh water.

Hiking/backpacking

Most dogs in good shape can carry up to one-third their body weight in a special dog pack. Start with an empty pack stuffed with newspaper to acclimate your dog to the pack before adding weight on successive hikes. Don't let him drink from streams, which may contain parasites such as giardia. After the hike, check him for ticks, burrs, and dreaded foxtails.

Earthdog

In earthdog events, small terriers and dachshunds navigate an underground trench constructed especially for the event. At the end, they "confront" their prey—a tame rat protected in a cage. The dog can see the cage but cannot touch it, as it is safely placed behind strong vertical bars.

Don't worry about the rats. I've seen earthdog competitions and quite frankly, the rats seem totally bored by the proceedings. See akc.org/sports/earthdog/

Obedience

Obedience is an activity in which your dog follows your commands to Heel, Sit, Down, Stand, Stay, Come, and in more advanced classes, Fetch, Jump, and hand signals. See akc.org/sports/obedience/ and akc.org/sports/rally/

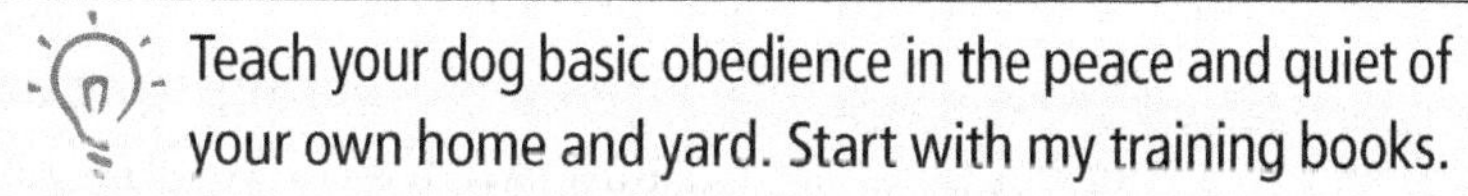

Don't try to teach your dog new things in a public (group) obedience class. These classes can be hectic and stressful and dogs have a hard time learning when overwhelmed by distracting sights and sounds. Safety is a major concern. Beginners often can't control their dogs, who may growl or lunge at your dog, negatively affecting his own temperament.

Musical freestyle

Also known as *dancing with dogs*, you and your dog perform your own individualized, choreographed routine that includes obedience exercises and tricks, all set to music. See canine-freestyle.org/

Tricks

When your dog discovers that certain behaviors make you laugh and applaud and offer treats, he is happy to repeat those behaviors. Popular tricks include shake hands, speak, play dead, roll over, sit up and beg, dance, spin, catch, and back up.

Tracking

In this activity, your dog uses his nose to follow a stranger's track to a glove or wallet dropped at the end of the track.

There's something magical about watching your dog put his nose to the ground and follow something invisible. Also you might keep in the back of your mind the dream that your dog will rescue someone and you'll be interviewed on the 6 o'clock news! See akc.org/sports/tracking/

Scent Work

In this AKC event, a dog must search for cotton swabs saturated with an essential oil or with the scent of his owner. The dog uses his nose to find the hidden object, then alerts you by sitting, lying down, barking, or any other behavior that communicates the location of the target odor. See akc.org/sports/akc-scent-work/

Lure coursing

This high-speed activity has sighthounds (Greyhounds, Salukis, Whippets, and others) rocketing across an open field trying to grab an artificial lure pulled just ahead of them. *Lure coursing* allows these dogs to use their incredible speed and chasing instincts in a constructive way. See akc.org/sports/coursing/lure-coursing/

Herding

If your dog likes to round up the kids, put him to work on real livestock (sheep, cattle, goats, and ducks). Herding clubs provide the animals for your dog to practice with, and an instructor will show you how to control your dog around the livestock.

The most popular herding dogs in the US are Border Collies and Australian Shepherds, but other breeds with herding instincts can also participate. See akc.org/sports/herding/

Protection sports

Combining obedience and protection work, these challenging activities demonstrate a working dog's mental stability, physical endurance, structural soundness, courage, and trainability.

The most popular breeds in protection sports are German Shepherds, Belgian Malinois, Dutch Shepherds, Rottweilers, American Bulldogs, and Dobermans. See Protection Sports Association (psak9.org), Schutzhund/IPO/IGP (schutzhund-training.com), and Mondio Ring (usmondioring.org)

Field/Hunting Tests

If you own a hunting breed but have no desire to hunt, the two of you can still participate in casual field/hunting tests that measure your dog's instincts and abilities.

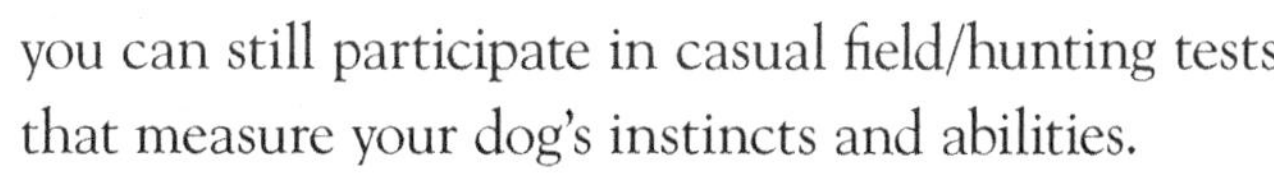

There are field tests for pointing breeds, for retrievers, and for spaniels. Even Beagles, Basset Hounds, and Dachshunds have their own field tests. Don't worry, no animal is ever harmed during these activities!

There are also basic field tests offered by national breed clubs. To see if there's one for your breed, do a search for **breed-name working certificate**

Jogging

Jogging can be very risky for dogs.

When they run around on their own, ***THEY*** control the pace—sometimes faster, sometimes slower, pausing or stopping whenever ***THEY*** feel like it.

But running beside you, or running beside your bicycle, where they must maintain the pace ***YOU*** set, is not natural for dogs.

It's especially bad to do this on a hard surface (sidewalk or road), where each step creates a jarring shockwave that travels up your dog's leg and must be absorbed by his bones, tendons, and joints. Yes, lots of people do jog/bike with their dogs, but those dogs typically pay the price with joint problems later in life.

If you do decide to jog with an athletic dog:

- ✓ *WAIT* until your pup's bones and joints are mature—at least 10 months in small breeds like terriers, at least 14 months in medium breeds like Border Collies, at least 18 months in large breeds like retrievers.
- ✓ Jog *ONLY* on a soft surface like a dirt track. Never jog your dog on pavement.
- ✓ Build up to a maximum of 4 or 5 miles.
- ✓ Jog only during cool weather.
- ✓ Stop regularly to give him a rest and a drink of water.

Exercise for active breeds

Many dogs described as hyperactive, over-exuberant, or destructive are dogs who aren't getting enough exercise.

> A hyperactive, destructive dog is trying to vent bottled-up energy. You can't fix this kind of "misbehavior" with training. You must provide more exercise.

Many breeds were developed for working purposes. They were NOT intended to be simply pets.

Owners make a huge mistake when they get, for example, a Border Collie, Weimaraner, American Bulldog, or Siberian Husky, and think that the dog will be happy with minimal exercise.

A breed with a working background may bounce off the walls because you're walking him around the block a few times or assuming that he'll exercise himself if you just put him outside in the back yard.

For active dogs, choose vigorous activities from the **Master List of Exercise Options** at the beginning of this chapter.

Exercise for puppies and adolescents

Puppies and adolescent dogs ***SHOULD NOT*** be vigorously exercised. They shouldn't accompany you when you go jogging or cycling, and they should not jump over anything higher than their own height at the shoulder.

> When immature dogs are allowed to do too much, their growing bones, joints, and tender tissues can be seriously damaged.

You must wait until the "growth plates" in their legs have closed and their bones and joints are settled and mature: roughly 8–10 months in small breeds, 12–14 months in medium breeds, 14–18 months in large breeds, and 18–24 months in giant breeds.

Safe exercise for puppies and adolescents

- ✓ interactive play sessions (with you) every day so they tone their muscles safely while learning controlled play (such as short, moderate-intensity games of Fetch or Tug)
- ✓ short walks (up to 20–30 minutes) so their joints aren't jarred for too long
- ✓ swimming, which provides wonderful exercise with no jarring of their tender bones or joints
- ✓ playing with a (well-known to you) dog who won't overpower the puppy or goad him into endless running games
- ✓ negotiating an obstacle course (low jumps, tunnels, a raised catwalk) that develops coordination and self-confidence

Exercise for old dogs

Though it may seem kind to let your old dog lie around and rest, it isn't. *Exercise is very important for elderly dogs.*

Exercise helps maintain a trim shape. Being overweight is especially dangerous for middle-aged and elderly dogs because it places extra stress on their weakening joints and heart. If the joints break down, painful arthritis will set in. If the heart breaks down, the lungs, liver, and kidneys will follow.

Obesity inevitably leads to a downward spiral in health. Slim dogs are healthier and live longer.

Exercise also helps maintain MENTAL health. Physical activity keeps oxygen and blood sugar at optimum levels in the brain. Without these nutrients, older dogs become dull and disinterested in the world.

Exercise allows you and your old dog to spend time together. It's important for his sense of well-being that he continue to feel special.

Safe exercise for older dogs

- ✓ Swimming (ideally in ***warm*** water). Tones the muscles and strengthens the heart, with no wear and tear on his old joints.
- ✓ Limited fetch. Toss a loved ball or toy *across a soft surface* (such as grass or carpet). Do only a few throws per session.
- ✓ Walking. Limit walks to 10–20 minutes. Try to walk on *soft surfaces* and in *pleasant weather.* Cold or damp weather aggravates old joints.
- ✓ Supervised play with another (well-known to you) dog. Gentle, controlled play can be rejuvenating for an older dog. But make sure a younger, stronger dog doesn't goad your old fellow into vigorous running games.

Exercise for overweight dogs

Chubby dogs are more likely to develop heart disease, lung disease, diabetes, and tendon, ligament, and joint injuries. So you need to get that extra weight off. That means less food (but also the right KIND of food—see Chapter 1) and more exercise.

Safe exercise for overweight dogs

- ✓ Walking. Start with two 10-minute walks each day, gradually increasing time and distance.
- ✓ Playing with another (well-known to you) dog.
- ✓ Swimming. Keep sessions short and stay close to your chubby dog in case he gets tired and needs assistance. (Also consider a canine life preserver).
- ✓ Fetch. Toss the ball less than 30 feet and repeat only a few times per session.

Exercise for toy dogs

Toy breeds are often billed as "Perfect apartment dogs because they never need to go outside."

This is wrong and sad. Most toy dogs are little athletes who love to romp on grass, chase butterflies, and sniff out the latest doggy news around telephone poles… just like larger dogs.

> Toy dogs who are confined to their house and yard tend to be unsocialized and can be the noisiest, nastiest, or most timid representatives of their breeds. So try to get your toy dog out into the world as much as possible.

But you do need to be careful.

A tiny creature can be seriously injured by something that a bigger dog would barely feel, such as being accidentally conked on the head by a thrown ball at the park.

Keep toy dogs ***on-leash*** outside your yard. They are too quick to dash off, and **virtually everything is a potential danger to them.** I have personally witnessed the horrifying spectacle of a large dog suddenly appearing out of nowhere, grabbing, shaking, and killing a friend's toy dog.

> Owning a toy breed means constant supervision and surveillance of what's going on around your tiny dog. Too much can happen to these little guys in the blink of an eye.

Safe exercise for toy dogs

- ✓ Walking. For 15–30 minutes at a time, in pleasant weather. Most toy dogs don't like cold or damp.
- ✓ Free running. In a safe enclosed area.
- ✓ Fetch, with soft toys or or balls or squeaky toys.
- ✓ Playing with other small dogs. Toy dogs love to chase and wrestle with other toy dogs. Allowing them to play with a larger dog is very risky. Even if the larger dog means well, a friendly head butt, playful pawing, or a misplaced step can injure a toy dog.
- ✓ Negotiating an obstacle course of small jumps, tunnels, and raised catwalks.

Exercise for giant breeds

- Bone cancer is one of the leading killers of giant dogs.
- Joint diseases are a major health problem in giant dogs.

Therefore the bones and joints of giant breeds should be carefully protected, especially when they're still growing.

> Giant breed puppies are much more fragile than they look. Slow growth and no forced exercise when young (up to 24 months old) can help prevent orthopedic diseases in giant breeds.

Now, that doesn't mean NO exercise.

> Giant breeds who are ***under***-exercised will end up with muscles, ligaments, and tendons that are too weak to support all the weight they need to carry as adults. That leaves them more vulnerable to injury.

Safe exercise for giant breeds up to 24 months old

✓ Free play with another (well-known to you) dog. Free play is the best exercise for young giant breeds because they tend to flop down and rest when they've had enough. Don't let young giants play with bossy dogs who try to goad the clumsy youngster into vigorous games that go on and on.

- ✓ Swimming. Tones your giant pup's muscles with no impact or concussion from the hard ground.
- ✓ Walking. Limit walks to 20 minutes, which minimizes the stress of repeatedly jarring their long gangly legs and immature joints. Once mature, longer walks are fine, but you should never jog or bicycle with these dogs.

Exercise for flat-faced breeds

Flat-faced breeds have inherited deformities in their face, nasal passages, and respiratory system.

This makes it difficult for them to breathe easily, especially in hot, humid weather. In the summer they should be kept indoors in air-conditioning and supervised during outside activity so they don't become overheated and suffer heatstroke.

To safely exercise these dogs, stick with moderate walks in cool weather, moderate games of fetch (if they're willing), and playing with a compatible (and well-known to you) dog who won't push the flat-faced dog to the point of dangerous panting and overheating.

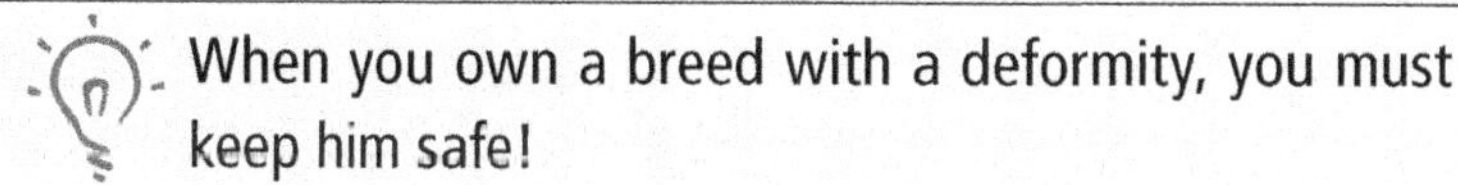
When you own a breed with a deformity, you must keep him safe!

Chapter 6

The 6th Thing You Must Do Right: Provide Emotional Security

We've talked about keeping your dog healthy by:

1. feeding real food
2. minimizing vaccinations
3. protecting his immune system by providing a non-toxic environment
4. preventing fleas, ticks, and heartworm
5. keeping his body and mind fit through physical exercise and mental stimulation

Your dog's physical and mental health are also affected by his *emotional health.*

There are two basic emotional states in dogs:

✓ calm/relaxed/secure

✗ or anxious/insecure

When your dog feels anxious and insecure, his body produces defensive biochemicals such as adrenaline and cortisol.

These potent biochemicals make his mind and body feel perpetually stressed and "wired", which can lead to digestive upsets, inflammatory health issues, and overreactive or obsessive behaviors.

Causes of anxiety and insecurity in dogs

- ✗ Dogs feel anxious and insecure when their daily schedule is unpredictable and different things happen at different times in different ways.
- ✗ Dogs feel anxious and insecure when you haven't established black-and-white rules. The dog isn't sure which of his behaviors will result in a reward and which behaviors will result in a correction.
- ✗ Dogs feel anxious and insecure when you (or your spouse or kids) enforce the rules inconsistently or in different ways.
- ✗ Dogs feel anxious and insecure when they haven't been taught many words or skills so they can't understand what you want them to do or how to do it.
- ✗ Dogs feel anxious and insecure when they spend a lot of time outside alone.
- ✗ Dogs feel anxious and insecure when everyone works or goes to school all day. Canines are sociable animals, not solitary animals. Dogs left alone for 6+ hours a day are lonely and bored.
- ✗ Dogs feel anxious and insecure when their household becomes unharmonious. Family problems are hard on both children and sensitive dogs. Emotionally charged conversations or loud arguments should take place without children or dogs present.
- ✗ Dogs feel anxious and insecure when they're frequently petted, carried around, or cuddled on your lap. Over-dependency

can lead to ***separation anxiety*** when you leave the dog alone. Dependent dogs are so accustomed to being the center of attention that they may become jealous (another form of anxiety and insecurity) when you pay attention to anyone else. Neediness and dependency are terrible for a dog's emotional health.

✗ Dogs feel anxious and insecure when you fail to protect them from kids or other pets who are pestering or bullying them.

✗ Dogs feel anxious and insecure when they haven't been taken out into the world and taught how to behave around strangers, strange dogs, or unfamiliar places. When a dog acts inappropriately in public and you don't respond properly, he will progress from anxiety and insecurity to neurotic or aggressive behavior.

✗ Dogs feel anxious and insecure when they don't see you as the competent leader of the household. If you're not comfortable providing guidance and direction and setting firm boundaries, if you feel guilty about saying "No" to your dog and making it stick… your dog will think that ***HE*** needs to take charge of every situation and make all the decisions. This is a stressful mind-set for any dog because he isn't equipped to make decisions in our complicated world.

How to provide emotional security so your dog has a calm, relaxed state of mind

Establish routines.

As much as possible, your dog's daily schedule should be a series of established routines that happen the same way every day. Familiar routines reassure him that everything in his little world is predictable—the same as it was yesterday, and the same as it will be tomorrow. Routines reassure him that YOU are dependable, that he can count on you to say and do things that he understands. A dog feels calm, relaxed, and secure when he knows what happens next.

Set firm boundaries—Yes to this, No to that.

Show your dog which of his behaviors will result in a reward and which behaviors will result in a correction. A dog feels calm, relaxed, and secure when he knows which behaviors are expected of him, and which behaviors he is NOT allowed to do.

Be completely consistent.

If you tell your dog to do something (or not to do something), you must make absolutely sure he does it, or stops doing it. Family members should use the same words and commands, reward the same behaviors, and correct the same behaviors. Dogs feel uneasy with "maybes" and "sometimes." A dog feels calm, relaxed, and secure when he knows that the rules always apply, so he never needs to guess.

Teach your dog new words and skills.

Like anyone who learns a foreign language, when your dog learns what your human sounds mean, he feels more secure. Same with learning skills such as heel, sit, stand, stay, come, wait, fetch. Child psychologists say that telling a child he's "wonderful" isn't nearly as effective as praising something specific the child has accomplished. Kids prefer specific, earned praise to vague, gushy platitudes. So do dogs.

Keep your dog indoors with you.

A dog feels calm, relaxed, and secure when he's a true member of your family. That means he lives in your house with you. A dog should only be outdoors for potty breaks, interactive play or exercise, or to lounge in the sun on a pleasant day while you're outside with him or just inside the house keeping an eye on him. When he's done, he should come back in.

> Dogs who spend much of their day outdoors, or in the basement or garage, or separate kennel building are forced to live "outside" their pack, on the edge of it, never really immersed in day-to-day family life.

Provide a safe den.

A dog feels calm, relaxed, and secure when he has a sanctuary all his own. If he finds his own private place and it's acceptable to you, put his blanket or bed there to encourage him to keep using it. I leave the doors to my dogs' crates open all day and they go in and out to rest and "recharge".

Provide sufficient companionship.

Dogs are sociable animals, which means they feel calm, relaxed, and secure when they're with another member of their family most of the day. At the very least, a dog left alone for more than 6 hours a day should have canine companionship.

Encourage independence.

Providing sufficient companionship doesn't mean your dog should frequently be held or carried, or cuddled on your lap, or petted every time he nudges your hand. A dog feels calm, relaxed, and secure in your presence, yes—but he should be standing on his own four feet most of the time.

Socialize your dog.

A dog feels calm, relaxed, and secure when he knows how to behave in different social settings. Take him to the park, downtown, a shopping center and practice all the words and skills he knows ("Heel. Sit. Come."), providing treats and leash guidance to ensure that he pays attention to you and ignores everyone else.

> Your goal is NOT to make your dog "friendly." Your goal is to teach him to behave (to pay attention, no barking, jumping, lunging) in different social settings. You want him to focus on you and simply "share space" with everyone else as though they were harmless background noise. He might ***like*** other people and other dogs... or not. Either way, he must ***accept*** them without resorting to inappropriate behavior.

Protect the dog from children and other animals.

A dog feels calm, relaxed, and secure when he sees that you will intervene if anyone pesters or bullies him or steals his food or toy.

Maintain household harmony.

A dog feels calm, relaxed, and secure when family members get along and there is peace in your household.

Provide calm, confident leadership.

Show your dog that you're in charge of everything in his life, that everything good comes from you, and that he should look trustingly to you for guidance, direction, and permission. A relationship where you are the leader and he is the respectful follower is the relationship every dog thrives on. Step up and be the decision-maker. Show him the clear, black-and-white rules and routines he is to follow, and then make sure he does.

When he is confident that you have everything under control, he will feel calm, relaxed, and secure.

You can learn how to do everything in this chapter in my *Respect Training* book. Follow the advice in that book faithfully and you'll have a calm, relaxed, secure, and well-behaved dog!

Chapter 7

The 7th Thing You Must Do Right: Emphasize Safety

We've talked about keeping your dog healthy by:

1. feeding real food
2. minimizing vaccinations
3. protecting his immune system by providing a non-toxic environment
4. preventing fleas, ticks, and heartworm
5. keeping his body and mind fit through physical exercise and mental stimulation
6. providing emotional security so he feels calm and relaxed

Raising a toddler who never grows up

Now it's time to face a grim fact.

All of this time and effort can be undone in the twinkling of any eye if you lose your dog to some tragic accident. It only takes an instant for a dog to squeeze through a gap in your fence and be lost, to dash through an open door and be hit by a car, to drown in a pool, to choke on a tiny ball, to snatch a cooked chicken wing from the kitchen counter, to be attacked by another dog, to fall from an upstairs deck, to be stolen from your yard, to be flung through the windshield of your car during a crash.

The sheer number of bad things that can happen to your dog is sobering, but what's more sobering is that almost all of those things are preventable.

> Yet they happen every day to ***someone's*** dog. Usually because that owner didn't realize that something in their dog's environment was an accident waiting to happen. And one day, sure enough, it did.

Where safety is involved, a strong immune system won't do your dog any good. As responsible guardians, we need to open our eyes really wide and observe everything going on around our dogs. Is ***that*** safe? Is ***that?*** What about ***that?***

> If there's anything in his environment that isn't safe, we should change it right now to ***prevent*** tragedy from ever happening.

And we need to keep on doing that for the rest of our dog's life.

Because raising a dog is like raising a toddler… except that a dog never grows up.

Like toddlers, dogs are curious and impulsive. They run in every direction, oblivious to danger. They poke and prod and explore with their mouth.

Raising a dog is like raising a toddler who never grows up.

Just as we did back in Chapter 3 on providing a non-toxic environment, let's take a walking tour of your home and yard, this time looking at potential safety issues.

Confinement is a must

Dogs who run loose are hit by cars. Poisoned, accidentally or on purpose. Stolen. Injured or killed by other dogs. Caught in animal traps.

Dogs who run loose CAUSE accidents by dashing across the street and forcing drivers to swerve wildly.

> I don't believe anyone reading this book would let their dog run loose, but in case you know someone who does, they're being utterly irresponsible, both to the dog and to other people.

Do all dogs need a fenced yard?

In my opinion, yes. All dogs should have a fenced yard in which to stretch their legs and run around a little, every day. See the article on my website: *Do dogs need a fenced yard?*

You might think you're covered because there is a fenced dog park nearby. This isn't the same as having a yard that's always accessible right outside your door so your dog can enjoy a quick dash into the fresh air. You're not likely to dash to the dog park multiple times a day, especially in bad weather.

Invisible fencing

In the article on my website (*Do dogs need a fenced yard?*), you'll find my advice on invisible/electronic "containment systems." In short, I do not recommend them to keep your dog on your property. ***In my experience, invisible fencing is unsafe.***

A small potty yard

If you can't build a real fence out of board panels or chain link, there are other options.

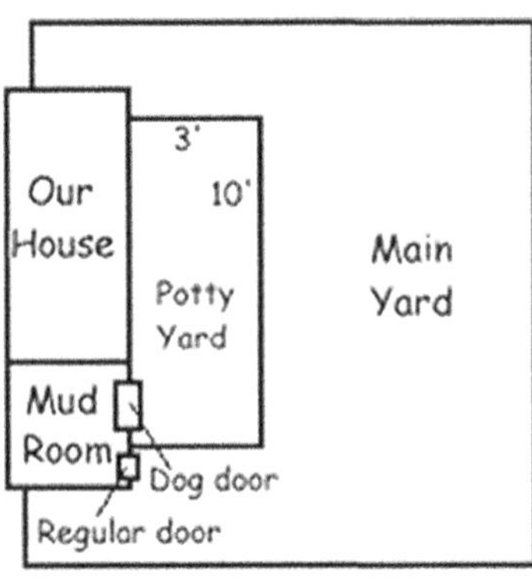

We have a mud room off our kitchen. In the mud room wall is a doggy door leading outside to a small, fenced **potty yard.** Our dogs can let themselves out to go to the bathroom—after which they can dash right back in.

Our main yard is also fenced, but if yours isn't, at least your dog would have an enclosed place to go to the bathroom without being leashed.

A makeshift pen for small dogs

Alternatively, you can pound some stakes into the ground, then run chicken wire or lightweight garden fencing around the stakes, attaching the fencing to the stakes with gardener's twisty ties. You could make quite a large enclosure at minimal expense that would be serviceable for a small dog—assuming, of course, that you're always supervising him in this somewhat "fragile" yard.

A commercial "exercise pen" or kennel run

A wire exercise pen or chain-link kennel run is freestanding and movable. But these small enclosures should not be a place to LEAVE your dog, except for perhaps an hour on a beautiful day. Instead, ex-pens and kennel runs serve as safe places where your dog can do his business off-leash.

I recommend searching for "Midwest exercise pen" on Amazon.

If your dog is medium-sized or large, buy several pens and hook them together to make a more spacious enclosure.

Close to the house

Any enclosure should be placed very close to your house. You will need to let your dog out multiple times a day—in bad weather, too—including very early in the morning and right before bedtime. So it needs to be close to the house.

> And you need to project into the future when a dog is older and needs to go out more often. One of my dogs is on medication that causes her to need quick bathroom access many times a day.

Tethering your dog to a swivel stake or cable/pulley system

This can work if you use it ONLY so your dog has some freedom to stretch his legs and sniff around so he can do his business. Then bring him back indoors. Never leave your dog tied outside on a tether.

Here's what can go wrong with tethers:

- Tied dogs can pull the stake out of the ground or the cable off the tree.
- They can chew through the rope.
- The rope or chain can break.
- They can get tangled in the rope/chain or wind it around something and hurt themselves trying to get loose.
- Tied dogs frequently become frustrated and aggressive, barking and lunging against their restraint when anyone passes by.

- NON-aggressive, sensitive dogs often feel trapped when the line becomes taut and then they may react with **defensive** ferocity, i.e. "I'll get YOU before you get ME!"

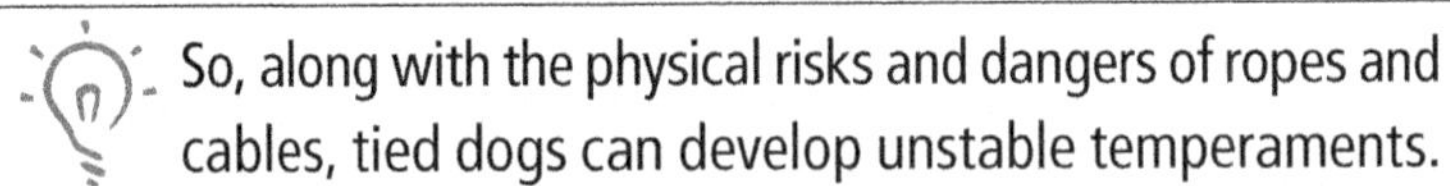

So, along with the physical risks and dangers of ropes and cables, tied dogs can develop unstable temperaments.

Make your yard escape-proof

Some escapes are deliberate. Your dog jumps or scrambles over the fence. He digs under or chews through. He opens the gate latch with his nose or paw. However he manages it, he tried to get out and now he's gone.

Dogs escape deliberately because they're bored or lonely, because they're tempted by something outside the fence (another dog or a squirrel), or because they're frightened (thunderstorm or fireworks).

Other escapes are accidental/opportunistic. Someone leaves the door or gate ajar. A child on a bicycle crashes into your fence, a board shatters, and your dog wanders through the gap. Down the driveway, across the street, and now he's gone.

To prevent escapes:

Know your own dog. Some dogs are clever ***escape artists*** who will go over, under, or through fences, gates, and doors. Other dogs seem to be homebodies—but then again, perhaps the chance hasn't yet presented itself, or the right temptation hasn't come along.

> Some of the most notorious escape artists include Siberian Huskies, Shiba Inus, Basenjis, Border Collies, Miniature Pinschers (small, yes, but incredibly agile and clever), Jack Russells (and other terriers), and Beagles.

Build appropriate fences ***for your particular dog.***

- 6-foot fences are safest for medium to large dogs, although some tall dogs will stay happily behind a 4-foot fence, while some small dogs will amaze (and dismay!) you by scrambling over a 7-foot fence.
- A solid fence is safest. If your dog can't see out, he is less likely to ***bark*** at things. If strangers can't see in, they are less likely to ***steal*** your dog. If kids can't see in, they are less likely to ***tease*** your dog. If passing dogs can't see in, they won't ***fence-fight*** with your dog. And solid fencing is ***harder to climb*** than wire or chain link. Pickets may also deter jumping, but they can be dangerous if a daring jumper tries to clear them—and misses.
- Are there low sections in the fence where your dog might be more tempted to jump? Are there any objects close to the fence (a tree stump or heavy-duty storage container) that your dog might scramble onto and use as a springboard?

- For serious jumpers and climbers, you may need to install an overhang around the top of the fence. This consists of 12- to 18-inch steel extension bars attached to the top of the fence, angled inward at 45-degrees, and strung with chicken wire. Think of prison-yard containment.

  Some determined dogs can only be secured in an enclosure completely roofed over with wire mesh.

- Can your dog dig under? Walk around the inside perimeter and study the bottom of the fence where it meets the ground.

  Some dogs can crawl under a surprisingly small gap. To deter serious diggers, line the inside perimeter with landscape timbers or patio blocks. Or dig a narrow trench along the inside perimeter, then fill it with concrete or attach a strip of chicken wire or garden fencing to the bottom of the fence, burying the lowest few inches in the trench.

- Can your dog squeeze through? If your fence is slats or pickets, make sure the ***spacing*** is narrow enough. If necessary, run a strip of small-mesh chicken wire or garden fencing across the slats.

- Are your gates secure? More dogs escape through open gates than by any other route. Self-closing gates are great, but might lull you into assuming that if a gate ***closes,*** it always ***latches.*** Not true! Also keep in mind that latches have two parts: the part that attaches to the gate, and the part that attaches to the gatepost. Make sure BOTH of these are firmly attached. Check periodically for loose screws or rotting wood. You might even opt for a double latch, especially if you have a dog who jumps against the gate. If one latch breaks down, the other is still there.

> Close everything behind you! Double-check to be sure everything has latched. Get into the habit of asking: "Are all of our doors closed? Are all of our gates closed? Where is my dog right now?"

Finally, don't put your dog in a ***position*** to escape. Don't leave your dog outdoors unless you're home AND watching him.

Secure your doors

Do all the doors of your house open into a fenced yard? If so, then even if your dog gets through the door, he'll still be safely confined in the yard.

But if you have a door that doesn't open into a fenced yard, I recommend that you add a screen/storm door to it, as a back-up barrier. That way, when you open the main door, your dog is still behind the screen/storm.

Beware of screen doors alone. On a pleasant day, it's tempting to leave your front door open and let fresh air in through the screen. But with screen doors that go all the way to the floor, this can be risky, as a clever dog might push open (or chew through) the screen in order to get to passing people, other dogs, or a squirrel. Again, you must know your own dog.

If you do trust a screen door to confine your dog, latch it tightly. Lock the latch. And DON'T trust your dog behind only a screen door when you leave the house.

> One last thing... don't rely ***only*** on physical barriers. Teach your dog NOT to go through open doors or gates without permission. I explain how to teach this in my Respect Training books.

Safety in the kitchen

Aside from cleaning products that irritate your dog's eyes, respiratory system, skin, and paws, the biggest dangers in kitchens are HEAT and DROPPED COOKWARE.

A dog underfoot could get burned by splattered fat or sauce, cut by a knife you knock off the counter, or hit on the head by a dropped pot.

Don't prop a small appliance on the edge of the counter with its *electrical cord hanging down* such that your dog could accidentally pull on the cord and bring down the appliance.

Keep your *wastebasket* under the sink or behind a closed pantry door, or use a heavy barrel with a snap-tight lid.

Food left within reach makes a tempting target. Small dogs are not exempt from this caution—plenty of small dogs will jump onto a chair and then onto the table to sample the food.

Most kitchens have a *slippery floor* of vinyl or tile on which your dog should not be allowed to romp vigorously. Sliding on a slick surface can cause ligament and joint injuries, in all dogs, but especially in youngsters whose bones and joints are still growing, and in older dogs whose joints are arthritic.

> Play active games only on carpets. If your whole house is vinyl or hardwood, add large area rugs for traction.

Don't spray *insecticide* along your baseboards or set ant traps on the floor where the dog can reach them.

Make sure *cupboard doors* close securely—don't tempt your dog by leaving a low cupboard door ajar. If you have a really nosy dog, you may even need child safety locks on lower cabinets. If you have a chowhound, the only food that should be in low cupboards should be in cans and jars (not cardboard boxes).

Safety in the living and family rooms

Some dogs find *electrical cords* to be irresistible and will chew happily on them. "Happily", that is, until their tongue is sliced open or burned from an electrical shock. If you have a puppy (or an adult chewer), hide electrical cords under rugs or furniture, or run them through protective PVC piping. You can also buy electrical cord "tamers" that keep cords jacketed inside protective sleeves.

Drapery cords can be another irresistible tug toy. Pups can chew off and swallow bits of the cord or become entangled in it and injure themselves trying to get free. Lift drapery cords out of reach until your puppy is older and more trustworthy.

If you have *indoor plants,* any plant material your dog eats may produce mild vomiting or diarrhea. But some plants are truly toxic to dogs. See the most current list of toxic and non-toxic plants on the Animal Poison Control Center website. (Some dogs will even chew on **silk** plants.)

Few dogs are so dumb as to actually stick their nose into the flames of your fireplace!

But a heat-loving dog might lie close enough for his hair to be struck by flying sparks. Or he may step on hot ashes. Use a fireplace screen so your dog must keep his distance. If he's a chewer, obviously keep your matches, kindling, and firewood where your dog can't get them.

On *low coffee tables,* food and other forbidden objects (cigarettes, pills, eyeglasses, breakables) can be easily stolen. Don't underestimate the reach of tiny dogs—they're often clever with their paws! If they can stand up on their hind legs and stretch far enough to touch something on the table with their paw, they may be able to pull it off.

And then there are the **tail waggers!** The vigorous wag of an enthusiastic, long-tailed dog can clear a coffee table with one sweep. Then everything on the floor becomes a potential chewable.

More about toy dogs… look critically at your furniture, from your tiny dog's eye-level, and consider whether it poses any danger. Some tables have sharp protrusions or crossbars running underneath. A romping toy dog could put out his eye or sustain a concussion if he races underneath and conks his head.

Safety in the bedrooms

Don't leave candles, matches, foam earplugs, antacids, etc. on your nightstand if your dog can reach them from the floor or bed.

Many dogs like to drag around your dirty clothes. That's fine, unless he actually chews the crotch out of your underwear and swallows it. Then he might end up in a veterinary emergency room with a blocked digestive tract. If you have a chewer, make sure your laundry basket has a lid and/or put it out of reach or behind a closed door.

Kids' bedrooms can be particularly dangerous, with swallowable marbles, action figures, blocks, and stuffed animals. Puppies and confirmed chewers must be kept out of these bedrooms.

Safety in the bathroom

Don't leave any ***pills*** on the edge of the sink. You might accidentally knock them off and if they land on the bath mat, you won't hear them fall. Even vitamins or ibuprofen can kill a dog.

Many dogs are drawn to smelly used tissues, adhesive bandages, and cotton balls. If your pup is a tissue shredder, put the wastebasket up on the back of the toilet, or in the tub behind the shower curtain.

Gentlemen, here's another reason to keep the toilet seat **down**—so your dog can't drink the water.

Safety in the yard and garden

A *chemically-treated yard* and *toxic plants* are the obvious dangers. There are plenty of hardy plants you can choose that don't need to be sprayed with insecticides or fungicides, or you can make organic solutions that won't harm your dog.

Is your compost pile secure from your dog rooting around in it?

For the same reason, secure your *garbage cans.* Use heavy-duty cans with tight lids and/or store the cans completely away from your dog.

Don't leave *garden tools* lying around with the tines pointed up so that your dog might step on them and cut his foot.

Safety on the driveway and walkways

Antifreeze can leak from your car's radiator or spill on the ground while you're pouring it, and pets may be drawn to its sweet taste. So I recommend using antifreeze with propylene glycol (much less toxic) instead of ethylene glycol (highly toxic).

Chemical ***ice-melting products*** are serious irritants to your dog's paws. The pellets get wedged between his toes and prolonged exposure can actually burn his feet. If he licks it off his paws, you may see vomiting or diarrhea, or worse.

The manufacturers of these products are sticking "Pet Friendly" assurances on the labels, but none of them are safe for pets. The ASPCA Animal Poison Control Center classifies all ice-melting products as toxic.

> The most dangerous products are those that contain chloride: *sodium chloride* (aka rock salt), *magnesium chloride, calcium chloride, potassium chloride.* The safest products are those that contain **urea.** Unfortunately, urea is lousy at melting ice, so you'll end up using a lot of it, which isn't good for surrounding vegetation.

Honestly, the best thing to do is shovel up as much snow as you can. Then apply a ***limited amount*** of ice melter to break the surface tension between the ice and pavement. Give it a little time to work, then use an ice pick to segment the remaining pieces, and a shovel to remove the slush.

> This quick removal process gets rid of those nasty chemicals that can burn the feet of passing dogs, cats, squirrels, etc.

Or… don't bother melting the ice and just use plain sand for traction.

Safety during walks

Since so many people don't shovel up their ice-melting products, you should expect that your dog's paws are walking through a toxic, salty slurry. Thus you should thoroughly rinse his feet after winter walks. Some owners put protective booties on their dogs.

Be aware that dogs can get frostbite just like people. A dog's ears, nose, and feet are especially susceptible. After a walk, check his feet for *snow and ice balls* embedded in the webs between his toes.

Put a sweater on your dog if he has a thin or sleek coat, if he has just been clipped, if he is elderly, or if he has an illness such as hypothyroidism where he has difficulty maintaining body heat.

Since so many people use the most toxic form of antifreeze, ethylene glycol, don't let your dog drink from a puddle where a car might have parked.

Since so many people use chemicals on their lawns, be wary of letting your dog romp across grass that looks perfect and pristine with no dandelions or weeds—it's been sprayed.

Be careful walking in hot weather. **Dogs don't sweat freely like people do.** Dogs can only release heat from their bodies through their tongue (by panting) and their footpads. So they are much more susceptible to heatstroke than we are. This is especially true of dogs with short faces, heavy coats, or black coats.

Before walking your dog across *blacktop* on a hot day, reach down and feel the surface with your hand. If it's hot to your bare hand, it will be hot to his bare feet. Pick up your small dog, or run across quickly (if it's a short distance), or find another route.

Safe collars and leashes

For most dogs, start with a flat buckle collar of nylon or leather. It simply buckles around your dog's neck. Some dogs never need anything more.

If you have a long-haired dog, a flat buckle collar might squash the hair, creating a depression around your dog's neck in much the same way as your wedding ring causes a depression on your finger. You might want to try a rolled leather collar, which is narrow and rounded and doesn't put as much pressure on the hair.

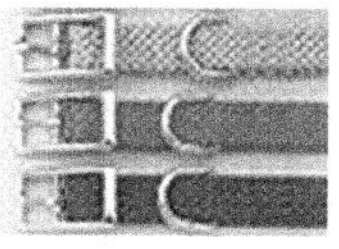

For toy dogs I recommend a Sunburst collar (Coastal Pet is the manufacturer). It is $^{3}/_{8}$ inch wide and made of very soft fabric where the buckle seeks its own hole so it's adjustable for perfect fit. It comes in lengths as short as 8".

Some toy dogs have a delicate windpipe and a collar makes them cough. If that happens, you can switch to a harness. I like a soft mesh harness like the Puppia® brand (pictured).

Strong pullers

Although a regular buckle collar **looks** mild, it exerts force on one concentrated point on your dog's throat if he's a hard puller. That puts a lot of pressure on his throat. You'll need to stop the pulling with a safer training collar and the proper leash handling techniques.

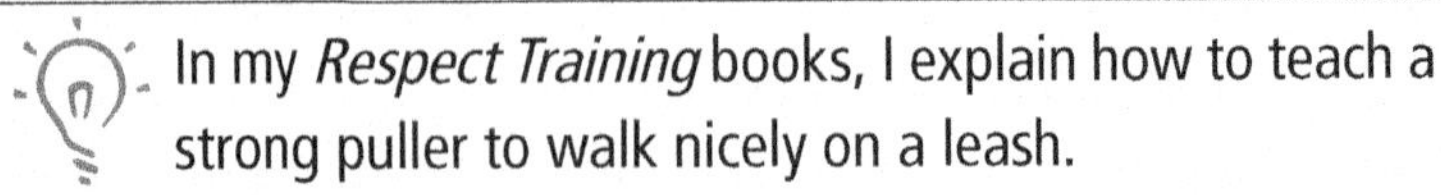

In my *Respect Training* books, I explain how to teach a strong puller to walk nicely on a leash.

Leashes

I recommend a 4-foot to 6-foot leash made of cotton cloth, leather, or nylon.

If you use a "retractable" leash, don't abuse it. I've seen people allow their dog to roam at the end of a long, retractable leash around other people or other dogs. The dog could approach individuals who didn't want to be approached, jump on them, or tangle the leash around them.

Use retractable leashes sensibly. You can allow full-leash length in open fields or parks or along quiet roads. But when people or other dogs are passing by, or when you're walking on or near a road with traffic, ***shorten the leash*** so that your dog is close beside you and fully under control.

Your dog should carry identification

ID Tag

When someone finds a loose dog, they look for an ID tag. If it has a personal phone number on it, they will usually take a minute to call.

A license or rabies tag is not enough! Most people will NOT call Animal Control or a vet to track down a license number or rabies tag number. It's too much hassle. They'll rationalize… "Ah, he probably lives down the street. His owner will be annoyed if he has to go to the pound to get his dog. And I'm supposed to hang around here waiting for Animal Control to show up? Nah, I'll let him go on his way, he'll probably find his way home."

So get your dog an ID tag with your phone number. I've had good luck with plastic reflective tags from Lucky Pet ID Tags. I prefer plastic because they make less noise than metal. I also prefer a very small tag, even on large dogs, so it doesn't annoy the dog by bumping against his neck.

Have the company engrave **"I'm lost!"** and your phone number. "I'm lost!" convinces the potential Good Samaritan that this dog shouldn't be wandering. Rather than my name and address, I prefer to include a second or even third phone number.

> Whether to include your dog's name is controversial. Hearing his name might reassure a nervous dog. On the other hand, if the dog becomes too responsive, the finder might decide to keep him!

Microchip

One weakness of an ID tag is that it doesn't do any good if your dog's collar comes off. A microchip, on the other hand, is **permanent identification** that stays with your dog forever.

A microchip:

- ✓ is a tiny transponder, about the size of a grain of rice
- ✓ is implanted (by your vet) with a hypodermic needle under the loose skin atop your dog's shoulders. No sedation is needed.
- ✓ has no power supply or battery. Its electronic circuitry is only activated if it is ***scanned.***
- ✓ bonds itself into place under your dog's skin, so it doesn't move around.
- ✓ is inexpensive—$25 to $75, plus about $20 for lifetime registration

How a microchip can bring your lost dog home

Most animal shelters have a microchip scanner which they wave across the back of each dog who comes in. The scanner emits safe, low-frequency radio waves that activate the microchip, which sends your dog's unique ID number to the scanner's viewing window. The shelter then contacts the national database where the ID number is registered, and you get a phone call!

The only microchips I recommend

There are a number of microchips, but many of them are flawed and inferior. I only use chips made by AKC Reunite (their Trovan chip), HomeAgain (their Destron chip), or Avid (their Avid chip). Most vets carry at least one of those three chips. Don't settle for less.

> Once the chip is implanted, it must be registered! This is a huge mistake some owners make—not registering the chip. A chip that isn't listed in one of the major databases is useless.

The only registries I recommend

There are lots of registries vying for your business, but most of them are fraught with problems. The free ones sound appealing, but who knows when they'll go out of business? I stick with the oldest registries that are tried and true.

- ✓ If my dog got the AKC Reunite chip, I register it in the AKC Reunite database for a one-time fee of $20.
- ✓ If my dog got the Avid chip, I register it in BOTH the AKC Reunite database (one-time fee of $20) AND in Avid's PETtrac database (one-time fee of $20).

✓ If my dog got the HomeAgain chip, I register it in the AKC Reunite database (one-time fee of $20). I do NOT register a HomeAgain chip in HomeAgain's own database. Why not? Because they charge ANNUAL fees, which is ridiculous.

Safety around other animals

OTHER DOGS

During your walks, you're bound to encounter other dogs.

One of the responsibilities of a leader is to protect followers. When your dog sees that ***you*** will step between him and an approaching dog, he will be more likely to relax when he sees other dogs. Often a dog who lunges or bellows threats at other dogs is feeling anxious and insecure because he thinks ***he*** needs to handle potential threats.

So when you and your dog go for a walk, especially in an area where you know other dogs run loose, take a sturdy walking stick.

If another dog actually approaches you and your dog, step firmly between them. Brandish your walking stick and order the other dog to get lost. If he keeps coming, drive him away with your stick. If there is a truly aggressive dog in your area, carry pepper spray.

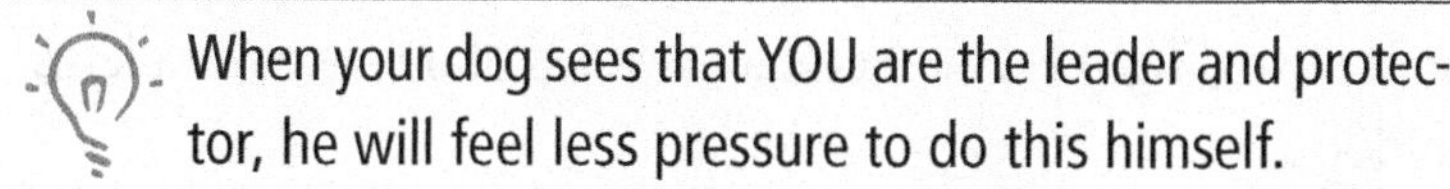
When your dog sees that YOU are the leader and protector, he will feel less pressure to do this himself.

If he continues to charge to the end of the leash, lunging and barking at other dogs, pick up my *Respect Training* book.

Should dogs be allowed to sniff each other?

I would need to know the other dog ***very well.*** Because if my dog is small, sensitive, or timid, a mistake here could have catastrophic consequences to his future attitude toward other dogs.

More dog fights ensue from sniffing noses and butts than at any other time.

This canine ritual is where crucial *social signals* are exchanged. Each dog uses subtle body language to say things such as:

- "I'm the boss!"
- "Oh yeah? Says who?"
- "I don't like the way you look or smell."
- "I don't mean any harm, please don't hurt me!"

Dogs can carry on quite a sophisticated conversation using the positioning of their head, ears, and tail, the tension of their muscles, the "hardness" or "softness" of their facial expression.

When this exchange communicates a pecking order that both dogs agree with, everything will probably be fine. But if that order is in doubt, a fight will likely ensue, either immediately or soon.

> The chances of a dog fight increase markedly when owners hold their dogs ***on tight leashes*** and let them sniff noses. Tight leashes lead to all kinds of behavior problems in dogs.

Even if an owner assures you that his dog is "good" with other dogs...

Take it with a grain of salt. Dog owners are always assuring people of their dog's "friendliness." Just ask any (bitten) vet, groomer, or mail carrier how many times he or she has been told, "Oh, my dog would never bite."

Sad to say, many owners know little or nothing about their own dog. Even worse, they have little or no control over its behavior.

Should you allow your small dog to play with a larger dog?

I don't. A larger dog can accidentally hurt a small dog simply by jumping up and down. Even playful pawing can harm or frighten a smaller dog.

And there is the ***prey instinct*** to think about. I have been the unhappy eyewitness to horrifying spectacles in which a large dog suddenly grabbed, shook, and seriously injured (and in one tragic case, killed) the smaller one.

The speed with which it happens is unbelievable.

The problem is that larger dogs may view toy dogs as *prey*. A sudden movement, such as your toy dog pouncing on a leaf, can trigger chasing and grabbing instincts even in a ***nice*** larger dog who means well.

For safety's sake, if you own a small dog, assume that:

- ✗ other owners don't understand the prey instinct.
- ✗ the efforts of other owners to control and restrain their dog may be slow, weak, and ineffective.

Err on the side of caution. Keep one eye peeled for larger dogs and move your small dog out of harm's way or pick him up.

CATS

When it comes to cats, there are three safety concerns.

Cat chasing can become an obsession.

Dogs who become enthusiastic about cat chasing will dash through open doors, leap from car windows, climb over fences, and rush heedlessly across the street. Since you never know when a cat may appear from the shadows, cat-chasing dogs are risky to take anywhere.

Your dog could injure or kill a cat.

Some dogs become deadly serious about stalking cats. If your neighbor's cat is injured or killed by your dog, not only is this a tragedy for the cat, but also you will end up paying the medical bills and your neighbor may retaliate by seeing that some "accident" befalls your dog when you're not home.

The cat could fight back.

Most dogs chase just for the fun of it and will put on the brakes and beat a hasty retreat if the cat suddenly turns to confront them. But if your dog can't get out of the way in time, a big ol' tomcat can cause nasty damage.

> Cat teeth and claws carry LOTS of bacteria, so cat scratches and bites are likely to become infected. And a dog who is hurt by a cat may develop psychological fears and neurotic behaviors.

OTHER ANIMALS

It's tempting to send your dog chasing after pesky squirrels or rabbits who dig holes in your garden or monopolize your bird feeders. But as we've just seen, chase-oriented dogs risk injury (or worse) when they forget their boundary training and self-control. They dash through open doors, pull you into the street, slip their collars, jump out of your car, and so on.

> Dogs who are allowed to chase other living things usually do so at the worst possible time. Then they never chase anything again.

Some animals fight back. A cornered raccoon can be absolutely ferocious. And need I mention the dismaying consequences resulting from encounters with **skunks** or **porcupines?**

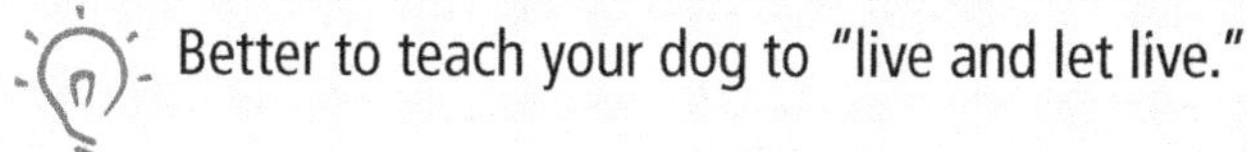

Better to teach your dog to "live and let live."

Birds of prey

- **Great Horned owls** are especially aggressive and will attack rabbits, skunks, kittens, puppies, and adult toy dogs. A friend of mine lost her Yorkshire Terrier to a Great Horned owl.
- **Golden eagles** weigh up to 10 pounds and will attack cats and small dogs. **Bald eagles** might go after a very small puppy or kitten.
- **Red-tailed hawks** weigh up to 3 pounds and might attack a pup of about the same size.

If these birds live in your area, don't let your toy dog (or a small puppy of any breed) run loose in a large open yard—**especially in the evening** when Great Horned owls are on the prowl. Stay right beside him if he needs to go outside at night.

Coyotes

In some parts of the country, coyotes are so prevalent that you should ***never*** let a small dog outside alone.

Toads

If your dog mouths a toad, the toad will protect itself by secreting a toxin from its skin. Toxins from most toads simply cause your dog to drool or vomit.

But the Colorado River toad (SW US) and the Marine Toad (Florida and South Texas) can kill a dog with their potent poison. If you live in these areas, be on the lookout for these toads.

Creepy crawly creatures

Dogs can be stung by bees, wasps, and scorpions, or bitten by spiders and snakes. And just as with people, the reaction varies from mild pain and swelling, to life-threatening anaphylactic shock and collapse. Clear away hives and nests, and also brush piles where scorpions and snakes might hide.

Car safety

If you allow your dog to ride loose in the car, you're putting the dog, yourself, your passengers, and every other person on the road in danger.

✗ In an accident, a loose dog's hurtling body smashes into the driver and other passengers with enough force to fracture a person's skull or neck.

> The Institute for Highway Safety reports that "after the collision ***outside,*** there are always collisions ***inside.*** Both wreak havoc."

- ✗ Your loose dog may CAUSE an accident by jostling your arm. Or his antics may distract you from paying full attention to the road.
- ✗ In an accident, your loose dog can be flung against the windshield, or through an open or shattered window, into the street, killing him on impact or setting him loose in traffic.
- ✗ In an accident, car doors pop open unexpectedly, or rescue personnel pull open the doors and your loose dog will take off in a panic.

> Always secure your dog in the REAR SEAT with a harness and seat belt, or in a crate that has itself been buckled into the rear seat. I recommend the Ruff Rider Safety Harness.

A dog should never ride in the front seat. Front airbags blast out of the dashboard at a fearsome speed and can kill a dog in the front seat.

Teach your dog to stay in the car even when the door is open

When you get out of the car, you should be able to open any car door without your dog immediately jumping out. He doesn't RIDE loose in the car, of course—we've already talked about that. But at some point, you will have to unbuckle his harness or open the door to his crate.

That's when the "Wait!" command comes in handy. It's taught in my *Respect Training* books.

Don't leave your dog in the car alone

You've heard all the warnings about not leaving your dog in a hot car. What you may not know is "How hot is too hot?"

On a mild 75-degree day, the temperature inside a car with the windows cracked can reach ***120 degrees in 30 minutes.***

A dog doesn't have all the sweat glands we have. He can only sweat through his tongue (by panting) and through his paw pads.

When he has only hot air to breathe, his body temperature climbs so rapidly that he is unable to lower it simply by sweating through his tongue and paws. That means he is going to overheat, and probably die.

If you see a dog panting in a car on a hot day, quickly check the closest store and ask the manager to page the vehicle's owner. Then call the police, who usually respond faster than Animal Control.

Other reasons not to leave your dog in the car alone:

- ✗ He could be stolen. Imagine what that would feel like to come outside and discover your dog gone from your car.
- ✗ He could annoy everyone by barking, especially if another car with a dog happens to park nearby.
- ✗ He could be harassed by passersby. Trapped in a small space where he can't escape, he may be terrified or become agitated and defensive.
- ✗ Or ***HE*** could be the one to initiate the aggression, lunging and barking at passersby. No, a lunging, barking dog is not "protecting his property" or "being a good watchdog." A sensible protective dog doesn't threaten people just because they walk near the car.

A dog who lunges and bellows at people simply because they walk by the car, or look at him through the window, or open the door of the car parked beside yours is an indiscriminate and undisciplined nuisance.

He is annoying everybody, he is creating a terrible impression for his breed, and he is forming a bad habit of mindless aggression.

Safety on airplanes

The only dogs who can fly in the cabin with you that way are service dogs, and very small dogs whose carriers can fit under the seat.

Every other dog must travel down in the belly of the plane as ***baggage*** or ***air cargo.*** Sometimes that works out okay. But you should know the risks:

- ✗ Flying is stressful for a dog. The baggage and cargo holds are temperature-controlled and pressurized, yes. But the experience is still frightening to a dog who is alone and cannot understand what is happening. Waiting in the terminal, with the rumble of forklifts and flinging of boxes and suitcases, bouncing along on the baggage cart, being loaded onto the plane, are especially stressful.
- ✗ Flights can be delayed or connecting flights missed. Your dog's crate may be misplaced, left behind, or loaded onto the wrong plane. He may be left in the sun on a hot tarmac runway. He may be left in a frigid warehouse.
- ✗ His kennel may be handled roughly or dropped. He may break out of his kennel and escape. He may be released from his kennel and disappear.

> Because these tragedies happen more often than you might think, I no longer allow a dog to fly unless he's in the cabin with me.

Safety during the holidays

The 4th of July

More dogs are lost around the 4th of July than any other time of year. Why? Fireworks.

There's something about the fizzing sparks and sudden explosion that terrifies many dogs. One of my own German Shepherds, who excelled in protection sports and paid no mind whatsoever to gunshots, disliked the sound of firecrackers.

It is the height of folly to leave your dog outside around the 4th of July. The calmest dog may hear a firecracker in the distance and panic—even if he has never reacted to firecrackers before—and flee over or under or through the fence.

> Keep your dog indoors around the 4th of July. If you must leave the house, lock him securely in his crate. Frightened dogs have broken through windows or torn up the house in their attempt to escape.

Halloween

If your dog is outgoing and trusting, he might find this holiday FUN because lots of children—new friends!—come to the door. My Miniature Poodle, Buffy, loves Halloween!

But if your dog is suspicious or timid, he might view these scary-looking creatures as threats. He might bark and bark and still the intruders keep coming, which makes his stress levels skyrocket.

A dog who is not fond of Trick-or-Treaters should be put in his crate in a back room. This will keep the kids safe and your dog calmer and under control.

> It's never a good idea to leave your dog outside alone. But it's especially risky on Halloween. He could become the target of juveniles playing "pranks."

Even worse, in some parts of the country, he could become the target of cults who engage in bizarre rituals in which animals are butchered. Black dogs, in particular, are at highest risk for "disappearing" around Halloween.

Thanksgiving

The obvious threat is your dog getting hold of a cooked turkey bone. Cooked bones can choke your dog, puncture his throat, or obstruct his digestive tract.

Close behind is eating rich, greasy leftovers that can cause a potentially life-threatening illness called *pancreatitis*. Veterinary emergency rooms see lots of pancreatitis victims over the Thanksgiving holidays.

That doesn't mean your dog can't partake of your holiday meal. As long as he is used to eating real food, his digestive system will have no difficulty digesting ***wholesome*** leftovers.

> ***Wholesome,*** I said! Plain turkey meat and a scoop of squash or sweet potato—unsalted and unbuttered.

NO gravy, **NO** stuffing, **NO** mashed potatoes, **NO** dinner rolls, **NO** pies, nothing with butter, sauces, or spices.

Christmas

Tipsy trees. Anchor the tree in a sturdy stand. Be aware that live needles cannot be digested and can puncture the throat or intestines.

Ornaments and tinsel. If you have a chewer, fasten decorations firmly to branches or hang them only on higher branches. Or surround the tree with a decorative fence, or keep your dog out of the room. Lots of ways here to ***prevent*** disasters!

Wrapping paper, bows, ribbons. Each Christmas, dogs are presented to emergency room vets with these festive items strangling their intestines.

> Speaking from experience… I recommend not allowing your dog to "unwrap" presents! It looks cute, but you might come home one day to a pile of shredded presents under the tree. It happened to me when I was a teenager with a young German Shepherd!

*UN*wrapped presents. After you open and admire a new gift, watch where you set it down. It may look like an inviting new toy to your dog. Children's toys are especially dangerous, as they often contain small parts that you might not notice are missing… until the dog starts vomiting.

Desserts, potpourri, incense… Don't leave your dog in a room unattended if there are tempting chocolate sweets or fragrant candles on the coffee table.

Christmas plants. If your dog nibbles on Christmas cactus, hemlock, holly, ivy, mistletoe, or poinsettia, the results can range from a mildly upset stomach to seizures and death. Keep these plants away from pets!

Unhealthy gifts given to your dog. Well-meaning friends and relatives may give your dog unsafe or unhealthy gifts, such as flimsy stuffed animals, rawhide chews, or a box of supermarket treats. Find a polite way to keep such things away from your dog.

Safety when you visit friends and relatives

Visiting is a major part of holidays… and other times of the year, as well. But if you bring your dog along, don't get so caught up with visiting that you forget his safety. Remember, a dog is a toddler!

For example, don't let him loose in someone else's house until you're sure that…

- ✓ All doors to the outside are closed and secure.
- ✓ The floors are not slick and slippery, especially if your dog is a clumsy adolescent or arthritic senior citizen.

✓ There isn't anything toxic or chewable that he could get hold of—mousetraps, kids' toys, rawhide chews, chocolates on the coffee table.

> It's always safest to keep your dog on-leash in other people's houses. There are too many potential dangers in a home that hasn't been carefully dog-proofed like yours has.

And don't let your dog loose in someone else's ***yard*** until you're sure that...

✓ fences and gates are high enough and secure.

✓ they haven't spread pesticides on the lawn or snail bait in the garden.

✓ garden tools or other sharp objects aren't lying about.

✓ garbage cans are lidded or out of reach.

✓ there isn't an aggressive dog next door.

> Walk around the yard and look for yourself. Don't accept reassurances from people who haven't read this book. They have good intentions, but they're unaware of important canine safety issues.

Safety when friends visit YOU

If you have guests, especially long-term guests, teach them about canine safety. Make sure they understand that they...

✓ should close all doors and gates firmly.

✓ should close all cabinets and cupboards firmly.

✓ should close their bedroom door to keep the dog out.

✓ shouldn't give your dog ***anything*** to eat.

But don't rely on them to remember. Keep tabs on them yourself. Check the floor to make sure they haven't dropped stuff that your dog may eat. Make sure the doors to their rooms are closed. Double-check that your front and back doors are closed, along with your outside gates.

When you cut the chocolate cake, look directly at your dog and say, "No, you can't have chocolate. Chocolate can kill a dog." Your guests hear it without feeling like you're lecturing them personally.

Don't let anyone take your dog for a walk unless you go with them.

- **Guests don't know** your dog. Maybe he's leery of passersby wearing beards or hats. Maybe he has a bad habit of trying to drink out of puddles (remember antifreeze?) or trying to eat junk off the sidewalk. Maybe he lunges after squirrels and could pull the leash right out of your startled guest's hand.

- **Guests may not know** how to control your dog properly around other dogs. What happens if your dog—or an approaching dog—acts aggressively?

- **Guests don't know** your neighborhood. They don't know where the loose dogs are, or the dogs who charge the fence when you walk by, or the teenagers at the corner of Elm Street who think it's funny to scare passing dogs by whooping it up and pretending to throw things.

Be especially vigilant with tiny dogs.

Leading causes of death in toy dogs are accidents and injuries. Small dogs are especially at risk when they're around people who don't understand just how **fragile** they are.

Remind your guests to watch their step. Most toy dog ***adults*** are quick and agile and have learned to avoid being stepped on. But toy dog ***puppies*** don't have that experience or coordination.

> **Safety tip:** Trade heavy boots for slippers and shuffle your feet low to the floor around toy breed puppies.

Remind your guests to NOT give your dog anything to eat without checking with you first. Most people offer bits of food that are too large for a toy dog to swallow.

> Chocolate is especially deadly to tiny dogs. If your guest leaves a Hershey's Special Dark Bar on the arm of the sofa and your 5-pound dog eats it, he'll probably die.

Remind your guests to NOT pick up your toy dog. Toys tend to lie deceptively still in your arms, ***then suddenly push off*** with their hind feet against your chest, launching themselves into space and ending up with a broken leg or concussion.

> Instead, ask your guests to sit down on the couch and wait until your toy dog climbs into their lap of his own volition.

Protecting your dog from thieves

People who pay you a visit are not always friends and relatives.

Having someone take your dog is a nightmare that will leave you overcome with shock, grief, and guilt.

Why your dog might be stolen

- For money. The thief may sell the dog, or else wait for a reward to be posted, then call and report they "found" him. It's still a horrible experience, but at least you get your dog back.
- For the illegal, underground dog-fighting industry. Medium-sized and large dogs may be stolen to serve as "practice opponents" for seasoned fighting dogs. Small dogs may be stolen to serve as helpless "bait" to be ripped apart, thereby increasing a fighting dog's prey instinct and aggression.
- For breeding. The thief may want your dog for his own breeding purposes or he may deliver your dog to a puppy mill.
- For experimental research laboratories. The USDA gives people licenses to sell animals to research laboratories. USDA regulations require these people to obtain their animals from breeders or dog pounds, but some unscrupulous dealers get their dogs from thieves or from "scouts" who scour the country responding to "Free to good home" ads. The dealer then transports these unfortunate dogs to a research lab hundreds of miles away.
- For cult rituals. Dogs may be stolen for sacrificial rituals, especially around Halloween, and especially black dogs. Their butchered bodies are often found later in the woods.
- To keep for their own. Someone may simply notice your dog and find something about him appealing.
- Frustration. Upset neighbors may steal a dog who barks too much or who pees on their lawn. They may drive your dog to another city and set him loose or give him to a rescue group.

Honestly, dogs who bark all day are so annoying that normal law-abiding people can be driven crazy. If you go to work and leave your dog barking where YOU don't have to listen to him—but everyone else within earshot does—don't be surprised if you come home one day and he's gone.

How to prevent theft

Never leave your dog unattended in the yard. Dogs who are stolen are almost always outside, unsupervised.

With your dog safely indoors, lock your doors when you leave him alone. Drop a security brace into the channel of your sliding doors and windows.

Never leave your dog unattended in a car. He is vulnerable to heatstroke, harassment—and theft.

Never leave your dog unattended in front of a store or bank. Don't tie him to a lamppost while you go in "for just a minute." It ***takes*** only a minute to untie a dog and pop him inside a car.

Whether true or not, tell people your dog is neutered. Whenever anyone admires my dog, I try to work this into the conversation: "We had her spayed so she can never have puppies."

Never brag about your dog to strangers. Don't tell people how much your dog cost, how "rare" his breed or color is, or how many ribbons he has won at dog shows

> In other words, don't make your dog seem desirable to a would-be thief.

Protecting your dog also means keeping him quiet and well-behaved so he doesn't drive your neighbors to do dreadful things just so they can have some peace. Don't let him bark and bark. Don't let him go to the bathroom on your neighbor's property. Don't let him act aggressively toward your neighbor's kids or your neighbor's pets.

Don't give people a reason to want your dog ***gone.***

Have your dog microchipped. It won't ***prevent*** theft, but it may keep him out of research laboratories, which are supposed to scan dogs before accepting them. And if he somehow ends up in a shelter, they'll scan him.

Take current photos of your dog, which will help you find him and prove ownership. Go over him from head to toe and write down identifying traits: two white toenails on right front foot, heart-shaped white spot on chest, scar on left ear, crooked tooth in lower jaw. Take close-up photos of each unique trait.

Trying to find a stolen pet can consume most of your waking hours, day after day—for weeks, months, even years. Your family and friends will eventually encourage you to give up, adopt another dog, get on with your life.

But you will remain haunted by the endless questions and worries: Is your dog alive? Is he being abused? Is he cold? Hungry? Confined in a puppy mill cage? Being subjected to torturous research experiments? Does he ever think about you and the wonderful home he had? Does he wonder why you've abandoned him?

Your grief and guilt will never go away.

The only guarantee against pet theft is to watch your dog just as carefully as you would watch your child.

Safety amidst natural disasters

Hurricanes, tornadoes, wildfires, floods, earthquakes. In the wake of natural disasters, rescue organizations move swiftly to assist ***people,*** but pets may be left to fend for themselves.

Many emergency shelters don't allow pets. Small wonder, then, that so many people refuse to evacuate their homes if it means leaving their pet behind. Our pets are part of our family. They depend upon us to protect them. Don't abandon your pets!

Fortunately, more and more shelters are allowing pets. You should also make up a list of pet-friendly motels in your area.

Your OWN accident or death

What will happen to your beloved dog if you're seriously injured in an accident? You may be unconscious or otherwise unable to communicate, so you should take steps ***right now*** to arrange for your dog's care.

- ✓ Find at least two friends or relatives who assure you that they'll provide emergency care for your dog or will contact caregivers (such as your pet sitter). Give them keys to your home, or tell them where keys are hidden.
- ✓ Write out your feeding and care instructions (including medications) and post it on your fridge.
- ✓ If you have multiple pets, include a picture and identifying information beside each name so they can be easily distinguished by people who don't know them.

- ✓ Make a brightly colored "Pet Alert" card and carry it in your wallet so it can be found by emergency personnel. List the types and names of your pets, and the phone numbers of your vet and emergency caregivers.

What will happen to your dog if you DIE?

In their wills, many pet owners leave money to a friend or relative who has agreed to care for their pet. But there's no guarantee the money will be used that way. Some caretakers have actually euthanized pets and used the money for themselves.

A safer method of leaving money for your pet's care is to set up a legal trust fund. All 50 states now allow this. You write out specific care instructions and appoint a trustee who oversees your chosen caretaker to make sure he is taking care of your pet in the manner you specified.

This can be expensive, though. You need to pay an attorney to set it up, and there will be annual administrative costs for the trustee to monitor your caregiver.

> How much money should you leave? Add up your dog's feeding and health care costs per year, and multiply by the remainder of your dog's expected lifespan.

Miscellaneous things to worry about!

Falling objects

Dogs can be injured by things that fall or things that are dropped. Hold pots and pans firmly so they don't fall on your dog's head. Don't prop shovels or rakes where they could be knocked over. Walk through your rooms looking for things that might fall—tipsy pedestals, for example.

If you live in earthquake country, make sure there's nothing immediately over your dog's regular sleeping area that could fall—for example, a shelf of heavy knickknacks, a heavy painting, or a mirror on the wall above his bed.

Falling DOGS

Every year dogs suffer broken ribs, broken legs, and concussions from falling off balconies, decks, and open stairwells. If possible, put up protective fencing. If it's already fenced but the openings between the slats are wide enough for your dog to squeeze through, add a strip of plexiglass or lightweight mesh/netting.

Swimming pools

The ***dog paddle*** is an instinctive swimming motion for most living creatures who find themselves in deep water. Most dogs don't drown because they can't SWIM—they drown because they can't get out of the water.

"But my pool has steps… a ladder… a ramp…"

> Well, that's all well and good if your dog doesn't panic… which he is very likely to do.

> When a dog falls into deep water, he usually turns around and tries to get out the SAME way he got in. It is NOT natural for a dog to paddle calmly around looking for the "right" way out.

When he is suddenly swamped with adrenaline, he is unable to think clearly and will simply flail his front paws at the spot where he fell in. If that's a steep, slippery wall, he is likely to stay right there, flailing desperately until he becomes exhausted and drowns, never once having looked across the pool at the steps, ladder, or ramp.

So if you own a dog and a pool…

- ✓ Show him the way out of your pool and have him ***practice*** using it. Repeatedly.
- ✓ If possible, fence your pool. Or fence your DOG so he can't go near the pool when you're not right there to supervise.
- ✓ Consider buying a ***Safety Turtle,*** a small electronic device that attaches to your dog's collar. If it becomes immersed in water (i.e., if he falls in the pool), an alarm sounds in your house. It's around $200, but may be worth it to you.

Boating

Every dog should wear a life jacket on a boat. It's just too easy for him to fall overboard.

ONE LAST CAUTION about neighbors

I'd like to repeat my warnings NOT to let your dog irritate the neighbors. In this day and age, people are so harried that they "snap" more easily than in the past.

Annoyed neighbors…

- ✗ WILL let dogs out of their yards, to be lost or hit by cars.
- ✗ WILL steal dogs and release them in another city.
- ✗ WILL poison dogs with meat soaked in rat poison.
- ✗ WILL shoot dogs with BBs or bullets.

> Keep your dog quiet. Keep him on your own property. Don't let him harass the neighbors, their kids, or their pets. Don't let him damage anything that belongs to them.

And ONE FINAL SCAN for chewables

Develop the habit of automatically scanning the floor and ground. Train your eye to spot the most innocuous things: safety pins, rubber bands, staples, tacks, string.

> Dogs are curious and impulsive. They run in every direction, oblivious to danger. They poke and explore. Remember… raising a dog is like raising a toddler who never grows up.

Chapter 8

The 8th Thing You Must Do Right: Groom Your Dog for Maximum Comfort

By maximum comfort, I mean grooming based ***entirely*** on what is healthiest and most comfortable for your dog, and easiest for you to maintain on a regular basis.

I don't care a whit about a breed's "official standard" for grooming. Cocker Spaniels at a dog show might have coats dragging on the floor. Old English Sheepdogs might have hair covering their faces. Poodles might be sculptured, manicured, and fluffed.

But we're not showing our dogs at the Westminster Kennel Club Show. We should simply want them to be comfortable around the house and when romping in the yard.

This is bizarre.

Trim hair across the eyes.

If your dog has hair hanging across his eyes, ***cut it short*** so he has an unobstructed view of the world.

- ✗ A dog with hair hanging across his eyes may become anxious, shy, or suspicious because he can't see the world clearly.
- ✗ He may bark more because he can hear sounds, but he can't see well enough to locate the source.
- ✗ He may have a short attention span because he can't focus clearly on you.
- ✗ He may move in a slow or clumsy way because he can't see where he's going.
- ✗ And as that hanging hair shifts and blows around, the world appears to change right in front of his eyes. Talk about startling and confusing.

> *No dog should have hair hanging across his eyes.* Ignore the fancy show dogs and trim the hair short across your dog's eyes. Dogs need to SEE.

Or if you don't want to cut the hair, you can lift it off his eyes and bunch it over his head, secured by an elastic band or pretty bow. Unfortunately, that band or bow might be pulling on his skin and making him uncomfortable and he doesn't know how to tell you. Nope, I cut that hair clean off.

Caution when cutting bangs—don't cut your dog's eyelashes! They help protect his eyes from dirt and debris.

Trim hair around your dog's private parts.

For sanitary reasons, keep the hair around your dog's private parts trimmed short.

- ✓ Female dogs need excess hair around their vulva trimmed, and male dogs need excess hair around their penis trimmed. But do leave a few long hairs that act as "wicks" for directing urine away from their body and toward the ground. Trim any urine-soaked hairs that have fused into mats; these pull on the skin when your dog moves around.
- ✓ Both males and females need their ***anal region*** thoroughly trimmed so that fecal matter doesn't have anything to cling to. Also trim the groin, stomach, and underarm hair short, as these areas are prime candidates for matting.

Trim hair on your dog's feet.

Trim ***around*** your dog's feet and ***between*** the foot pads.

Long hairs on your dog's feet pick up dirt and debris and track it around your house. Long hair between the toes and pads can mat, and in the winter, provides a perfect place for painful ice balls to form.

> Trim long hair all around the foot so that each foot appears nice and round. Then turn the foot so the PAD is facing up and trim the hair across the bottom of the foot, including between the toes and pads so the hair is flush with the pads.

Trim the overall coat shorter.

How can this dog run and play comfortably in grass, leaves, or snow?

Just clip the coat short.

- ✓ Shorter hair is easier to brush and comb, which is easier on you and easier on the dog.

- ✓ Shorter hair is easier to bathe and dry, which is easier on you and easier on the dog.
- ✓ Shorter hair mats and tangles less (if at all), which is easier on you and easier on the dog.
- ✓ Shorter hair doesn't attract as much dirt, leaves, and debris, so your dog can run and play like a normal dog, without you worrying about him "messing up" his coat.

You can trim the entire coat short, or just those areas that tend to tangle or pick up debris.

Grooming cheat sheet

1. Clean your dog's ***eyes.***
2. Clean your dog's ***ears.***
3. Clean your dog's ***teeth.***
4. Cut your dog's ***toenails.***

> Clean eyes, ears, teeth, and toenails BEFORE brushing and bathing. You want to loosen eye gunk, ear wax, toe crud, etc.—which can then be brushed/washed away.

5. Brush and comb your dog's ***coat.*** Brushing and combing removes tangles in longhaired dogs. In ***ALL*** dogs, brushing removes dirt, dander, and shed hair, and stimulates skin oils to flow, which helps keep hair healthy. So even short-coated dogs should be brushed.

> Brush BEFORE bathing. Otherwise dirt, dander, and loose hair will make the water filthy and clog up your drain. Also, if you try to bathe ***tangled*** hair, the water will fuse the tangles into a horrible mat. And if you don't remove loose undercoat before bathing, it will whirl into a blizzard all over the room when you turn on the blow dryer. So brush BEFORE bathing!

6. Trim or clip the coat—but just a "rough cut." It's hard to evaluate how much hair to cut from a dirty coat, so you can't do final styling until the hair has been bathed and dried. But there's no point in bathing hair that you KNOW you're going to be clipping off. A shorter coat is quicker and easier to wash and dry.

7. BATHE ONLY WHEN NECESSARY. Your dog should NOT be bathed every time you brush him. Too much bathing dries out the skin and leads to itching.

> Dogs who need frequent clipping, such as Poodles, Bichons, and Schnauzers, may be bathed every time you clip them (roughly every 6–8 weeks). But most dogs should only be bathed every 6+ months. Many dogs do fine with a bath only ***once*** a year.

8. Dry your dog with a towel, blotting up most of the water. Then allow his coat to air-dry or use a ***hand dryer*** on LOW HEAT. Dogs who are put in cages with a hot dryer blowing on them have died of heatstroke. If your grooming shop is still drying dogs this way, find another groomer.

9. Finish trimming or clipping. With the coat clean and dry, you can see it more clearly and do final styling with scissors or electric clippers.

How to clean your dog's eyes

Moisten a soft cloth or cotton ball with warm water and carefully remove mucous strands and debris from around the eyes. Don't poke the eyeball! Pay special attention to the ***inner corner*** of each eye, where spilled tears collect and form brownish "sleepy seeds" and "tear stains."

With blunt-nosed scissors, trim long hairs around the eye (but not eyelashes!) that might otherwise curl toward (and poke) the eyeball. Long hairs also act as undesirable "wicks" for moisture to run down and onto the hair ***under*** the eyes, creating tear stains.

How to clean your dog's ears

Remove excess hair from inside the ears. Hair inhibits air circulation and attracts wax, moisture, and dirt, clogging up the ears and providing a breeding ground for mites, yeast, and fungi.

You can CLIP the hair with blunt-nosed scissors (carefully), or PULL each hair entirely out. To pull hair, you can use your fingers or tweezers, but a ***hemostat*** or ***forceps*** gives you a much firmer grip on the hair.

Pull only a few hairs at a time, slowly, rotating the hair clockwise and pulling in the direction of hair growth. The ears are sensitive, so if there's a lot to pull, do some now and some later.

> Consider this... pulling hair can inflame the skin and lead to the very ear infection you were trying to avoid. In the end, you may decide to just regularly trim the hair short with scissors.

Clean the ears. Moisten a soft cloth or cotton ball (not a Q-tip) with warm water. Squeeze it thoroughly to remove excess water. You don't want water dripping into the ear canals, as too much moisture attracts parasites.

> Swab the inside of the ears, but only the parts you can see. Don't push down the ear canal or you might damage his ear drum; this is why I don't recommend using a Q-tip. Occasionally clean with a mild herbal ear wash such as *Halo,* which contains cleansing herbs such as clove oil, calendula, and chamomile.

How to clean your dog's teeth

Bad teeth are a ***serious*** problem in dogs. Dogs don't experience cavities like we do, but they are VERY prone to plaque and tartar buildup. When tartar wedges under the gumline, the inflamed gum becomes a breeding spot for bacteria. The result is gingivitis (gum disease) and infection. An infection in the gums can quickly make its way to your dog's brain or heart.

- Bad teeth can be inherited. Many breeds are well-known for having teeth that build up lots of tartar: tiny breeds such as Chihuahuas and Maltese, flat-faced breeds such as Pugs, and breeds with a long, narrow muzzle such as Greyhounds and Shelties.
- Bad teeth can develop when dogs don't eat the raw meaty bones they were designed to eat. Gnawing on raw bones scrapes off plaque and tartar, and the stringy meat and tissues attached to the bone provides a natural flossing action between the teeth.

- Bad teeth can develop when you don't brush and scrape the teeth on a regular basis.

Evaluate your dog's teeth right now

If his teeth simply have a coating of clear, sticky plaque or a bit of hard yellow tartar, you can start a regular, at-home cleaning program right away.

> But if his teeth have a yellowish tint, or if thick tartar is coating many teeth, or if you see a red line at the base of any tooth (suggesting inflammation or infection ***under*** the gum line), you need to see the vet.

Unfortunately, dental cleaning at the vet's requires general anesthesia, which is always risky. The good news is that once the teeth have been professionally cleaned, you can start your dog's regular, at-home tooth-cleaning program and hopefully never need to schedule another veterinary cleaning.

Dental cleaning is a significant part of your vet's income, so he might try to convince you to come back every year. Sure, **WE** go for dental cleanings once or twice a year, but **WE** don't need general anesthesia! If you keep your dog's teeth clean, you can hopefully prevent him from undergoing anesthesia again.

Regular, at-home dental cleaning program

1) Brush the teeth. You can use a regular toothbrush (some owners even use an electric toothbrush) or just wrap a piece of gauze around your index finger.

Use a toothpaste made especially for dogs. Human toothpaste contains fluoride, sodium lauryl sulfate, alcohol, propylene glycol, etc. Because dogs can't spit, these ingredients can seriously upset their stomach when they swallow it.

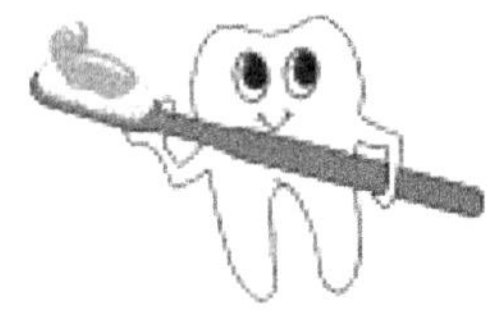

The best canine toothpastes contain enzymes that actually EAT plaque and tartar so that you'll need to do much less brushing. I like *Virbac CET Plaque & Tartar* or *Zymox Oratene Gel,* but there are others.

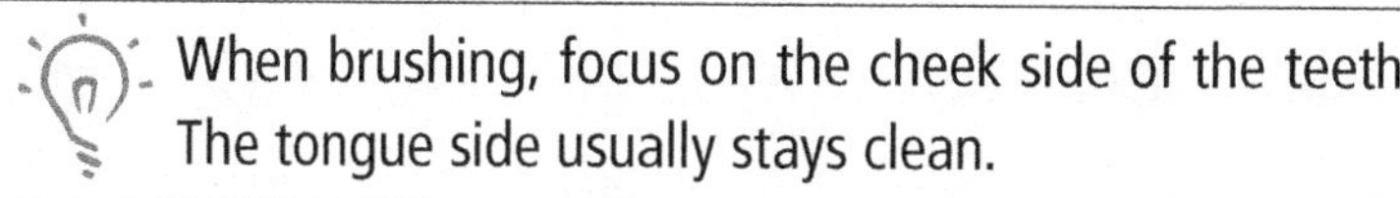

When brushing, focus on the cheek side of the teeth. The tongue side usually stays clean.

2) Use enzymatic sprays or powders. Just as toothpaste can contain tartar-eating enzymes, so can pump sprays that you spritz onto the teeth or powder that you sprinkle into his food. I recommend *Leba 3* spray or *VetriScience Perio Support* powder.

3) Scrape off tartar. Depending on how easygoing your dog is, you might use a dental scaler to scrape off bits of hard tartar.

Dental scalers are sharp, so even when you're careful, you might nick the gums and make them bleed. Same thing happens to us when the dental hygienist is scraping and flossing our teeth. It's not a tragedy. The bleeding will quickly stop.

More concerning is that a scaler can scratch the enamel on the teeth, producing shallow nooks and crannies where plaque and tartar may accumulate more quickly. So when you use a scaler, you need to stay on top of the tartar.

4) Give your dog "teeth-cleaning" toys. In theory, it sounds smart to encourage your dog to chew on toys that might scrape his teeth clean. Unfortunately, most of these toys have horrible ingredients that your dog shouldn't be ingesting. I don't give my dogs any so-called "teeth-cleaning" chewables.

You might try a *Bristly* brushing stick. It's natural rubber with grooves and ridges that help clean the teeth when the dog gnaws on it. Buy only the original product from the manufacturer, as the many knock-offs can be dangerous.

5) Consider giving your dog a raw meaty bone. The best natural toothbrush in the world is a real bone with a little meat and gristle still attached. The bone scrapes against the sides of your dog's teeth and the meat gristle flosses under the gum line.

A number of veterinarians, such as Dr. Richard Pitcairn DVM, say, "There is no better natural cleaner for teeth."

But are bones safe?

The best answer is that nothing a dog puts into his mouth is completely safe. Sticks, balls… dogs have even choked on kibble. There are different kinds of bones and each has its own pluses and minuses.

- The best bones for dental health are soft, flexible bones like chicken necks with the meat still attached. On the negative side, those can cause gagging or choking in dogs who try to swallow them whole. There might also be the risk of salmonella in raw chicken bones.

- Large knuckle or soup bones (from beef) aren't going to cause choking unless the dog breaks off a small piece of it. That might not even cause choking, but it could obstruct the digestive tract, or cause constipation. In addition, these big beef bones are very hard and could cause a fractured tooth in powerful chewers.

- Bones filled with marrow (pure fat) can cause pancreatitis in some dogs, especially small, middle-aged, sedentary dogs.

> Generally, I give soup bones to my large dogs for a few minutes a couple of times a week, with supervision. I don't give bones to my small dogs.

Isn't kibble good for the teeth?

No. This myth probably began in the marketing department of a pet food company. Kibble doesn't clean the teeth. Kibble is crunched with the bottom surfaces of the teeth, *not the sides of the teeth where plaque and tartar form.*

> In fact, kibble can ***cause*** dental issues when tiny shards of kibble get wedged between the teeth or under the gum line, where they decompose into convenient landing spots for bacteria.

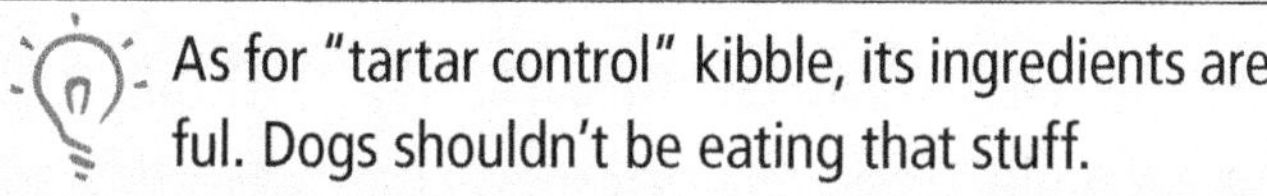

How to cut your dog's toenails

Your dog's nails should not be touching the ground when he walks. Imagine yourself trying to walk with your toenails pressing into the ground. You would need to rock back on your heels to take the pressure off. The same thing happens with your dog, and this unnatural shifting of weight can cause splayed feet and sore foot pads.

- ✗ If you can hear your dog's nails clicking when he walks on a hard surface, his nails are too long.
- ✗ If the tip of your dog's toenails extend well beyond the ***quick,*** his nails are too long.

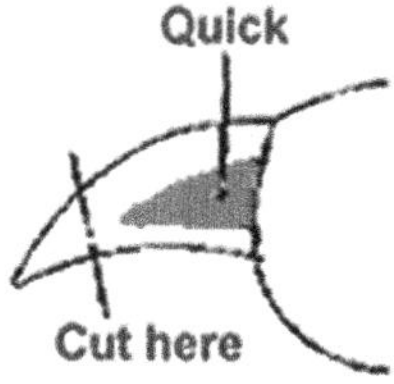

The ***quick*** is the big, central blood vessel in each nail. Usually the quick stops just before the nail starts to curl downward. In light-colored nails, you can see the reddish/pinkish blotch of the quick.

In dark nails, you have to guess. Basically there should be no sharply curved part of the nail.

Tools for cutting toenails

This is the nail clipper I use for very small dogs.

This is the nail clipper I use for most dogs.

This is the nail clipper I use for dogs with large, thick, strong nails.

Styptic powder stops bleeding quickly in case you cut a toenail too short. Always have it ready when cutting nails. The most popular brand is Kwik-Stop.

Your dog must be under control for cutting nails

Since dogs feel less confident when they're up high on a raised surface, a grooming table or sturdy wooden box is especially helpful for reluctant or uncooperative dogs. A helper can steady your dog's head if necessary.

> But if your dog is really fussy about having his nails cut, you have a problem that goes much deeper than simply grooming. To have a healthy relationship with your dog, you must be able to handle him in any way that you see fit. A dog who protests when you try to do something that he doesn't like, is making a statement that he doesn't trust you to be in charge.

> If your dog won't sit or stand or lie still for grooming, my *Respect Training* books are all about establishing a healthy leader/follower relationship with your dog. You'll also learn how to teach the vocabulary words your dog should know for routine grooming.

How to cut toenails

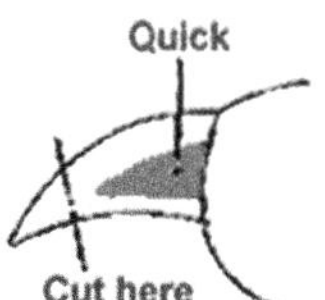

Each of your dog's toenails has a ***nerve and a blood vein,*** called the ***quick.*** If you cut into the quick, it hurts and bleeds.

So your goal is to cut the DEAD part of the nail that protrudes BEYOND the quick. There's no more feeling there than when you cut your own nails.

> The trick is to ***locate*** the quick so you'll know where to cut. In white toenails, you can see it. In dark nails, you can't.

Fortunately, in nails of any color, if you turn your dog's paw so the pad is UP, you'll see a groove along the bottom side of the nail.

> This groove is deep and distinct at the tip of the nail and becomes wider and shallower toward the toe. The part of the nail with the deep distinct groove is dead. There's no nerve or vein there, so you can safely cut it off.

In print, it's hard to describe the technique of cutting a nail. It's easier to watch a few tutorials on YouTube.

If your dog's nails are very long…

…the quick is likely to be very long, too, since it grows along with the nail. With a long quick, if you try to cut enough nail to make it comfortable for your dog to walk, you would end up cutting into the quick.

> So cut off only a little bit of the nail. Wait a few days, during which the quick will recede away from the end of the nail and you'll be able to cut a bit more.

What happens if you cut into the quick?

It stings. Some dogs barely notice, while others say "Yipe!" Blood will well out, and be forewarned, nails tend to bleed a LOT. Don't let it alarm you. It's not dangerous.

> Dab a chunk of styptic powder onto the cut and apply pressure for a few seconds. The powder will stop the bleeding, although the powder itself stings a bit when applied. Don't fuss over your dog or he'll make a mountain out of a molehill. A cheerful "Sorry about that" is enough. Once you've dabbed on the powder, leave the ouchy foot alone while you work on other feet. Then go back to the ouchy foot and finish the other nails on that foot.

How often do you need to cut toenails?

Every dog is different. Most need their nails clipped every 2–3 weeks. Some breeds have faster-growing nails than others. For example, Chihuahuas tend to have nails that sprout new growth every few days!

> You can help keep nails worn down by walking your dog regularly on pavement. The hard surface encourages the quick to recede away from the tip of the nail and discourages nail growth.

Caution: On hard surfaces, your dog should be ***walking,*** not running. Vigorous exercise should only be done on dirt or grass. Hard surfaces can seriously damage bones, muscles, joints, and paw pads, especially in young or senior dogs.

Don't forget DEWCLAWS!

A dewclaw is an extra (fifth) toenail on the inside of your dog's front legs (very common) or hind legs (much less common).

Some dogs are born with dewclaws, while other dogs are born without. If your dog doesn't have declaws ***now,*** he might have started out with them. Some breeders have any dewclaws on their puppies removed by their vet a few days after birth.

The reason usually given for dewclaw removal is that dewclaws "can get caught on things and possibly rip off." This rarely happens. But what ***is*** common is having owners forget to clip dewclaws when the other nails are cut. Since dewclaws don't touch the ground, they don't become worn by walking. If you forget to cut them, dewclaws will keep growing, eventually curling around in a complete circle that's difficult to fix.

What about electric nail grinders?

Instead of clipping nails, some owners grind the nails with a cordless Dremel from the hardware store, or an Oster grinder from the pet store. Make sure the grinder has a low speed setting and a sandpaper drum (not stone). The noise may bother some dogs, but most of them get used to it. Be careful not to burn the nail bed by grinding too long on one nail.

> Oh, and one last thing about nails... please don't use nail polish on your dog's toenails. The chemical ingredients and artificial fragrances aren't good for him.

How to brush and comb your dog's coat

Remember, brush BEFORE bathing so you can remove tangles before the water fuses them into mats, and so you can remove dirt, hair, and other debris that might clog up your drain.

Grooming tools for a sleek coat

A smooth coat that lies close to the body (Doberman, Great Dane) is the easiest to care for. Simply brush once a month with a **round curry brush** or **natural bristle brush.**

Grooming tools for a short, dense coat

A short, dense coat (Labrador, Rottweiler, Smooth Fox Terrier) should be brushed every couple of weeks with a **bristle brush.** Also use a special **shedding blade** to remove dead undercoat.

Grooming tools for a medium-length thick coat

Dogs like German Shepherds and Siberian Huskies have a thick shedding undercoat. I use a **slicker brush** every couple of weeks, plus a **shedding blade** to remove all the dead hair.

Grooming tools for a long, thick coat

A longish top coat PLUS a thick undercoat (Rough Collie, Newfoundland, Old English Sheepdog) is a high-maintenance coat. The top coat should be brushed and combed twice a week to prevent matting. I use a **slicker brush, wire pin brush,** and **steel comb.** The thick undercoat should be brushed with a **shedding blade** every day during shedding seasons.

Grooming tools for a long single coat

A single coat means no undercoat. Longhaired coats ***without an undercoat*** (Maltese, Yorkshire Terrier) need to be brushed and combed once or twice a week to prevent mats. But at least you don't need to deal with a heavy-shedding undercoat!

Remember that you can seriously cut down on brushing and combing if you trim the coat shorter.

Grooming tools for a silky, feathered coat

Some dogs have a shortish to medium-length coat on their torso, with longer, silky feathering on their ears, chest, stomach, legs, and tail. Think of a Golden Retriever, Border Collie, or Cocker Spaniel. These coats shed a goodly amount. Once or twice a week, they should be brushed **(pin brush)** and combed, focusing on the feathering to prevent mats and tangles.

Grooming tools for a curly coat

Curly/wavy coats (Poodle, Bichon Frise) need very little brushing when clipped short. If you leave longer hair on the ears, legs, tail, etc., that should be combed and brushed (slicker or pin brush) once or twice a week to prevent mats.

Grooming tools for a wiry coat

When clipped short, wiry (terrier) coats are reasonably easy to brush with a slicker or pin brush once or twice a week.

Best positions for brushing

When I'm brushing my dog's head, shoulders, chest, and front legs, I have her "Sit." When I'm brushing her back, sides, hindquarters, rear legs, and tail, I have her "Stand." Both of these grooming exercises are taught in my *Respect Training* books.

Brushing out tangles, and de-matting techniques

Many owners dutifully brush their dog's back and sides, but don't pay enough attention to the most tangle-prone areas: *behind* the ears, armpits, stomach, groin, feet, and the anal area.

> These areas are very sensitive, so brush and comb slowly and carefully as you search for tangles to tease out. To ***avoid*** tangles, brush and comb these mat-prone areas every couple of days, or else keep them trimmed short.

> Remove mats immediately. A mat can range from a few hairs fused together to a hard, knotted ball. Mats hurt your dog by tugging on his sensitive skin whenever he tries to move.

To remove a mat, isolate it by taking the base of the mat between your fingers and moving it *toward* the skin, to reduce pulling. Then use your fingers or a wide-tooth steel comb to try to separate the mat into smaller pieces, which you can then try to brush out.

If trying to remove the mat hurts your dog, just cut the thing out with scissors or use a dematter (essentially a comb with a razor blade between each tine) to slice up the mat. The coat will always grow back.

If your dog's coat has been neglected...

If your dog has a ton of mats, don't think you can just drop him at the groomer's and have those mats disappear with no muss and no fuss. It doesn't work that way.

> De-matting hurts. Under solid mats, the skin, deprived of air circulation, becomes red and sore. Trying to force a de-matting tool into those mats could cause the inflamed skin to peel away, which could lead to a staph infection.

> Any responsible groomer will tell you that de-matting should only be done with a few small mats that can be removed in less than 15 minutes. More than that and you should quit for that day and do more tomorrow. Or just cut the mats out. Or clip the whole coat short. It will grow back and meanwhile your dog will be comfortable while his skin heals.

Brushing the anal area

The anal area often collects dried fecal matter. DON'T brush or comb forcefully through this. Anal skin is very fragile and tears easily. Either trim away the junk with scissors, or soak it with water until it softens and breaks up. To avoid this problem happening again, keep the hair in the anal area trimmed or clipped short.

Brushing a whiskery beard

In whiskery dogs, the beard can become wet and sticky simply by eating and drinking. Fungi and bacteria love colonizing the skin under wet, sticky hair.

So keep your dog's beard clean, neat, and healthy. Trim it short and wipe it with a wet washcloth after meals. When combing the beard, start with a wide-tooth comb to suss out the most obvious tangles, and finish with a fine-tooth comb to find the baby tangles.

How to trim/clip your dog's coat

Blunt-nosed scissors are safest. Thinning shears have ragged teeth on one or both blades. Thinning shears "blend" the trim line so it looks soft rather than sharply defined, but you need some experience to do it right.

Electric clippers make overall body hair shorter. Oster is a popular brand.

Some clippers come packaged with useful blades, and some don't. So you might need to buy your blades separately. Blades are categorized by numbers, such as #3, #5, #10, etc. The ***higher*** the number, the ***more hair*** the blade takes off.

For most dogs, I recommend a #3F or #5F blade for the body. (The **F** means a fine cut.) For the stomach, groin, and anal areas, you can use a #5F or if you want that hair even shorter, try a #10.

Important things to know about using clippers

- Generally you should clip in the same direction the hair grows, i.e. clip WITH the grain, not against it.

- Clipper blades must be kept well-lubricated. Dry blades get hot, and then your dog can end up with ***clipper burn,*** which is itchy and uncomfortable and can lead to infection. Your first bottle of lubricating oil usually comes with the clippers. If you do notice redness or itchiness after clipping, apply aloe vera gel or vitamin E oil to soothe the skin.

- Clipper blades must be kept sharp. Dull blades pull and tear the hair. You can get your blades sharpened by mail order. Do an internet search for "clipper blade sharpening".

- When clipping loose skin around the neck and shoulders, keep the skin taut by stretching it with your other hand while you're making your pass with the clippers. This keeps the skin from bunching up, so the blade can pass over this area smoothly without getting rucked up.

Shaving dogs in the summer

Many owners ask about shaving their long-coated or thick-coated dog for the hot summer.

Yes, you can do that, but there are two concerns:

✗ **Sunburn.** To guard against sunburn, leave the coat at least two inches long. Yes, Dobermans have coats that are shorter than that, but Doberman skin is used to the sun. Whereas the skin of a long-coated or thick-coated dog is used to being protected from the sun. If you suddenly throw that skin open to the sun, it's likely to burn.

✗ **Alopecia.** If you cut a thick coat too short, you can damage the hair follicles and then an odd skin condition caused alopecia *(al-lo-PEE-shee-ah)* can develop. It's characterized by *hair loss* and then abnormal hair growth. Typically the coat doesn't become normal again for six to twelve months, and sometimes never.

> Post-clipping alopecia is most common in furry "spitz" breeds such as Pomeranians, Malamutes, Chows, etc. But it's also common in hairy breeds such as Golden Retrievers and Newfoundlands. It's safer to use air conditioning, fans, and cool, wet towels to keep these breeds comfortable in the summer.

Stripping terrier coats

If you have a wirehaired terrier, the breeder probably told you to have its coat *stripped* or *plucked*, rather than clipping it with electric clippers.

Stripping means you use a special grooming tool to pull dead hairs out by their roots so new hairs can grow fresh from the root. *Plucking* means doing the same thing with your fingers.

> Stripping/plucking is the only way to maintain the crisp, hard coat and rich colors that wirehaired terriers are supposed to have for the show ring.

Clipping, on the other hand, means removing only the TIPS of each dead hair. This makes the coat shorter, which is good, but also softer (and thus more prone to matting) and more bland in color. So clipping produces a less proper terrier coat.

HOWEVER…

The big problem with stripping is that it's ***uncomfortable*** for your dog. Most groomers won't do it because it takes so much time and because they don't want to put your pet dog through it. I don't do it either, but the choice is up to you.

How to bathe your dog

You've cleaned your dog's eyes, ears, and teeth, and clipped his nails. You've brushed his coat and removed tangles and dead hair. You've done a rough trimming/clipping so you won't need to bathe a lot of hair that was going to come off anyway.

Now he's ready for a bath. Maybe. When was the last time he had a bath? Too much bathing can cause dry skin and itchy skin conditions.

> Dogs who need frequent clipping, such as Poodles, Bichons, and Schnauzers, can be bathed every time you clip them (roughly every 6–8 weeks). But most dogs should only be bathed every 6+ months. Many dogs do just fine with a bath only ***once*** a year.

Where to bathe your dog

Sink, bathtub, or outdoors with the hose.

For sink and tub bathing, I recommend that you:

- ✓ install a hand-held sprayer so you can ***rinse thoroughly.*** Trying to rinse by pouring cupfuls of water over his coat seldom does a good enough job. Shampoo left on the skin is one of the major causes of skin problems in dogs.
- ✓ put a rubber bath mat in the sink or tub to prevent slipping.
- ✓ place a hair-catcher plug into the drain to prevent hair from running down the drain and clogging it.

How to bathe your dog

1. Remove his collar. A wet collar can lead to a rash.
2. Protect his ears. You can put a cotton ball into each ear or just be sure not to spray or pour water over his face/ears.
3. Use lukewarm water. Hot water can dry out the skin and cause itching.
4. Use a safe shampoo. I use a brand called *Earthbath* but only their *Fragrance-Free, Hypoallergenic* version. Avoid shampoos with tea tree oil, pennyroyal, or D-limonene, all of which can be toxic to dogs, especially small dogs.

5. Shampoo and scrub the dirtiest parts (legs, feet, stomach, anal region) first. Let that shampoo soak in for a couple of minutes while you work on the rest of the dog.

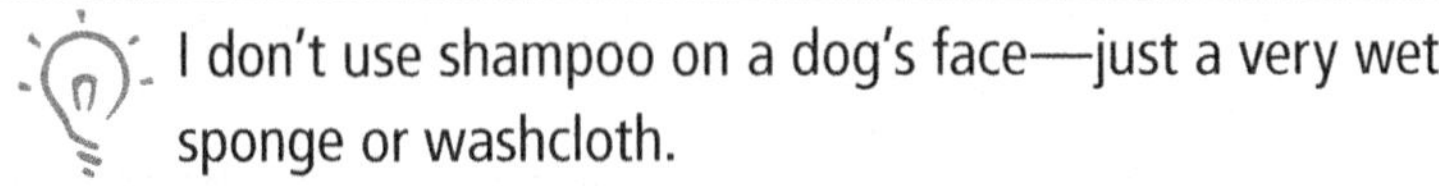

I don't use shampoo on a dog's face—just a very wet sponge or washcloth.

6. Rinse the coat. **Rinse, rinse, rinse!** Your dog is not rinsed until the water runs absolutely clear. I can't emphasize enough the importance of thorough rinsing, including the armpits, between the toes, and under the tail. Shampoo left on the body can cause itchy skin conditions. ***Rinse the feet last*** to remove shampoo residues that have been draining off the body.

7. Use a conditioner (optional). If your dog is prone to flyaway hair or itchy skin, make a conditioner by mixing 1 part **raw apple cider vinegar** with 3 or 4 parts water. After shampooing and rinsing, run your hands over your dog and gently squeeze out as much water as you can, so he's no longer dripping. Pour the conditioner over his damp coat (not on his face). Give it a minute or two, then towel-dry the coat. Don't rinse off this conditioner.

8. After your dog has had a good shake, blot the coat with thick towels. If the hair is short, rub briskly. If the hair is long, don't rub it or you might tangle it up. Don't forget to remove cotton from the ears and dry the ears well. Damp ears can lead to ear infections.

9. Finish drying the coat. Air-drying is fine for most dogs. But don't let them out in cold weather until ***completely*** dry.

Thick- or long-coated dogs are more vulnerable to developing "hot spots" (acute moist dermatitis) if you leave their coat wet after a bath. I use a hand-held blow dryer on LOW, not too close to the skin.

Keep the dryer in constant slow motion so that it never focuses on one part of the skin too long. Occasionally rest your other hand on your dog's body so that your hand is between his skin and the dryer. This keeps you in touch with the amount of heat his skin is experiencing.

The coat will dry faster if you use a brush (or your fingers) ***to lift and separate the hair*** you're drying with the blower.

Never put your dog in a crate with a dryer blowing on it. Too many dogs have died of heatstroke this way. Dogs also feel stressed when confined in a small space with hot air blasting on them.

10. Once your dog is all clean and dry, do any final brushing and trimming/clipping.

Three greatest risks of taking your dog to a professional groomer...

✗ **Chemical products.** "Specialty" shampoos (whitening, darkening, medicated...), colognes, hair sprays... Ask the groomer, "If I provide the shampoo, can you guarantee me that you'll use only that shampoo and nothing else?" Tell the groomer that your dog is extremely allergic or recovering from cancer, or whatever. Make sure the person you speak with is the SAME person who will actually be grooming your dog. Phone receptionists may agree to anything.

✗ **Tranquilizers.** "Do you have tranquilizers or sedatives available in case a dog acts up on the table?" I don't use a groomer who has sedatives available, because having them on hand makes it too easy to use them. If my dog got a little fussy on the table and they were running behind schedule and thought a small dose of a sedative might move things along more quickly…

✗ **Cage drying.** Cage-drying leads to heatstroke. Make absolutely sure your grooming shop dries ALL dogs by hand with a blow dryer. If a groomer says they "sometimes" cage-dry, but that they'll use a hand dryer on your dog, I wouldn't risk it. If they have cage dryers available, it's too easy to forget and stick *your* dog in a cage.

Chapter 9

The 9th Thing You Must Do Right: Control Your Dog's Reproduction

We've talked about keeping your dog healthy by:

> feeding real food, minimizing vaccinations, protecting his immune system by providing a non-toxic environment, preventing parasites, providing physical exercise and mental stimulation, providing emotional security, emphasizing safety, and grooming for maximum comfort and health.

Next, you need to take steps to control your dog's reproductive life. So let's have a thoughtful discussion about breeding and spaying/neutering.

We're going to start by talking about females, so if you have a female dog, keep reading. If you have a male dog, skip ahead to the section on Male Dogs.

Female dogs—breeding (pros and cons)

Here are the pros (pluses) of breeding your dog:

✓ You might get cute puppies.

Here are the cons (negatives):

✗ Responsible breeding is expensive.

✗ Responsible breeding takes a lot of time and effort.

✗ Breeding can be stressful and heartbreaking.

✗ Breeding won't improve your female's personality.

✗ Breeding won't produce puppies just like your female.

✗ Breeding takes homes away from needy dogs already born.

Let's look at those negatives in more detail.

Responsible breeding is expensive

Official health tests. You must find out if your female has any genetic health problems that could be passed on to her puppies. Different tests are recommended for different breeds, but include hip and elbow X-rays and specialized tests for eye, cardiac, liver, kidney, thyroid, or bleeding disorders.

> The proper tests can cost hundreds of dollars. But hereditary health problems have become epidemic in many breeds because so many people are breeding their dogs without doing these required health tests.

Stud fee. You might promise a puppy to the stud dog owner instead of a fee... but then you're out what someone else would have paid for that pup. Or you might think you can save money by using your own male as the stud dog. But then you have to pay for all the official health screenings for HIM, too.

Veterinary costs. Infections can occur during pregnancy and after whelping. A C-section may be required—super expensive. In some breeds, ***fragile puppies*** (needing expensive medical care to save their lives) are very common and the puppy mortality rate is high.

> Even if all goes WELL, puppies need exams and vaccinations.

And your costs don't necessarily end once you've sold the puppies! Depending on your contract, you'll need to pay for the treatment of puppies who develop health problems covered by your guarantee. If you refuse to pay, the new owner may sue you. Win or lose, lawsuits cost time and money to defend.

Food costs. A nursing female eats twice as much meat as normal, and weaning puppies gobble up meat like there's no tomorrow.

Responsible breeding takes time and effort

You'll need to spend time **learning about genetics.** If you don't know what *coefficient of inbreeding* means, you're not ready to produce a litter of puppies.

You'll need to spend time **researching pedigrees.** A pedigree is only a written list of names. You need to learn about the actual ***dogs*** behind those names. What health problems did they have? What was their temperament like?

You'll need to spend time finding a suitable male. His pedigree must be compared with your female's. When bred together, what will the coefficient of inbreeding be for the litter? The male should have the same excellent temperament and health tests as your female. The sad fact is that 99% of the so-called "stud dogs" you'll find have not been tested for ANYTHING. All they might have is a *general health certificate*, which is worthless. It says nothing about genetic health problems that can be passed on to the puppies.

You'll need to spend time facilitating the actual breeding. Often it takes several trips to the stud dog's home to make sure the breeding "takes". In dogs, there's only a small fertility window of a few days twice a year.

You'll need to spend time at the vet's. According to Murphy's Law, problems during pregnancy and whelping usually occur in the middle of the night on a holiday weekend. During a blizzard. When your car won't start.

You'll need to spend time tending to the puppies. Preparing food. Replacing dirty newspapers all through the day. You may need to get up at night to do supplemental feeding by tube or bottle.

You'll need to spend time doing paperwork. Registration applications, advertisements to sell the pups, sales contracts and health guarantees so you're covered legally.

You'll need to spend time "qualifying" prospective owners. That means answering emails and phone calls. You must ask the right questions: "Are you willing to feed this puppy real food? Do you have toddlers? A fenced yard? Is someone home all day? What happened to your past dogs?" Some of your questions will annoy prospective buyers and your conversations may become arguments. This can be stressful, to say the least.

> You will find it very difficult to find buyers who will care for your beloved puppies the way you now know they should be cared for. Too many buyers let their vet make all the decisions, subjecting the pups to feeding and vaccination practices which you now know are not best.

You'll need to spend time meeting prospective owners. You'll wait all day for people who never show up. Others will make it past your qualifying questions on the phone, but when they show up, you don't like them. They reek of alcohol and cigarette smoke. They handle the puppies roughly. Their kids are spoiled brats. Their other dog is standing in the open bed of their pick-up truck, barking his head off.

> When your goal is to place puppies carefully, you will have to turn some people down. Do you have the social skills to get them out of your house tactfully, without finding your tires slashed the next morning?

You'll need to spend time **handling problems after the sale.** When their new puppy is misbehaving, buyers will call you for help. When they have to move, or they lose their job, or they bring home a new baby, or their mother-in-law moves into their spare bedroom, they might want you to take the dog back.

> Are you willing and able to take all your pups back (at whatever age, complete with health or behavioral problems) and find new homes for them?

Breeding can be stressful and heartbreaking

You may lose your female. Dogs die trying to give birth, or shortly thereafter. Can you really handle this kind of guilt? Your dog was happy and healthy and full of life… until you decided that you wanted puppies.

Puppies may be born dead or deformed. *Mummy puppies* are all shriveled. *Water puppies* have no skeleton and appear full of gelatin. Puppies can be born with missing eyes or limbs, or cleft palates (a hole in the roof of their mouth so they can't eat), or hydrocephalus (fluid on their brain). It's sad to see.

Puppies may be born okay, then slowly weaken and die. It's heartbreaking trying to save *fading puppies* who die for no apparent reason.

The worst anxiety is when a puppy leaves. What if the home you chose isn't as good as it seems? What if they neglect this puppy who knew nothing but loving care in your home? What if they sell him to someone else? What if they feed him crappy food? What if they leave the front door open, or the gate near the pool?

> It's hard to find homes as careful and responsible as yours. ***You're*** reading a book about caring properly for your dog. Most people who want a dog don't even bother.

Breeding won't improve your female's personality

It's a myth that a shy or nervous female will become more confident if you "let her be a mother." Females who show increased confidence when they're caring for a litter do so because of maternal hormones… which don't last. Once their hormonal levels subside, shy females become shy again.

Even worse, many nervous females *continue to act nervous* while caring for their litter. Since pups tend to mimic their mother's behavior, this sets a terrible example for them.

Finally, if shyness is *part of your female's genes*, she may pass those genes along to her puppies. The pups won't show it for many months, but eventually they will.

> The moral is this… a timid, nervous, insecure, or shy female should NEVER be bred.

Breeding won't produce puppies just like your female

If you're hoping to get a puppy just like your female, the chances are slim to none. In each puppy, half of its genes come from its father. So unless the male is a genetic clone of your female, you can only get half of your female in each puppy.

> If you want another dog who looks like your female, go back to the breeder and get another pup from the same parents.

Also, much of what you love about your female is her ***personality*** (her habits, quirks, idiosyncrasies). **Personality is not inherited.** Certain *behavioral skills* (herding, hunting) can be inherited. *General temperament* (confident, shy, outgoing, nervous, independent) can be inherited. But *PERSONALITY* is mostly unique to each individual dog. You can't reproduce personality.

Breeding takes homes away from needy dogs already born

- Visit your humane society and walk along the rows of cages.
- Attend one of the "Adopt a Dog" days sponsored by your local pet store, where local rescue groups bring some of their dogs who need homes.
- Visit the websites of rescue groups and animal shelters and look at the photos.
- Watch a few videos on the Hope For Paws rescue channel on YouTube.

After looking at the hopeful faces and wagging tails of all those dogs who desperately need homes…

Do you really need to create more lives and take homes away from these wonderful dogs who are already here?

Female dogs–spaying (pros and cons)

You can call it *spaying* or *neutering* or *desexing.* All three refer to a hysterectomy—removing the ovaries and uterus so your female no longer comes into heat and cannot have puppies. Don't mispronounce it as *spading*… that's a gardening term!

A dog who is NOT spayed is also called *intact* (meaning her reproductive organs are still intact). So you can have a spayed female or an intact female.

Should a dog have one litter before being spayed?

No. Your female does not… absolutely does not… need to have puppies in order to be happy or healthy.

Quite the opposite, actually. A female who is allowed to have puppies can suffer infections and complications that can cost a fortune while making her miserable or even killing her.

So if you're not going to breed her, does that automatically mean you should spay her?

Not necessarily. As with most things in life, there are pros and cons.

Good reasons to spay your female

Spaying prevents the nuisance of heat periods.

✗ **Heat periods can be messy and embarrassing.** Your dog's genitals swell. She will have a bloody discharge, which can stain your carpets and furniture. She may spend a lot of time licking her private parts. She may flirt with other dogs (male or female), presenting her rump and encouraging other dogs to mount her. She may mount other dogs herself or hump pillows or stuffed toys. Even when Grandma is visiting.

✗ **Heat periods require vigilant confinement.** A female in heat can be smelled from a long distance away and fences mean nothing to a lust-crazed male. You shouldn't leave her alone in the yard for a single minute. Indeed, you may have to stop walking her completely.

✗ **Heat periods can upset your own plans.** Vacations and trips may have to wait. Friends and relatives won't appreciate a visit when your dog is bleeding or will leave tempting scents in their yard. And leaving an unspayed female with a pet sitter or boarding kennel is very risky because of the extreme requirements for vigilance.

Spaying prevents deadly infections of the uterus.

Nearly one in four ***intact*** females will develop an infection called ***pyometra*** at some point in their life.

The uterus swells up with toxic pus and the only cure is an emergency spay. The surgery is dangerous when a middle-aged or elderly dog is already sick from the infection.

> Many beloved dogs are lost to pyometra, which is completely preventable by spaying while your dog is still young and healthy.

Spaying offers partial protection against breast cancer.

If your dog is spayed before 2½ years old, she is less likely to develop mammary tumors (about half are malignant).

Spaying prevents not only real pregnancy, but also false pregnancy.

A few weeks after a heat period, some intact females act as though they're going to have pups. Their nipples produce milk and they may become obsessed with stuffed toys as puppy substitutes. It sounds harmless, even amusing. But the hormonal changes associated with false pregnancy can throw your dog's metabolism all out of whack, causing health problems.

> A 9-year-old dog named Caina developed a false pregnancy, followed by infection of her mammary glands. The infection spread through her bloodstream and even with antibiotics, Caina died.

Possible disadvantages of spaying your female

Most of the following statistics come from a ten-year study at the University of California (Davis) Veterinary Teaching Hospital. The study was headed by Dr. Benjamin Hart, and the study results were published in 2013.

Spaying doubles the risk of obesity.

Extra weight leads to debilitating joint disease, arthritis, heart disease, pancreatitis, and diabetes.

> Spayed dogs become overweight when owners feed the same amount of food as before their dog was spayed. Spaying, you see, changes a dog's hormonal make-up and metabolism so she doesn't require as much food.

Monitor your dog's shape and keep adjusting the amount you feed so she stays on the slender side, and provide plenty of exercise. Then your spayed dog will not become fat.

Spaying increases the risk of a deadly cancer called hemangiosarcoma.

Apparently the reproductive hormones offer some protection against this cancer, because spayed females are ***twice as likely*** to develop hemangiosarcoma of the spleen and ***5 times as likely*** to develop hemangiosarcoma of the heart, compared to intact females.

Hemangiosarcoma can affect any breed, but is far more common in these breeds: Afghan Hound, Belgian Shepherds, Bernese Mountain Dog, Bouvier des Flandres, Boston Terrier, Boxer, Bulldog, Doberman, English Setter, Flat-Coated Retriever, French Bulldog, German Shepherd, Golden Retriever, Greater Swiss Mtn Dog, Labrador Retriever, Rhodesian Ridgeback, Rottweiler, Saluki, Scottish Terrier, Skye Terrier, and Vizsla.

Spaying triples the risk of hypothyroidism.

The loss of reproductive hormones appears to upset the endocrine system. This can result in low thyroid levels, which causes weight gain, thinning hair, and lethargy. Fortunately it can be treated with a daily thyroid supplement for the rest of your dog's life.

Spaying increases the risk of "doggy dementia."

Older dogs suffering from *Canine Cognitive Dysfunction* become disoriented in their own house, interact differently with their human family, and/or forget their training. Intact dogs are less likely to suffer this disease, probably because the reproductive hormones in some way help protect the brain.

Spaying is major surgery requiring general anesthesia.

Studies show that about 20% of spay procedures have at least one complication, such as a bad reaction to the anesthesia, infection, abscess, etc. Most of these complications are minor. Less than 5% are serious, and the death rate is less than 1%.

If done at the wrong age, spaying increases the risk of hip dysplasia, torn ligaments, bone cancer, and urinary incontinence.

Reproductive hormones help your dog's bones, joints, and internal organs to develop properly. If you remove those reproductive hormones too early, they don't have enough time to complete their valuable work.

- ✗ Early spaying causes ***uneven growth*** in the leg bones. This leaves your dog more vulnerable to hip dysplasia and torn ligaments.

- ✗ Early spaying **TRIPLES** the risk of ***bone cancer,*** which can occur in any dog but is a major threat in large and especially giant breeds. Dogs spayed early are ***3 times more likely*** to develop it, compared to dogs spayed later or not at all.

- ✗ Early spaying causes ***urinary incontinence*** in up to 20% of spayed females. Weak bladder muscles start to leak in middle age. This is stressful for both you and the dog, who is understandably upset at "having accidents." Estrogen supplements will be required to manage the leakage, but getting the dose right takes trial and error.

- ✗ Early spaying can adversely affect ***the size and shape of a female's vulva.*** Sometimes the vulva is even recessed inside her body instead of protruding as it should. Abnormal vulvas have folds of skin that trap bacteria, leading to dermatitis, vaginal infections, or urinary tract infections.

My advice... should you spay your female?

Reading through all those pros and cons may have left you a little uncertain about whether spaying is the right thing to do, or not.

My opinion is that the vast majority of female dogs should be spayed.

- ✗ Uterine infections are bad.
- ✗ Mammary tumors are bad.
- ✗ False pregnancies are bad.
- ✗ Heat periods are a nuisance to live with.
- ✗ And it can be much harder than you think to prevent accidental breeding. Females in heat are driven by instinct to escape and meet up with males, who can smell a female in heat from long distances. And I wouldn't risk my dog's health (or life) just to bring more puppies into a world that already has enough dogs.

So I recommend spaying.

The only breeds I might hesitate to spay are those most prone to hemangiosarcoma, since spayed females are the most likely to develop this cancer. Unless you can read the tea leaves and predict the future, there's just no way to know which risk is greater for your individual dog. But I would probably still spay—***at the right age***—and then cross my fingers.

WHEN to spay your female

We've talked about how spaying too early can have unwanted consequences for your dog's health. She needs her reproductive hormones for some time so that her bones, joints, and internal organs can develop normally.

How long it takes for the reproductive hormones to do their work depends to some extent upon ***breed,*** but can be estimated fairly accurately by ***size.***

- Dogs less than 30 lbs should be at least 9 months old.
- Dogs between 30 and 50 lbs should be at least 12 months.
- Dogs over 50 lbs should be at least 15 months.

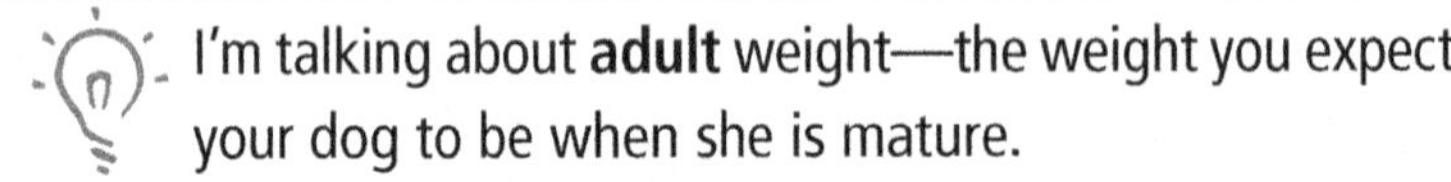

As you can see, these time frames are far removed from the "Spay at 6 months!" advice routinely given by many vets, animal shelters, and rescue groups. Their "hurry up and spay" advice is predisposing young dogs to health risks that could have been avoided simply by waiting until maturity.

> Even worse, some shelters and rescue groups are actually spaying puppies as young as 8 weeks (!) because they don't trust the adoptive parents to follow through with the surgery.

The intentions of these groups are good. They're trying to ensure that their dogs don't end up adding to the overpopulation problem.

Unfortunately, the owners who adopt those dogs will be forced to deal with any resulting health problems. And if those owners are responsible people who ***would*** have had their dog spayed (at a safer age), they're understandably upset at seeing their beloved dog now struggling with a health problem.

Some ***breeders*** have also hopped onto the "pediatric spay and neuter" bandwagon. Mostly their motives are aligned with the animal shelters and rescue groups—honestly trying to curb pet overpopulation.

> Some breeders, however, do not have entirely pure motives. From a marketing perspective, it's better to be the only people producing a given breed in a given area. So it's good for ***them*** to require their buyers to spay at an early age. But again it's the new owners (and of course the unfortunate dog) who will have to deal with any health problems that result from the too-early spay.

How your dog's heat periods affect when to spay

Most female dogs have a heat period every **6** months. But some have a heat period every **5** months, or every **7** months.

Each heat period lasts about three weeks, during which there is a discharge (varying from bloody to clear) and you need to keep your dog away from intact males. But even after that 3-week period is over, it takes some time for her reproductive system to completely settle down.

> Don't spay a dog during her heat period, or immediately before, or immediately after. There's too much activity going on in her reproductive system. Give her body time to settle down (I wait a full 6 weeks after the heat period is over) before spaying.

Thus, when deciding ***when*** to spay your dog, you must take her heat periods into account.

For example, suppose you decide to spay your small dog, Pumpkin, at the safe age of 9 months old. You make an appointment at the vet's.

> Except… the day before her surgery, Pumpkin comes into heat for the first time. Cancel the surgery. Allow 3 weeks for the heat period and another 6 weeks for her reproductive system to settle down. That means Pumpkin won't be spayed for another couple of months.

That's fine! In fact, now the surgery will be ***easy*** to schedule because her second heat won't arrive for another 5 to 7 months. You can fit the spay easily between the first and second heats.

Spaying between heats is much easier than trying to schedule the spay ***before*** your dog's first heat… because you can't know ***when*** that first heat will occur. Typically it's between 8 and 15 months old, but that's too great a range to guess at.

> It's easier to simply WAIT until the first heat has come and gone. Then WAIT another 6 weeks. Then spay. Perfect timing.

Let's see how that works for Ashley, a medium-sized dog. You want to spay her after 12 months old. Ashley has her first heat at 10 months. You wait out those 3 weeks. You give her another 6 weeks to settle down and spay at just over 12 months old.

Next is Rae, a very big girl! You don't want to spay Rae until at least 15 months old. She has her first heat at 9 months. You wait out those 3 weeks and another 6 weeks to settle down. So now Rae is 11 months, still too young to spay. You want her to be at least 15 months.

> Should you make a vet appointment for 15 months? Wait… oh no!… since Rae had her first heat at 9 months, her second one is ***due*** at 15 months—exactly when you were hoping to spay her. Rats!

But the solution is simple. Wait through Rae's second heat period, too. Then give her 6 weeks to settle down, and you'll be spaying her around 18 months old. That's fine.

Don't be in a rush to spay. Let your dog's heat periods guide you to the best time for surgery. Let her have at least one—even two if necessary—so you can ensure that the surgery is scheduled in-between them.

And make sure the surgery takes place ***after 9 months*** for small dogs (less than 30 lbs at maturity), ***after 12 months*** for medium-sized dogs (30–50 lbs at maturity), and ***after 15 months*** for large dogs (over 50 lbs at maturity). The numbers aren't cast in stone, but they're pretty good.

Dr. Lynne Friday, DVM, says about early spaying:

"Many female dogs are spayed too young, resulting in underdeveloped muscles and supporting tissue that control the bladder. In these cases, the muscles and excretory openings from the bladder may not mature sufficiently for a lifetime of control. The muscles are matured by ovarian hormones. They become stronger if the female is allowed to have its first season before being spayed."

And Dr. Richard Pitcairn, DVM, says:

"The best time for surgery is after sexual maturity, which ensures the least effect on the neuro-endocrine/metabolic system and allows full development of a normal adult body shape. For a female, this means after her first heat."

Male dogs–breeding (pros and cons)

Here are the pros (pluses) of breeding your male dog:

✓ You'll get a stud fee or maybe a puppy.

And here are the cons (negatives):

✗ His behavior may change—for the worse.

✗ You'll need to pay to have your male tested for specific health issues before breeding.

✗ Responsible breeding takes a lot of time and effort.

✗ The puppies will be half your responsibility, too.

✗ Breeding won't produce a puppy just like your male.

✗ Breeding takes homes away from needy dogs already born.

Let's look at those negatives in more detail.

His behavior may change for the worse.

✗ **Marking territory.** Many male dogs who have been bred become obsessive about *marking* their territory. To announce their masculinity to the world, they lift their leg and spray their urine as high as possible—sometimes indoors, as well as out.

> Toy dogs are especially notorious for hiking their leg on every vertical object larger than a blade of grass. After breeding, this bad habit usually gets worse.

- ✗ **Mounting other dogs.** Male dogs who have been bred may embarrass you by mounting other dogs or people's legs and generally acting "more humpy."

- ✗ **Fighting.** Some male dogs who have been bred are more likely to pick fights with other male dogs.

- ✗ **Ignoring you.** Male dogs who have been bred may ignore you when other dogs are around because they're too busy checking out whether the other dogs might be potential partners—or potential rivals.

- ✗ **Challenging you.** Some male dogs who have been bred may try to assert themselves by challenging your rules.

You'll need to pay to have your male tested for specific health issues before breeding.

You must find out if your male has any genetic health problems that could be passed on to his puppies.

Different tests are recommended for different breeds, but include hip and elbow X-rays and specialized tests for eye, cardiac, liver, kidney, thyroid, or bleeding disorders.

> The proper tests can cost hundreds of dollars. But hereditary health problems have become epidemic in many breeds because so many people are breeding their dogs without doing these specific health tests.

Responsible breeding takes a lot of time and effort.

You'll need to put in time and effort **learning about genetics** and the actual breeding process. If you don't know what *coefficient of inbreeding* means, you're not ready to create a litter of puppies. Traditionally, breeding is done at the stud dog's home, where his confidence is highest. But what if he is confused or reluctant? Do you know what to do? Do you know how to tell whether a female dog is truly fertile? There's a learning curve here!

You'll need to put in time and effort **researching pedigrees.** A pedigree is only a written list of names. You need to learn about the actual ***dogs*** behind those names. What health problems did they have? What was their temperament like?

You'll need to put in time and effort evaluating (and rejecting) female dogs whose owners are eager to breed them. The female's pedigree must be compared with your male's. When bred together, what will the coefficient of inbreeding be for the litter? The female should have the same excellent temperament and health tests as your male.

> Sadly, 99% of the female dogs presented to you as "potential mothers" have not been tested for ANYTHING. All they might have is a *general health certificate,* which is worthless. It says nothing about genetic health problems that can be passed on to the puppies. These would-be "mothers" are not ready for breeding.

You'll need to put in time and effort evaluating (and rejecting) **OWNERS,** too.

✓ Does the owner of the female have ***time*** to care for puppies all day? If the adults in that family work all day, raising puppies shouldn't even be considered.

✓ Does the owner of the female have the ***knowledge*** to screen buyers and the ***confidence*** to turn down unsuitable buyers? Or will the owner sell to anyone with cash in their hands?

✓ Does the owner have a sales contract that you can look at. should say specifically that they will take a puppy back at any time and find a new home for it.

These puppies will be half YOUR responsibility.

Sure, you can write your stud dog contract so it states that you wash your hands of all further responsibility for the puppies' lives, blah, blah, blah...

But puppies don't know anything about contracts. Puppies are innocent and helpless. They deserve to be well cared for. If it weren't for your male, they wouldn't have been born so, like it or not, they're kind of... your ***granddogs.*** So to speak.

> What if one of those pups needs help 5 years from now. If the owner of the female fails to help, will you step up?

> Whether you own the male parent or the female parent, bringing new lives into the world is a serious responsibility and can be a heavy weight on your shoulders if things don't go well.

Male dogs—neutering (pros and cons)

You can call it *neutering* or *castration* or *desexing*. All three refer to the removal of the testicles so your male can't breed or sire puppies.

> A dog who is NOT neutered is also called *intact*. So you can have a neutered male or an intact male.

Have you been told that neutering is a must for your male dog?

Absolutely necessary? All positives... no negatives?

Also that neutering should be done as early as possible, certainly by 6 months old?

It sounds so definitive.

But current research on neutering shows that the issue is not so simple. *There are a number of risks associated with neutering male dogs that pet owners are not being told about.*

First, let's look at the positives—the advantages of neutering

Good reasons to neuter your male

Neutering reduces leg-lifting and marking territory.

Intact males, driven by testosterone, usually lift their leg when they pee, to "mark" their territory. The higher they spray their urine, the more impressive they appear to other dogs. Some intact males become obsessed with marking territory and will tow you toward every tree and telephone pole. Some dominant, bossy dogs will even mark inside your house.

> Now, neutering isn't a cure-all for marking, because testosterone is also produced elsewhere in the body, not only in the testicles. Many dogs, even when neutered, will still lift their leg, but less obsessively. However, a dominant bossy attitude will need to be addressed through *Respect Training*.

Neutering reduces dominance and aggression.

This is due to the reduction of testosterone, but remember, NOT ALL testosterone is removed by neutering. If your dog has ***inherited*** his dominance or aggression, or if it's caused by ***improper socialization or training,*** then neutering can be helpful, but by itself it won't work.

Neutering reduces the risk of your dog being attacked by other males.

Even if your dog isn't aggressive himself, being intact makes him a target for other intact males who might see him as a potential rival.

Neutering helps re-focus your dog's attention.

Intact males often pay too much attention to other dogs as potential mates and rivals. Neutering can (maybe) break your dog's over-focus on other dogs, but it is *Respect Training* that will teach him to re-focus on YOU.

Neutering can reduce sexual behaviors.

Intact males are more likely to hump other dogs, pillows, stuffed animals, sometimes people's legs or ankles. Now, these behaviors can also occur in neutered dogs and can stem from over-excitement, lack of exercise, or the dog simply not being taught that these behaviors are unacceptable.

Neutering keeps your dog from pestering or chasing females in heat.

A female in heat gives off chemicals that can be scented from a mile away. If your dog is intact, he may become very agitated: whining, pacing, drooling, sometimes escaping his house or yard. Neutering puts an end to all that.

Neutering reduces the risk of prostate disorders.

I don't mean prostate cancer, which is uncommon in dogs. But dogs can develop prostate cysts or infection. More commonly, an ***enlarged prostate*** occurs in up to 80% of intact male dogs past the age of 7 or 8. No symptoms? Great, just keep monitoring. But if your dog has pain or difficulty peeing or pooping, it's time to neuter him. Neutering (reduction of testosterone) will cause the prostate will shrink naturally and the symptoms will stop.

Neutering prevents testicular cancer.

About 7% of intact males develop a testicular tumor. It seldom spreads and has a cure rate over 90%, but neutering prevents it.

> If your dog is at least a year old and still has one or both testicles tucked up inside his body (called *cryptorchidism*), the retained testicle is *14 times as likely to develop a tumor* compared to a normal descended testicle. I would absolutely neuter this dog… but not until he's old enough (I'll talk about that in a minute).

Neutering reduces the risk of perianal fistula.

In this painful skin disease, infected boils develop around a dog's anus and are extremely difficult to treat. It can appear in any dog, but is most common in intact German Shepherds, Irish Setters, and Leonbergers.

Neutering prevents your dog from breeding.

The dog population in the United States is out of control. Every day dogs are put to sleep because there are not enough homes for them. If you breed your male dog, his puppies would take homes away from the poor dogs who are already here.

What if your male passed along genes for a health problem? A dog who is allowed to breed must first be tested and cleared of certain health problems known to be hereditary.

> It's a big responsibility to own an intact male dog. You must be extra careful to keep him away from intact females.

Possible reasons not to neuter your male dog

Most of the following statistics come from a ten-year study at the University of California (Davis) Veterinary Teaching Hospital. The study was headed by Dr. Benjamin Hart and study results published in 2013.

Neutering doubles the risk of obesity.

Extra weight leads to debilitating joint disease, arthritis, heart disease, pancreatitis, and diabetes.

> Neutered dogs become overweight when owners feed the same amount of food as before their dog was neutered. Neutering, you see, changes a dog's hormonal make-up and metabolism so he doesn't require as much food.

Monitor your dog's shape and keep adjusting the amount you feed so he stays on the slender side, and provide plenty of exercise. Then your neutered dog will not become fat.

Neutering increases the risk of a deadly cancer called hemangiosarcoma.

Apparently the reproductive hormones offer some protection against this cancer, which usually strikes the spleen or heart. Neutered males are nearly twice as likely to develop hemangiosarcoma, compared to intact males.

Hemangiosarcoma can affect any breed, but is far more common in these breeds: Afghan Hound, Belgian Shepherds, Bernese Mountain Dog, Bouvier des Flandres, Boston Terrier, Boxer, Bulldog, Doberman,

English Setter, Flat-Coated Retriever, French Bulldog, German Shepherd, Golden Retriever, Greater Swiss Mtn Dog, Labrador Retriever, Rhodesian Ridgeback, Rottweiler, Saluki, Scottish Terrier, Skye Terrier, and Vizsla.

Neutering triples the risk of hypothyroidism.

The loss of reproductive hormones appears to upset the endocrine system. This can result in low thyroid levels, which causes weight gain, thinning hair, and lethargy. Fortunately it can be treated with a daily thyroid supplement for the rest of your dog's life.

Neutering increases the risk of "doggy dementia."

Older dogs suffering from *Canine Cognitive Dysfunction* become disoriented in their own house, interact differently with their human family, and/or forget their training. Intact dogs are less likely to suffer this disease, probably because the reproductive hormones in some way help protect the brain.

Neutering is major surgery requiring general anesthesia.

Studies show that about 20% of neutering procedures have at least one complication, such as a bad reaction to the anesthesia, infection, abscess, etc. Most of these complications are minor. Less than 5% are serious, and the death rate is less than 1%.

If done at the wrong age, neutering increases the risk of hip dysplasia, torn ligaments, and bone cancer.

Reproductive hormones help your dog's bones, joints, and internal organs to develop properly. If you remove those reproductive hormones too early, they don't have enough time to complete their valuable work.

- ✗ Early neutering causes ***uneven growth*** in the leg bones. This leaves your dog more vulnerable to hip dysplasia and torn ligaments.

✗ Early neutering QUADRUPLES the risk of ***bone cancer,*** which can occur in any dog but is a major threat in large and especially giant breeds. Dogs neutered early are ***4 times more likely*** to develop bone cancer, compared to dogs neutered later or not at all.

So... should you neuter your male dog?

Let me ask you some questions:

1. Does your dog have any of these behavior problems?
    - Does he mark (lift his leg) a great deal?
    - Is he aggressive toward people or other dogs?
    - Does he mount/hump other dogs a lot, or even your leg?
    - Does he pay more attention to other dogs than to you?

> If he has any of those behavior problems, begin Respect Training immediately and neuter at the right age. (We'll get to *the right age* in a moment.)

2. Does your dog interact with a lot of other dogs? If so, neutering would be wise. He will be less inclined to pick fights with other males, less inclined to be *picked on* **by** other males, and less inclined to pester females in embarrassing ways.
3. Is your dog a German Shepherd, Irish Setter, or Leonberger? These breeds are overly prone to perianal fistula and neutering reduces the risk of that.
4. Does your dog have two testicles in his scrotum, or is one (or both) missing? Missing testicles are up inside his body. In a puppy, it's not uncommon for them to go up and down for some months. But if they have never dropped by a year of age, they're

probably not going to. Since retained testicles can develop cancer, neutering is a must… but at the right age.

5. Is there a real risk that your male dog might encounter an unspayed female in heat? If so, you should neuter him.

If none of the above issues applies to your dog, you might decide not to neuter.

WHEN to neuter your male dog

If you do decide to neuter, remember that your dog needs his reproductive hormones for some time so that his bones, joints, and tendons develop normally.

How long it takes for the reproductive hormones to do their work depends to some extent upon ***breed,*** but can be estimated fairly accurately by ***size.***

- Dogs less than 30 lbs should be at least 9 months old.
- Dogs between 30 and 50 lbs should be at least 12 months.
- Dogs over 50 lbs should be at least 15 months.

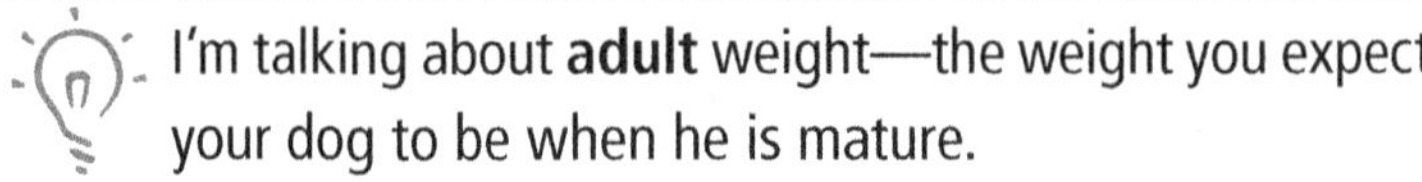

I'm talking about **adult** weight—the weight you expect your dog to be when he is mature.

As you can see, these time frames are far removed from the "Neuter at 6 months!" advice routinely given by many vets, animal shelters, and rescue groups. Their "hurry up and neuter" advice is predisposing young dogs to health risks that could have been avoided simply by waiting until maturity.

> Even worse, some shelters and rescue groups are actually spaying puppies as young as 8 weeks (!) because they don't trust the adoptive parents to follow through with the surgery.

The intentions of these groups is good. They're trying to ensure that their dogs don't end up adding to the overpopulation problem.

Unfortunately, the owners who adopt those dogs will be forced to deal with any resulting health problems. And if those owners are responsible people who ***would*** have had their dog neutered (at a safer age), they're understandably upset at seeing their beloved dog now struggling with a health problem.

Some ***breeders*** have also hopped onto the "pediatric spay and neuter" bandwagon. Mostly their motives are aligned with the animal shelters and rescue groups—honestly trying to curb pet overpopulation.

> Some breeders, however, do not have entirely pure motives. From a marketing perspective, it's better to be the only people producing a given breed in a given area. So it's good for ***them*** to require their buyers to neuter at an early age. But again it's the new owners (and of course the unfortunate dog) who will have to deal with any health problems that result from the too-early surgery.

Does neutering solve behavior problems?

No, neutering ***by itself*** does not solve behavior problems. It does decrease the chances of some behavior problems developing in the first place, because it removes testosterone that pushes some dogs to be bossy and disrespectful. But once bad habits have been established, behavior problems require ***training.***

"Will neutering stop my dog from lifting his leg when he urinates?"

Sometimes. Sometimes not. Whether or not a neutered dog lifts his leg when he urinates is influenced by these factors:

- ✓ **His personal levels of dominance and territoriality.** The point of leg-lifting is to spray urine as high as possible. If your male has a *Top Dog On The Totem Pole* attitude, he may lift his leg, whether neutered or not.
- ✓ **His personal level of hormones.** Testosterone is produced elsewhere in the body, not just in the testicles. So a neutered male still has some male hormones. These may or may not be enough to compel him to lift his leg.
- ✓ **Habit.** If he had been lifting his leg for some time before neutering, it might be enough of a behavioral habit that he will continue to do so, at least sometimes.

Safe surgery and anesthesia

For convenience, I'm going to use the pronouns for a female dog in this section (she, her), but the information is applicable to both males AND females.

Spaying and neutering are major surgeries requiring general anesthesia. General anesthesia is never routine.

There are steps your vet can take to make anesthesia much safer and more comfortable for your dog. But many vets won't take all these steps unless you specifically request them.

Seven questions to ask your vet

Ask the vet... "Will you use isoflurane or sevoflurane as the anesthetic?"

You want sevoflurane (see-vo-FLOOR-ane) or isoflurane (eye-so-FLOOR-ane), both of which are inhaled gases.

The gas is delivered through a tube down the dog's windpipe and the dog just drifts asleep. The vet can continuously adjust how much anesthetic your dog is getting by turning the vaporizer knob.

As soon as the vaporizer is turned off, 99% of the gas in your dog's body is quickly exhaled through her mouth. She will be awake within a few minutes and moving around within a half hour.

This is a huge improvement over older gases such as halothane, which hung around for hours, delayed recovery, and eventually had to be processed through the liver, where it could do damage if your dog got too much.

> Sevoflurane or isoflurane. Those are the only two acceptable answers for me.

Ask the vet... "Which sedatives do you use for induction?"

Inducing anesthesia means "getting it started." You can't just turn on the gas and aim the nozzle at the dog's face! Instead, the dog needs a tube down her throat, through which the gas can be continuously administered.

The problem is, to insert this tube, your dog must be very relaxed. One way to relax a dog long enough to get the breathing tube down her throat is to administer a very short-acting ***sedative,*** either by injection or through an IV.

> The sedative I prefer is **propofol** *(PRO-po-fol).* My second choice of sedative is a combination of diazepam (also known as valium) and ketamine.

Unfortunately, even good sedatives occasionally cause problems:

✗ Propofol can cause some dogs to stop breathing.

✗ Ketamine can cause some dogs to have seizures.

Some vets use other sedatives such as acepromazine, xylazine, or medetomidine. I'm not comfortable with the safety profile of those sedatives and I don't want them used on my dog.

Finally, no barbiturate sedatives. Barbiturates have ***al*** at the end of their name: Thiopent***al.*** Thiamyl***al.*** Methohexit***al.*** Pentobarbit***al.*** Barbiturates are too easy to overdose, too hard on the liver and kidneys, and recovery time is unnecessarily long.

"Masking" means no sedative required

It might be possible for the vet to sedate your dog (just long enough to insert the tube) without using an injected or IV sedative. For some dogs, the best "sedative" is just the inhalant gas (sevoflurane or isoflurane) itself.

Yes, the inhalant gas can be used as BOTH the sedative and the actual anesthetic. Here's how:

The gas mask is held over your dog's face for a few seconds. She will breathe in the gas and doze off enough for the vet to insert the breathing tube. Then he can maintain her the rest of the way with the gas from the vaporizer. Thus, from beginning to end, your dog is never injected with anything. My vet does this with my dogs.

This technique is called ***masking.*** The vet might say, "I won't need to give her a sedative if I induce by masking."

> So instead of this: sedative → throat tube → gas,
> the vet does this: gas → throat tube → gas.

A potential problem with "masking" is this:

Some dogs struggle if the gas mask is placed over their face. A struggling dog can be hard to control and her heart rate and blood pressure will go up. Fear and stress are not what you want right before surgery!

> However, masking can work very well for calm, quiet dogs. Ask your vet if he believes your dog could be masked with gas quickly and easily. If he is reluctant to do so and he has propofol or ketamine/diazepam for the sedative, that's fine.

Ask the vet… "How will you maintain my dog's body temperature during surgery & afterwards in recovery?"

Anesthesia and surgery cause your dog's temperature to fall, sometimes dangerously low.

It's very important that your vet take precautions to keep your dog's body temperature UP.

Typically this is done by performing the surgery on a heated table, and/or by wrapping your dog in thermal blankets both during the surgery and recovery. Make sure this will happen.

Ask the vet… "Which monitoring devices do you use during surgery?"

Your dog is less likely to die under anesthesia when the most modern technology is used to monitor her vital signs. These are the monitoring devices I want my vet to use:

- ✓ pulse oximeter—monitors pulse rate and oxygen level
- ✓ ECG heart monitor—monitors heart ***rate*** and heart ***rhythm***

✓ blood pressure monitor

✓ body temperature monitor

My dogs don't go under anesthesia without these monitors. And speaking of monitors, ask the vet…

"Will there be a vet tech in the room watching the monitors?"

Major surgery should not be a one-man job.

Ask the vet… "Will you run a blood panel before surgery?"

Running a blood panel simply means drawing blood to make sure your dog's liver, kidneys, and other organs are healthy enough to withstand the double stresses of anesthesia and surgery.

The blood panel can be done the same day as the surgery if the vet has a testing lab right there at his office. Otherwise the blood will need to be sent to a third-party lab and the results will take a day or two to come back.

Always, always, always have your vet run a blood panel before anesthesia and surgery.

Ask the vet… "Can I bring my dog home the same day?"

✓ If your dog did fine through the spay surgery, and

✓ if your dog wakes up okay, and

✓ if you will be home 24/7 to watch over her for the rest of the day and the following day…

You ***SHOULD NOT*** need to leave her at the vet's overnight.

Think about your dog. She will be feeling discomfort from the surgery. She will be feeling confused and anxious. Even if there IS someone at the vet's office overnight (and often there isn't!)... that person would simply check your dog's vital signs and move on.

No, I want my dogs home, in familiar surroundings, where they feel calmest and most secure. I put them in their crate right beside my bed so they know I'm there.

> "But my vet told me it was office policy for all dogs to stay overnight after neutering!"

Yes, some vets have office policies that are one-size-fits-all, and most owners follow them without question.

- ✓ But YOU are a special owner.
- ✓ YOU have done research that other owners haven't.
- ✓ YOU are more involved in your dog's safety and welfare.
- ✓ YOU don't just hand your dog over and wave goodbye, giving up all participation in decisions about what's best for her.

Unless your dog did poorly during the surgery and needs ***treatment***... or unless no one will be home at your house to watch over her... she doesn't need to stay at the vet's overnight for "routine monitoring."

Chapter 10

The 10th Thing You Must Do Right: Choose the Right Vet

When it comes to ***preventing*** health problems, the bulk of the responsibility falls on YOU—your dog's guardian and primary caregiver. ***Preventing*** health problems is the focus of this book.

But once you've detected something awry, you need to work with a vet to diagnose and treat health problems.

But which veterinarian? This is a crucial decision.

> All the effort you've put into keeping your dog healthy can be undone by a vet who scoffs at your nutritious meals, who chastises you for not vaccinating your dog "enough," or who tries to inject your dog with steroids for minor health problems.

You might think you've already found a good veterinarian for your dog. He or she is a friendly person. The office is not far away. The fees are reasonable. And the office staff greets your dog with smiles and petting.

Nice, certainly! But not the best reasons for choosing a vet.

> **The number one thing you want to know about a veterinarian is their *philosophy* of health care.**

The most sensible philosophy of health care

...is holistic. Now, don't roll your eyes! Holistic doesn't mean *New Age crystals* or *chanting*. Holistic means "whole." A vet with a (w)holistic philosophy looks at the ***whole*** picture of what's going on with your dog and offers a ***whole*** range of healing treatments.

> For example, if Molly has an ear infection, a holistic vet will prescribe an antibacterial or antifungal med. But he will also prescribe nutritional supplements or medicinal herbs to make Molly's immune system stronger so that it can resist future infections.

> A vet with a (w)holistic philosophy offers guidance on how you can make ***everything*** in your dog's daily life health-promoting.

Don't we all want this kind of forward-looking, whole-picture health care for our dogs? Yes, of course.

(W)holistic vets offer a wide range of treatment options:

- ✓ drugs and medications
- ✓ medicinal herbs
- ✓ nutritional supplements
- ✓ homemade diets

- ✓ acupuncture
- ✓ chiropractic adjustment
- ✓ laser therapy

> A vet with so many options can choose the gentlest and safest treatment that will do the job with the fewest side effects.

The problem with a "conventional" philosophy of health care

Sadly, most owners limit themselves (and their dog) to a vet who doesn't have such broad-based training and expertise and so doesn't offer many treatment options.

Of course owners don't do this on purpose. But if you open the phone book and start calling vets, it's likely that all of them will have a ***conventional*** philosophy of health care, rather than holistic.

> What is a conventional philosophy of health care? Feed kibble or canned. Annual shots. And for almost every health issue, the only treatment options are medications, surgery, or a (dreadful) prescription diet.

Now, don't misunderstand… those are lifesavers when really needed! The problem is that conventional vets have to use those treatments for ***EVERYTHING*** because they haven't learned how to use any alternatives—many of which are just as effective and with fewer side effects.

Dr. Richard Pitcairn DVM can tell you more:

"In our eagerness for quick and easy solutions, we seize on a certain drug that may just cover

> up symptoms without addressing underlying causes. For example, synthetic cortisone is powerful enough to stop a wide variety of symptoms in their tracks. But inside, the disturbance continues unseen. Animals vigorously treated with such drugs (apparently successfully) go on to develop another condition within a few weeks or months."
> *Dr. Pitcairn's Complete Guide To Natural Health For Dogs and Cats*

Drugs and medications can have side effects that you don't see; side effects that happen deep inside the body and take time to cause problems.

Dr. Nino Aloro, DVM, agrees:

> "Sometimes the side effects are worse than the disease. Standard medications have the potential to cause frightening problems with the liver, heart, kidneys, skin, immune system, and digestive tract."

Why don't conventional vets offer more kinds of treatments? Because they haven't been trained for it. Veterinary colleges teach classes that rely on medications, surgery, and prescription diets.

Vets who want to add more skills, such as acupuncture or herbology, need to take extra courses. Holistic vets have chosen to do that. Conventional vets have chosen not to.

A conventional-only philosophy deprives your dog of valuable treatment options that might really help his long-term health.

The other major problem with most conventional vets is that they don't give good advice about your dog's all-important general care.

- ✗ For example, most conventional vets recommend dog food that isn't suited to a dog's digestive tract. Their nutrition classes were taught by the representatives of commercial dog food companies—hardly objective sources.
- ✗ Most conventional vets give too many vaccinations, even though the research is clear that over-vaccinating can damage your dog's health.
- ✗ And most conventional vets suggest spaying and neutering too early, despite studies that show the health risks.

> So… most conventional vets simply don't give good advice about your dog's general care. (W)holistic vets do much better in this all-important area.

What is a holistic vet?

Quite a few vets CALL themselves holistic, but they're really not. **Holistic,** you see, has become a "fad" word, sort of like **organic** or **all-natural,** where the definition depends on who you ask.

Here's my definition of a truly holistic vet…

> A truly holistic vet offers a full range of treatments (conventional and alternative). And a truly holistic vet helps you make your dog's daily life as health-promoting as possible, which starts with a canine-appropriate diet.

Based on my definition, vets who offer only a few types of treatments aren't truly holistic.

- If all they offer are medications, surgery, and prescription diets, those vets are ***conventional***.
- If all they offer are medicinal herbs, nutritional supplements, chiropractic adjustment, acupuncture, or some other healing method, I call those vets ***alternative***.

Only when a vet ***integrates*** both conventional and alternative treatments do I call him or her truly holistic (***integrative*** is another good word.) Some veterinary practices might be called integrative if they include both conventional vets and alternative vets. That's good, but not as convenient as having a single vet who can do it all.

Assembling your vet team

If you don't live near a truly holistic or integrated vet… don't despair. Most pet owners (including myself) don't. So let me tell you how I still obtain excellent veterinary care for my dogs.

I have a wonderful ***alternative*** vet certified in herbal medicine and acupuncture. She also prescribes drugs (such as antibiotics and pain medications) and does blood work and basic diagnostic tests.

She comes very close to being a true holistic vet. But she does not offer vaccinations, dental cleaning, surgery, or advanced diagnostic tests such as X-rays.

> For those, I turn to my wonderful ***conventional*** vet—the best I've ever found.

Both vets share the essential trait of *open-mindedness.* They appreciate what the other has to offer, and though they've never met, they work cooperatively through me. The three of us are a team that provides the best ***integrated*** (holistic) care for my dogs.

There have been times when other vets needed to join our team. As when my Papillon needed a quick X-ray and of course it was a holiday weekend (isn't it always?!)

Fortunately I had already chosen a 24-hour emergency practice. It pays to plan ahead and know who you will call if X or Y should happen. You don't want to spend valuable minutes making frantic phone calls to find someone who is open.

> If you don't live near a holistic/integrated vet who "does it all," you should look for both an alternative vet and a conventional vet, so your dog can be treated in an integrated manner with all possible treatments available. You want both vets to be open-minded and supportive.

If your current vet isn't supportive

Do you think your current vet will be accepting of your ideas about your dog's health care? If that's true, excellent! But it's more common that a conventional vet is friendly and smiling *as long as you agree to everything they want to do.*

But suppose you say,

- "I'm interested in feeding a homemade diet."
- "I've learned that annual booster shots aren't necessary and I want to check titers instead."
- "I'd like to do a little research before I agree with your treatment plan."
- "I'd like to run this by my other vet and get her take on it."

Then those smiles might vanish.

If a vet doesn't "believe in" alternative treatments and keeps giving you skeptical looks or making condescending remarks, please consider finding another vet who IS supportive or at least open-minded.

Do it politely, so as not to burn any bridges. You might need this vet for emergency care where conventional medicine is at its best.

YOU are in charge of your vet team

The conventional vets I use are smart and dedicated. I very much appreciate their skills.

> But they have conventional mind-sets, so their advice always includes medications, surgery, and prescription diets.

When I mention alternative treatments such as herbal medicine, or acupuncture, or adjusting my dog's homemade diet, or anything else outside their training and expertise, they're okay with it... but they never bring up these options themselves.

Remember… when a conventional vet gives advice, you're getting only some of the possible options.

So when my dog has tests done, I listen to what my conventional vet has to say about the results. I listen to his recommendations for treatment. But then I do some research on my own. And I ask my alternative vet for HER recommendations.

> Often I decide to follow some of the recommendations from each one, combining the wisdom each brings to the table.

You can see why a single holistic vet is your ideal choice! Then you won't need to go back and forth between two vets. That takes time and money, unless you find a vet who encourages communication by phone and email, as my own vets do.

> But however you need to do it, valuable treatments that can make a difference to your dog's health should not be overlooked.

Finding an integrated or holistic vet

Your mission… to find a ***holistic*** or ***integrative*** vet in your area who practices both alternative and conventional medicine.

Most veterinarians who graduate from veterinary school join the American Veterinary Medical Association (AVMA) and go on to practice conventional medicine. Those vets are a dime a dozen and are not the vets you're looking for right now.

You want vets who have graduated from veterinary school and ***also*** completed courses in alternative medicine. These vets not only join the AVMA, but also typically join the A***H***VMA, as well. The ***H*** stands for holistic.

> To find these vets, visit the AHVMA website and click on the link that says *Find a Vet.*

If there's a vet within driving distance, make sure it says the vet treats *Small Animals.* Some vets only treat *Equines* (horses).

Also check the healing techniques (or *modalities*) offered by the vet. Some will be familiar (nutrition, herbs, acupuncture), while others (applied kinesiology?) will make you scrunch up your face and say, "What's THAT?"

I'm dubious about some techniques myself, so I stick to those that have been successful for my own dogs, or for dogs owned by trusted friends and colleagues.

Specifically, the techniques I look for (in alphabetical order, not order of preference) are:

- ✓ acupuncture
- ✓ Chinese herbs
- ✓ chiropractic
- ✓ conventional medicine
- ✓ nutrition
- ✓ western herbs

Keep in mind that if a vet does practice some or all of these techniques, but NOT conventional medicine, I consider that vet ***alternative.*** With that vet on your team, you would also want a ***conventional*** vet in order to have an ***integrated*** team.

Back to your list of vets… some listings include a website, which you should certainly visit.

To add more vets to your list, do a Google search for:

> holistic vet YourState

Interviewing holistic vets

If you have found some integrated or alternative candidates, your next step is to find out whether you want to work with them. Holistic vets are individuals, just like everyone else.

- Some graduated at the top of their class. Others graduated at the bottom.
- Some are highly skilled. Others are less than competent.
- Some are friendly and easy to work with. Others are brusque, arrogant, or intimidating.

And beware… some vets who bill themselves as holistic don't really have holistic attitudes. Dr. Crumpet may have taken a few courses in natural health care, then joined the AHVMA. But if he continues to practice conventional medicine, with a few herbal remedies thrown in when the owner insists on it, Dr. Crumpet is certainly not a holistic (or even an alternative) vet.

But if you can't find a truly holistic vet and you need to assemble a team, Dr. Crumpet might serve as the ***conventional*** half of your team. He's obviously open-minded about alternative treatments and that's a big plus in a conventional vet.

But for now, let's keep looking for a truly holistic/integrated vet.

You have the phone number of one or more candidates? Call them. Tell the receptionist you're looking for a holistic vet and that you'd like to ask just **three questions** about Dr. X. The receptionist might be happy to talk to you herself, or she may pass the phone to someone who is better equipped to answer.

Initial telephone questions

"Does the vet offer both conventional and alternative treatments? What kinds of alternative treatments?"

You've already seen the vet's listing on the AHVMA website, which included their modalities, but ask anyway. The vet may have added (or stopped offering) a modality that you're interested in. Might as well find out now!

The receptionist might tell you that the office is composed of several vets who each specialize in one or more modalities. There might be a vet who specializes in acupuncture and medicinal herbs, plus a vet who practices conventional medicine.

> This kind of veterinary practice is often called ***integrated*** because they're under one roof and can easily communicate with each other, which is good… but it's less convenient than one vet who "does it all."

? Does the vet support homemade feeding? Raw feeding? "What kind of dog food do you sell in the office?"

From my feeding chapter, you should know whether you want to make your dog's food from scratch or feed a pre-made diet. You should know whether you want to feed cooked or raw. You want a vet who supports your feeding method. If a vet is claiming to be holistic, but is selling Science Diet, that would end the phone conversation for me right there!

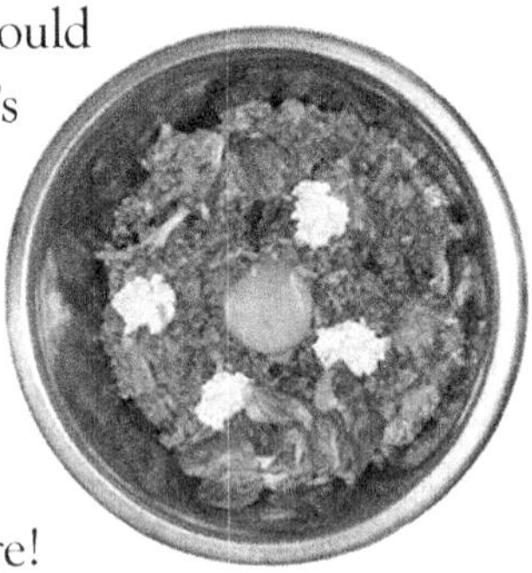

? "What does the vet generally recommend for vaccinations, for puppies and for adult dogs?"

You want a vet who recommends minimal puppy vaccinations and no annual boosters. Some vets will recommend boosters every 3–5 years, but I would insist on testing titers first.

So those are your initial telephone questions. If you receive answers that sound promising, you should schedule a **Wellness Appointment** so you can all meet.

A word about fees...

An office visit with a holistic (or alternative) vet usually costs more than an office visit with a conventional vet. Often considerably more.

There are two reasons for this:

- Unlike a conventional vet, a holistic vet does not receive income from unnecessary annual vaccinations. That lost income must be made up somewhere so the vet can stay in business. Holistic vets make up that income in higher consultation fees.

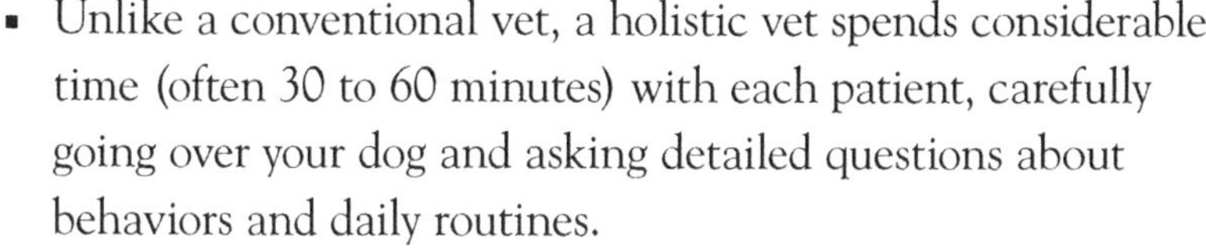

- Unlike a conventional vet, a holistic vet spends considerable time (often 30 to 60 minutes) with each patient, carefully going over your dog and asking detailed questions about behaviors and daily routines.

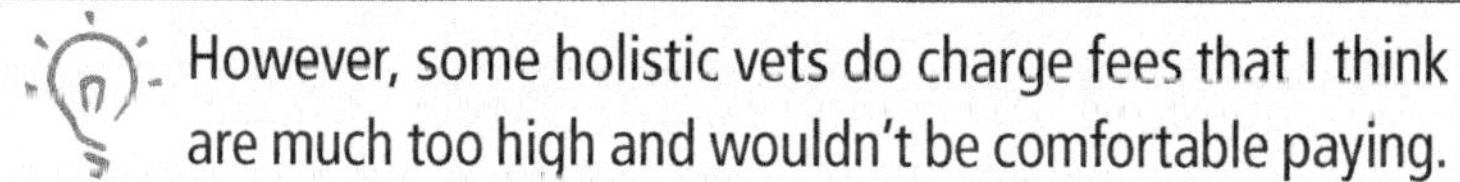

However, some holistic vets do charge fees that I think are much too high and wouldn't be comfortable paying.

In-person questions for the vet

First I look around the office. I'm not so much looking FOR certain things as I'm hoping that I ***don't*** see those things.

For example, in a ***conventional*** vet's office, virtually everything you see is tied to pharmaceutical or pet food manufacturers.

Brochures and posters on the wall hawk medications. The shelves are typically stocked with Science Diet. On the walls are certificates proclaiming the vet's assistants to be Certified Nutritionists (based on a nutrition course sponsored by the Hill's Company, makers of Science Diet).

I ***don't*** want to see these things in the office of a holistic or alternative vet!

When you meet the vet:

- Repeat the questions you asked on the phone about feeding, vaccinations, and the treatments he offers. You want to hear these answers from the vet himself.
- If he does acupuncture or chiropractic, ask what his certifications are. Ideally he will be a member of IVAS (Int. Veterinary Acupuncture Society) or AVCA (American Veterinary Chiropractic Association).
- Ask how long it takes to get an appointment if your dog is ill. Holistic vets are often in high demand and this can mean waiting too long for your dog to be seen. If this is the case, you will need to scope out a secondary vet to have on hand.
- Ask the vet what days and hours he keeps. Ask how he handles problems that come up outside of those hours. Unless it's a multi-vet practice, you'll probably be referred to a 24/7 emergency clinic, which are expensive and totally conventional. I only use them for true emergencies.
- Ask if he does vaccinations. Titer tests? Dental cleaning? Neutering? What kinds of diagnostics can be done? X-rays? Ultrasounds? Does he have his own bloodwork lab in the office or does he send blood out?

> Alternative vets often focus on their specialties and may not offer all the services you might need. Hence the need for having more than one vet on your dog's health care team.

- Ask about the vet's typical fees.
- If he is ***alternative-only*** (doesn't offer conventional medicine), tell him that you would like to take advantage of conventional medicine as well as his own expertise. Ask him if he is comfortable with that.
- Finally, ask the vet, "What does 'holistic' mean to you?" There's no right answer to this question. It just gets the vet talking so you can see if his explanation resonates with you, and if you understand it. If you're going to be working with someone, you want them to speak so that you understand.

> Of course, you also want the vet to do a nose-to-tail checkup of your dog, so you can see how they interact with each other.

Finding an open-minded CONVENTIONAL vet

Suppose you can't find a good holistic/integrated vet, but you DO find an alternative vet. Very good!

Next you'll need a conventional vet who is open-minded and supportive of your desire to raise your dog on a natural diet, minimal vaccinations, alternative treatments such as acupuncture and herbal medicine, and so on.

If you think your current vet will be supportive, excellent! If not, start with the phone book or visit vetstreet.com and type your zip code into their "Find a Vet" box. Then start calling. Say something like:

> "I'm looking for a new vet for my dog and I'd like to ask a few questions about your veterinary practice. Are you the right person to talk to?"

Continue with:

> "I'm looking for a vet who will be comfortable working with me. I use alternative medicine as well as conventional. I feed (a homemade diet) (raw diet) and I do titer tests, not regular booster shots. Do you think one of the vets at your practice might be a good fit for me?"

If you receive a positive answer, schedule an appointment to meet the vet. In the previous section, I recommended questions to ask a holistic vet. You can ask a conventional vet variations of these same questions.

Also ask about high-tech diagnostic equipment. One of the advantages of a conventional vet is that they're more likely to have sophisticated diagnostic tests such as digital X-rays or ultrasounds.

Working ONLY with a conventional vet

You're disappointed. After searching diligently, you haven't been able to find a vet who is holistic/integrated or alternative.

You're going to have to work exclusively with a conventional vet.

That means you must be an alert advocate for your dog.

✗ At the vet's office, don't turn your dog over to anyone. You want to be a ***participant*** in his care, not a passive onlooker who just pays the bill.

✗ Don't let anyone take your dog "into the back" where you can't see what's happening.

✗ Don't sit in the waiting room while the vet examines or "does stuff" with your dog. Stay with your dog.

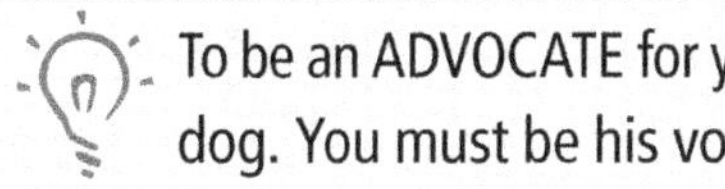
To be an ADVOCATE for your dog, you must be WITH your dog. You must be his voice, his guardian, his protector.

Also don't feel rushed to make decisions in the vet's office. If he is suggesting a long-term course of treatment—for example, if he wants to put your dog on meds for low thyroid, or allergies, or scratching… you can always tell him that you want to think about it and that you'll call back.

THEN GO HOME. Learn about the health issue online. There are even holistic vets online who offer phone consultations. Do a Google search for *holistic vets phone consultations*

Holistic health care is a complete way of living with your dog.

To raise your dog holistically, you need to do many little things on a daily basis. Real food, minimal vaccinations, a non-toxic environment (look everywhere!), parasite control, a clean, well-groomed body, plenty of exercise and mental stimulation, emotional security, and SAFETY (look everywhere!).

All these little things add up to protect and strengthen your dog's body and mind and immune system. If he does

> become sick, the chosen treatment should be the most effective one with the fewest side effects.

Instead, many dog owners raise their dog ***conventionally*** while occasionally dabbling in a bit of "natural medicine"—only to find that it doesn't work.

That's right. It doesn't. If a dog is eating kibble every day... if he is vaccinated each year... if his bed is washed with chemical-laden detergents... if he is bathed with fragrant flea shampoos... if he is treated with steroids for allergies or with repeated courses of antibiotics for chronic ear infections... if his home contains air fresheners or cigarette smoke...

> ...natural remedies will probably not work. You can't undo a whole bunch of bad stuff with a few herbs.

Raise your dog in all the ways I recommend in this book—holistically. Then use a combination of conventional and alternative medicine to treat health problems. That's what I do.

Chapter 11

The 11th Thing You Must Do Right: Recognize When Something Is Wrong With Your Dog

Even when you've followed the guidelines in this book and done your best to prevent things from going wrong...

> ...they still might go wrong. That's just the nature of living creatures.

> At that point, the quicker you notice something wrong with your dog, the quicker and easier the problem can be resolved.

That means you should observe and examine your dog on a regular basis, looking at each part of his body and noting whether it looks normal or abnormal.

> It is vitally important that ***YOU*** keep tabs on your dog's health. The vet can't do it. He's way the heck over there in the animal hospital. You're the one living with your

dog, looking at him, feeding him, grooming him, petting him, taking him out to potty and play.

Those interactions are your opportunities to notice things. Get in the habit of turning on your ***Health Radar*** whenever you interact with your dog.

- ✓ Petting him gives you a quick feel of his skin and coat.
- ✓ Grooming him gives you a quick look at his eyes, ears, nose mouth, feet, toenails, and private parts.
- ✓ Taking him for a walk or playing with him gives you a quick look at how his legs and joints are functioning.
- ✓ Taking him out to potty or cleaning his yard gives you a quick look at his stool.

> These quick little observations can pick up the very beginnings of health problems when treatment will be most effective.

So this chapter is about knowing what to look for when you look at or interact with your dog. Remember, you're the only one who can do this, so he's depending on you!

This chapter will walk you through a ***quick*** list of things to look for on your dog. A ***quick*** list. I can't cover this topic comprehensively in one chapter. In fact, I've written entire books on this topic, which you can find on my website. It's obviously impossible to cram an entire book into a single chapter! But I can give you some of the key highlights.

Nose

May be moist or dry, cool or warm. It's a myth that a dog's nose must be moist and cool to be healthy.

Abnormal: Crusty or scabby ulcerations on the nose. Hairless patches around the nose. Chronic discharge, especially combined with persistent sneezing and watery or crusty eyes. Thick, yellowish-green discharge. Chronic nosebleeds. For a dry nose with cracks, soothe with aloe vera gel, calendula, or vitamin E oil.

Mouth

Gums should be pinkish (or pinkish with black or brown pigment). A healthy shade of pink suggests that your dog's heart is pumping blood efficiently through his body. Press your index finger against the gums; they should ***blanch*** (fade to a paler shade), then return to normal within two seconds after you stop pressing. This test is called ***capillary refill*** and can be very valuable in assessing your dog's health.

Abnormal: Whitish or yellowish gums. Slow to return to pink after pressing. Any growth or swelling on the gums, tongue, roof or floor of the mouth, which may be combined with drooling or difficulty chewing. Horrible breath—a dog's mouth does have odor from his food, but it should not be putrid.

Teeth

Should be white, clean, straight, and firmly rooted in the gum.

Abnormal: A broken or fractured tooth. A tooth that wiggles in the gum. A crooked tooth that interferes with other teeth or pokes into the soft tissues of the mouth when the dog chews.

Teeth should not have:

- ✗ an off-white, sticky film—that's **plaque,** which is made up of bacteria.
- ✗ a yellow-brown, hard calculus—that's **tartar,** which is hardened plaque.

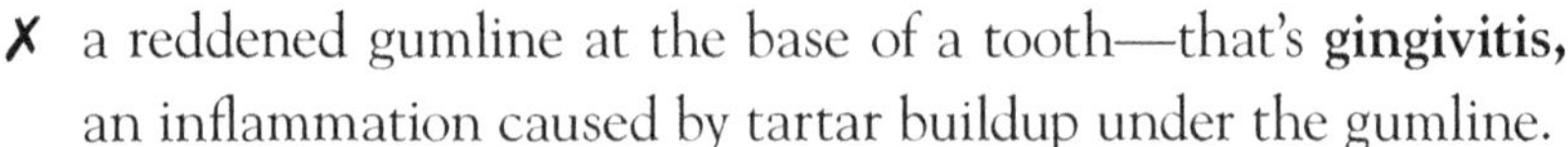

- ✗ a reddened gumline at the base of a tooth—that's **gingivitis,** an inflammation caused by tartar buildup under the gumline.

Lips

Abnormal: Skin lesions, raw patches, cracking, or hair loss on (or around) the lips. Especially common with loose lips or facial folds.

Breathing

No chronic coughing. However, if you have a small dog, it's normal for him to experience periodic episodes of snorting, wheezing, or honking, especially during or after eating, drinking, or excitement. This is harmless *reverse sneezing.*

Eyes

Abnormal: Squinting, watering, yellowish-green mucous. Pawing at the eyes. Hair loss or skin lesions around the eyes. In the white area of the eye, there should be no yellow or orange tinge, brown pigment strands, or tiny red spots. On the colored area or black pupil, there should be no cloudy/whitish spot (cataract). The eyeball should not be enlarged, especially if whitish, bluish, or reddened (glaucoma).

Abnormal: Eyelids should not be swollen, reddened, or rolling inward so that the eyelashes irritate the eyeball. The lower eyelid should not droop, sag, or roll outward.

Abnormal: Signs of vision impairment include reluctance to go outside at night, move around in a dark room, or use stairs.

Ears

Abnormal: Brownish, waxy discharge. Black specks like coffee grounds. Red flush (inflammation). Head-shaking or holding the head tilted to one side. Persistent scratching of the ears. Flinching when you rub the ears. A fluid-filled swelling on the inside of the ear flap (hematoma). A growth on or inside the ear.

Long ears (Basset Hound, Poodle, spaniels, setters) are more susceptible to ear problems because the long, narrow ear canal traps wax, providing a sticky medium in which fungi can grow and parasites can feed. Dogs with profuse hair inside their ears are doubly susceptible because the hair acts as a magnet for moisture, dirt, and wax.

Head and neck

Abnormal: A growth or lump, which could be an attached tick, a non-tumorous growth (such as a fatty lipoma), or a tumor (benign or malignant). A small lump in your dog's neck, just behind and below his jawbone at the junction of his jaw and throat, could be a swollen lymph node, suggesting an infection, tick disease, or cancer (lymphoma).

Front legs and feet

Abnormal: Small hairless patches on the front legs of a puppy or adolescent are a symptom of demodectic mange, especially with similar patches on the face. Reddish-brown stains on the front feet are caused by saliva from chronic licking and chewing, which are symptoms of allergies, injury, or a foreign body lodged in the foot (such as a splinter or foxtail).

All four paws

Abnormal: A growth, swelling, or mat between the toes or around the footpad.

There should be four toenails on each foot. They should not be long, brittle, misshapen, or loose/wiggly/missing. Also check the dewclaws if your dog has them. They're an extra (fifth) toenail that you may find on the inside of your dog's "wrists."

In middle-aged and senior dogs, lift one hind foot just off the floor and replace it so the TOP of the paw is resting on the floor. Let go of the paw. A dog with normal nerve reflexes will quickly flip his paw into its normal position. A dog who does this slowly could have a disk or spinal column disease impeding his reflexes.

Tail and anal area

Abnormal: At the base of the tail, dampness or hair loss due to chewing, usually from fleas or allergies.

Abnormal: A lump near the anus. Red or ulcerated skin. Fecal matter stuck to his hair—keep this area clipped short. Dreadful odor. If your dog has been "scooting" his behind across the floor or grass, his anal glands could be full and need to be expressed by the vet. Dogs also scoot when they're itchy, which could be caused by stuck fecal matter, fleas, or worms.

Vulva

Abnormal: Red irritated skin in the folds of the vulva, especially combined with frequent licking, particularly after urinating, because urine burns! Spayed females should have no discharge.

In intact females, a discharge means she's in heat... unless it occurs 4–6 weeks AFTER a heat period, when a discharge is bad news—*pyometra,* a serious uterine infection. She will need to be spayed immediately.

Testicles/scrotum

Abnormal: Any lump. One testicle larger than the other (but it's normal for one to hang slightly lower than the other). A warm, swollen testicle, especially combined with excessive licking and discomfort, suggests an infection or injury.

Groin/Breasts/Penis

Roll your dog onto his or her side or back.

Abnormal: In the groin, a lump or bulge under the skin suggests a hernia or swollen lymph gland.

Abnormal: Palpate your female's mammary glands (breasts), paying special attention to the **two rear breasts** (closest to her tail). A lump suggests a tumor. A discharge of milk 4–9 weeks after a heat period has ended, especially combined with enlarged breasts, abdominal distension, rooting into blankets (to make a den), or "mothering" stuffed toys, suggests ***false pregnancy*** (assuming you're sure she isn't actually pregnant).

Abnormal: Examine your male's penis. An occasional clear discharge is no cause for alarm. But a yellowish-green or bloody discharge, especially combined with excessive licking or swelling, is abnormal. In an older, intact male, a discharge plus difficulty pooping could signify an enlarged prostate.

Torso, Skin, Coat

Run your hands over your dog's shoulders and back, along his sides, and under his stomach and chest.

Abnormal: Tenderness. Lumps or growths. Itchiness. Raw weeping lesions that exude pus and serum. A greasy coat that smells rancid. A dry, dandruffy coat. Hair loss. Fleas or ticks.

To dog owners west of the Mississippi, wild grassy weeds called ***foxtails,*** with their sharply barbed seeds, are *dangerous scourges.* Foxtails contain a living bacterium that lets the seed burrow into the skin like a barbed fish hook, leaving a channel of pus. If it reaches the brain or heart or lungs, it can be fatal.

Foxtails grow during the spring rains and dry out in the summer. The dried seed at the top of the stalk hangs down like a fox's tail and sticks to your dog's fur if he brushes past it.

> During the summer and fall in foxtail country, check your dog's eyes, ears, nose, throat, paws, toes, and belly every day. You must catch these dangerous invaders quickly.

If you find a foxtail before it has burrowed completely beneath the skin, you can soak it with mineral oil to stop its burrowing, then remove it with tweezers. But if you notice any swelling or oozing/pus-filled break in the skin, it could be an ***already-burrowed-in*** foxtail and you should see the vet immediately so it can be removed (surgically, if necessary).

Gait/movement

Some health issues aren't evident until your dog moves. Observe him regularly as he walks around your house, runs around your yard, climbs stairs, or jumps onto the sofa.

Abnormal: Favoring a leg. Moving stiffly. Moving both rear legs together (like a bunny hop). Reluctance to jump. Sitting on one hip with one rear leg extended stiffly. Slowness/discomfort when sitting down or when rising from a sitting or lying position.

> A dog who isn't moving "right" may have simply pulled or sprained something. Could even be as minor as a mat pulling on the skin in his groin or armpit, or a thorn stuck in the pad of his foot, or a torn toenail. Or it could be a serious rupture of a ligament, or a degenerative disease (arthritis, dysplasia) in one of his joints, or a pinched spinal cord from disk disease.

Abnormal: Wobbliness. Loss of balance. Tremors. Dragging the back toes. Walking in circles or with the head tilted to one side. Shaky legs or sudden collapse after exercise or excitement.

Perhaps the most frightening abnormal movement to witness is a *seizure,* which is a sudden jolt of electrical activity in the brain. Some dogs might stare rigidly into space, snap at the air, or bite weirdly at their own body. But in a typical seizure, the dog falls onto his side, his body rigid, legs extended, feet paddling as though trying to run. He may drool or lose control of his bladder or bowels. He may lose consciousness. Fortunately, it's usually over in less than 90 seconds.

Energy level

We've been looking at your dog's individual body parts, but a dog isn't simply a collection of body parts. An essential part of his health is his energy, his vigor, his spirit.

How does your dog FEEL?

✓ Is there a light shining in his eyes?

✓ Is there a spring in his step?

✓ Is he interested in the world around him?

✓ Is he eating?

✓ Is he playing?

> Sometimes the very first symptom of a serious illness is nothing more than listlessness, lethargy, or loss of enthusiasm.

Vomiting and regurgitation

Both are abnormal, but they ***are*** different. Vomiting entails retching and heaving as the body actively expels partially-digested contents from the stomach.

Regurgitation is ***passive.*** The food never makes it down to the stomach, so it isn't forcefully expelled. A chunk of it simply sits in the esophagus until your dog lowers his head and it spills out of his mouth onto the floor.

Gas (flatulence)

- Dogs can be gassy when they eat kibble or canned food, or real food that's not easily digestible—grains, legumes such as peas and lentils, starchy potatoes and pasta, and milk/dairy. The solution is to feed only real meat, fish, eggs, and a few steamed veggies.

If the dog is still gassy, replace cauliflower, broccoli, brussels sprouts, asparagus, carrots, peas, and corn with less-gassy veggies such as zucchini and green beans.

- Short-faced breeds can be gassy because their deformed head and respiratory system forces them to snort and snuffle and swallow air… which must then escape from the body somehow.

- Dogs can be gassy when they eat too fast, which makes them swallow air. To slow down a gulper, feed multiple small meals per day. Or feed him in a private area with no other dogs lurking around as competition. Or place a good-sized rock or a chain with big links in his food dish so that he must pick slowly around the obstacle.

Peek at your dog's urine

His urine reveals a great deal about his health and can be ***the very first sign*** that something is wrong.

Normal urine is "well-concentrated" (meaning it has a strong yellow color and ammonia odor) first thing in the morning when your dog hasn't had a chance to potty all night. Normally, dogs urinate every 4–6 hours during the day. Puppies, with their immature bladders, may urinate every 2–3 hours during the day.

Abnormal: Orange or blood-tinged urine. Painful urination. Straining to urinate yet producing very little. Sudden urge to urinate where the dog rushes for the door every hour or so. Increased drinking resulting in increased urination (frequency and/or quantity).

Abnormal: "Leaking" urine occurs when your dog dribbles or produces wet spots and appears to have no control over it, even appearing surprised or embarrassed. In many dogs, especially youngsters, this is usually caused by excitability or submissiveness, not ill health. In other dogs, it's caused by a urinary tract infection, an orthopedic disease where it hurts the dog to get up and walk outside to potty, or senility. In middle-aged spayed females, it can be caused by lack of reproductive hormones that support strong muscles and tissues of the bladder; these dogs will need lifelong hormone administration.

> Urine burns the bladder, so working owners who make their dog "hold it" for 8–10 hours every day are doing the dog a disservice.

Peek at your dog's stools

This examination is getting worse and worse, isn't it? But what goes in must come out! The question is: Does it come out normally?

Abnormal: ***Chronic*** soft, loose stools, or more than 3 stools per day. These are common complaints in dogs eating kibble or canned food, which has ingredients dogs can't readily digest. Feed your dog digestible real food.

Abnormal: ***Sudden*** diarrhea usually means that your dog ate something that didn't agree with him (whether food or NON-food), or that he is experiencing some stress or excitement. Most of the time, diarrhea clears up on its own in a day or two... as long as you don't keep feeding the dog!

> A short fast gives the digestive system a rest. If food is going too rapidly through her, you're making things worse if you provide more food.

- ✓ For one full day, I stop feeding meals. Every few hours, I offer a couple of mouthfuls of chicken broth mixed with a little aloe vera juice, raw apple cider vinegar, raw honey, slippery elm, and/or decaffeinated herb tea (steeped for 20 minutes so it's both strong and cool). The next couple of days, I add a little cooked white rice and hamburger. Then some steamed veggies, etc.

Abnormal: Blood in the stool. If it's simply a tinge, I wait to see if it's repeated. If it's thick and copious blood, go to the vet.

Abnormal: Constipation (difficulty producing a stool). Check the anal area for irritated skin or matted hair. Feed only real food—its built-in moisture bathes and flushes the intestines. Canned pumpkin adds both moisture and fiber. More exercise makes the bowels move more easily. But consider... an orthopedic disease (hip dysplasia or disk disease) can make it painful for the dog to assume a crouched position, so he deliberately "holds it."

Abnormal: Bits of vegetables in the stool. Raw veggies often come out in recognizable form because your dog couldn't digest them. Always pulverize raw veggies, or cook them.

Abnormal: "Grains of rice" in the stool... but you're not feeding rice! These could be worms, or segments of worms.

Take your dog's temperature

Every owner should know how to do this. Different dogs have different "normal" temperatures, so it's a good idea to take your dog's temperature ***when he's healthy*** so you'll have something to compare it to if you ever need to take it ***when he's sick.***

1. You need a RECTAL thermometer.
2. "Shake it down" to about 95 degrees.
3. Grease the bulb end with KY jelly or vegetable oil.
4. Have your dog "Stand." You may need someone to hold him still.
5. Lift his tail and insert the bulb end slowly, with a twisting motion. If you meet resistance, you're probably hitting stool, so don't push any further.
6. Hold it there for 2 minutes or until it beeps (depends on your thermometer).

7. Remove it, wipe it clean with a tissue, and read the temperature.

Normal temp is 100 to 102.5 degrees (pups and small dogs tend to be on the high end). If below 99 or above 104, repeat, leaving the thermometer in a bit longer. If it's still low or high, do you have a second thermometer you can try? When multiple readings on multiple thermometers are low or high, call the vet.

Bloat: The 6-Hour Killer

I've decided to end this examination chapter with a group of symptoms that all dog owners should learn and know by heart.

These symptoms belong to an emergency gastrointestinal syndrome that strikes suddenly (in a matter of hours) and is often fatal. ***Bloat or gastric torsion is the second- or third-leading cause of death in many large and giant breeds.***

Even if ***you*** don't own a large breed, chances are that you know someone who does. If you happened to be visiting that person, your recognition of these symptoms could save their dog's life. That's a good reason to at least ***look*** at this list, right?

If a large dog:

- ✗ has a swollen (bloated) stomach that feels hard…
- ✗ is clearly uncomfortable, perhaps pacing restlessly…
- ✗ drools or retches or tries to throw up—but cannot…
- ✗ tries to go to the bathroom—but cannot…
- ✗ pants rapidly or assumes a "prayer position" with his front paws and chest on the ground, hindquarters in the air, as he tries to relieve the pressure in his stomach…

RUSH him to the vet. There's not a moment to lose.

Conclusion

At the beginning of this book, you learned that there are three major causes of health problems in dogs: heredity, abnormal structure, and environment.

Once you ***have*** your dog, you can't do anything about the first two causes of health problems.

> If his parents weren't tested for specific hereditary health problems or if he is inbred to a high degree, or if he has an exaggerated/unnatural build… you can't change that now.

So in this book, we focused on the ***LAST*** cause of health problems—the one you **CAN** do something about at this point—your dog's environment.

The good news is that there's a long list of health issues you can minimize or prevent simply by controlling, adjusting, and monitoring your dog's environment.

> ***YOU*** (not your veterinarian) are the primary driver of your dog's health.

The things ***YOU*** do with your dog at home will make all the difference in his short- and long-term health and lifespan.

1. Feed the right food.
2. Minimize vaccinations.
3. Protect your dog's immune system by providing a non-toxic environment.
4. Prevent fleas, ticks, and heartworm.
5. Provide physical exercise and mental stimulation.
6. Provide emotional security.
7. Emphasize safety.
8. Groom your dog for maximum comfort and health—not appearance.
9. Control reproduction.
10. Find the right vet.
11. Recognize when something is wrong with your dog.

In short, make ***everything*** in your dog's life health-promoting and his chances of living a long, healthy, happy life are hugely increased. I wish you both well!

Index

Made in the USA
Monee, IL
18 June 2021

71696861R00177